RSVP THE HOUGHTON MIFFLIN READING, STUDY, & VOCABULARY PROGRAM

RSVP THE HOUGHTON MIFFLIN READING, STUDY, & VOCABULARY PROGRAM

SECOND EDITION

James F. Shepherd
Queensborough Community College
The City University of New York

Houghton Mifflin Company   Boston
Dallas   Geneva, Illinois   Hopewell, New Jersey   Palo Alto

To my students

Cover design by Tom Powers

Part-opening photographs:

Part 1. Susan Lapides / Part 2. Joel Gordon / Part 3. Karen R. Preuss, Jeroboam / Part 4. J. D. Sloan, The Picture Cube / Part 5. Susan Lapides

Other credits:

Pages 5–41: Chapters 1–4 are based on material in *College Study Skills*, 2nd ed., 1983, by James F. Shepherd. Used by permission of Houghton Mifflin Company.

Pages 45–97: Chapters 5–7 are based on material in *College Vocabulary Skills*, 2nd ed., 1983, by James F. Shepherd. Used by permission of Houghton Mifflin Company.

(Credits continued on page 361)

Printed in the U.S.A.

Library of Congress Catalog Card Number: 83-80900

ISBN: 0-395-34260-0

ABCDEFGHIJ-M-89876543

CONTENTS

PREFACE

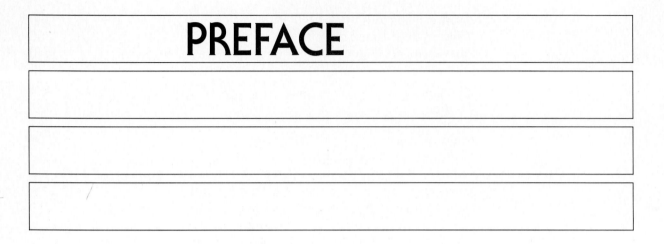

RSVP: The Houghton Mifflin Reading, Study, & Vocabulary Program orients students to college life and instructs them how to improve the vocabulary, reading, study, and test-taking skills that are essential for academic success. It is a complete text and workbook that was studied in its first edition by thousands of students in classrooms and learning centers.

The text features clear, concise, but complete explanations of skills and more than 150 practical exercises for the development of skills, which are motivating because they are in a great variety of formats and challenging without being frustratingly difficult.

The twenty-six chapters are arranged in the sequence most instructors have indicated they prefer; however, chapters are written so they may be taught in any sequence that is appropriate for specific students or groups of students. The text is comprised of five parts:

- Part I, "Prepare to Succeed," orients students to college life, explains course and degree requirements, and offers suggestions for scheduling study time and increasing concentration.
- Part II, "Improve Vocabulary," teaches how to determine word meanings by studying context, analyzing word structure, or using a dictionary, and it offers students the opportunity to learn the meanings of up to 267 words.
- Part III, "Read with Understanding," develops literal, inferential, and evaluative comprehension and it lays the foundation for improving underlining and note-taking skills.
- Part IV, "Study for Examinations," explains how to take good class notes, decide what to learn, underline textbooks, make notes for textbooks, and recite and review information in preparation for tests.
- Part V, "Use Good Test-Taking Methods," presents instruction for improving skill in answering true-false, multiple-choice, matching, fill-in, and essay questions.

The text concludes with a glossary, an index, and a form for scheduling study time.

RSVP has three features that, in sum, distinguish it from other study skills texts. First, it offers comprehensive instruction and practice in four essential skills areas: vocabulary, reading, studying, and test taking. Other texts are less comprehensive than *RSVP* in one or more of these areas, usually vocabulary or test taking.

Second, dozens of actual textbook selections are provided for the practice of skills. Instructors report that these selections have been skillfully selected to be representative of a wide range of college reading, to promote skills acquisition, *and* to be very interesting to students.

Third, instruction is integrated so that skills taught in earlier chapters are reinforced or refined in later chapters. For instance, vocabulary skills taught in Chapters 5–7 and reading skills taught in Chapters 10–12 are reinforced by exercises in Chapters 13 and 14. Also, skill in locating major details and minor details, taught in Chapters 10 and 11, is refined when students do underlining and note-taking exercises in Chapter 19.

This Second Edition of *RSVP* is a complete revision of the original and contains many improvements, including the following:

1. There is a fuller explanation of how to schedule study time (Chapter 2).
2. There are more exercises for using context to infer word meanings, and many of them are based on excerpts from college textbooks (Chapter 5).
3. There is instruction in a wider range of dictionary skills (Chapter 7).
4. There is the opportunity for students to learn the meanings of up to 267 words (Chapter 8).
5. There are exercises for locating minor details in textbook selections and for making notes in the outline format (Chapter 11).
6. There are more exercises in which textbook selections are followed by multiple-choice questions (Chapters 13 and 14).
7. There are more reading selections from technical and scientific textbooks (Chapters 10, 12, 13, and 14).
8. There are new exercises for interpreting tables and graphs (Chapter 15).
9. There is instruction for making notes in a greater variety of formats (Chapter 19).
10. There are more and improved exercises for answering true-false and multiple-choice questions (Chapters 22 and 23).

I am grateful to the faculty of Queensborough Community College for the partial leave that allowed me the time to write this revision and to the following reviewers for their useful comments:

William T. Anagnoson
Montgomery College

Liz Karzag
West Valley College

Marion L. Patterson
Coppin State College

Deborah Ann Rosecrans
University of Cincinnati

Edward F. Wightman
Hudson Valley Community College

Joseph Zielinski
Tarrant County Junior College

Also, in writing this revision I was encouraged and inspired by my students, to whom this book is dedicated, and by my friend and mentor Professor Emeritus Josephine P. Ives, of New York University.

I would like to know your reactions to *RSVP*. If you take the time to write to me, I will take the time to thank you. Address your letter to James F. Shepherd, c/o Marketing Services, College Division, Houghton Mifflin Company, One Beacon Street, Boston, Massachusetts 02108.

J.F.S.

TO
THE
STUDENT

I have been fascinated by textbooks for as long as I can remember. As a child I would read my school books wondering who wrote them and by what magic they were printed so that pictures were always exactly where they should be on pages. Later, in high school and college, I would puzzle over textbooks that were difficult for me to read and imagine to myself how they could be written to make them more understandable.

When I graduated from college, I did not know that I would become a teacher and one day write textbooks myself. But, of course, if I had not graduated from college, I would not be doing the work that I enjoy doing so much today—teaching and writing books for students.

My experiences are very similar to those of thousands of other college graduates; our lives are better because we went to college. I am pleased that you have joined us. I believe that you are wise to want a college education and that your successful experiences in college will make it possible for you to live a life that is better in ways that you cannot even imagine today.

I wrote *RSVP* so that you will improve your vocabulary and do your best when you read, study, and take tests in college. You can use the things you learn in this book to do your best in school; I sincerely hope you do. I, and many others you have never met, want you to enjoy the benefits of a college education.

The books I write for students have always benefited from students' reactions to them. If you take the time to write to me about *RSVP*, I will write to thank you. The address is on the preceding page.

J.F.S.

RSVP THE HOUGHTON MIFFLIN READING, STUDY, & VOCABULARY PROGRAM

1. PREPARE

TO

SUCCEED

One day while a construction worker was on his way home from work, he found a dollar bill on the sidewalk. He bought a lottery ticket with the money, won a million dollars, and invested his winnings. Today he is wealthy. By chance, he became a financially successful man.

There is an element of chance in all our lives, but most people who have what they want did not get it by chance. They got what they have by deciding what they would have and by working for it.

Many of the people who want a college education never get one because they don't know how to plan or exactly what to do to achieve their goal—a college degree.

RSVP was written to help you understand how to do well in your courses, stay in school, and thus acquire a college education. The first four chapters explain some strategies that are used by successful college students, basic information about degree requirements, and sources of help in case of academic difficulty. The remaining chapters explain and provide practice for improving vocabulary, reading, study, and test-taking skills.

1. DO WELL
IN
EACH
COURSE

Those who do well in college are determined to benefit from it as much as possible and to accumulate a good record that will help them when they apply for admission to other schools or seek employment. They are as serious about doing well in college as they are about doing good work on jobs they do not want to lose.

- They know what their teachers require.
- They attend class meetings faithfully.
- They keep up to date with course work.
- They turn in assignments on time.
- They are prepared for all tests.

This chapter explains these and other basic strategies for assuring academic success.

KNOW TEACHERS' REQUIREMENTS

Teachers ordinarily explain course requirements during the first few days of classes. When course requirements are presented orally, take accurate and complete notes; when they are distributed on printed pages, keep them in a safe place. In either case, understand them completely and follow them exactly.

EXERCISE 1

KNOWING TEACHERS' REQUIREMENTS

Write the names of your two most demanding courses over the columns on page 6. Referring to information about requirements for the courses, answer all the numbered questions, even if you must write "no," "none," or "I don't know." Answer the lettered questions only when they follow a numbered question you have answered "yes."

	1.	2.
1. What books, equipment, or other materials must you purchase?	_____	_____
2. Have you purchased the books or materials?	_____	_____
3. What materials must you take to class?	_____	_____
4. Do you know in advance the topics for class meetings?	_____	_____
5. Must you take notes during class?	_____	_____
6. Must you participate in class discussions?	_____	_____
7. Must you attend a laboratory?	_____	_____
a. Where is it located?	_____	_____
b. When must you attend?	_____	_____
8. Must you attend conferences with the teacher?	_____	_____
a. Where are they held?	_____	_____
b. When must you attend?	_____	_____
9. Must you write a major paper?	_____	_____
a. How many pages long must it be?	_____	_____
b. When is it due?	_____	_____

10. Must you do
    homework
    assignments?   _____   _____

11. How many tests must
    you take?   _____   _____

12. What is the date of the
    first test?   _____   _____

13. What material will be
    covered on the first
    test?   _____   _____

14. When you take tests,
    will you answer
    objective questions
    (multiple-choice, true-
    false, and so on)?   _____   _____

15. When you take tests,
    will you answer essay
    questions?   _____   _____

TAKE A NOTEBOOK TO CLASS

Use a notebook to keep class notes (see Chapter 16) and records of assignments, tests, instructors, and classmates.

- Information about *assignments* should explain exactly what they are, how they are to be done, and when they are due.
- Information about *tests* should include exactly what materials and topics will be covered on each test and the dates that the tests will be given.
- Information about *instructors* should include their names, office locations, office telephone numbers, and the times they are available in their offices.
- Information about *classmates* should include the names, addresses, and telephone numbers of at least two people in each class whom you can contact in case you must be absent from a class.

Most students use spiral notebooks because they are convenient to carry and to use on small desk tops. The 8½-by-11-inch size is preferred because it is large enough to organize notes so that information about a single topic usually fits on one page rather than on two or three pages.

Some spiral notebooks have pockets on inside covers or dividers for the safekeeping of papers that teachers distribute.

Ring binders, on the other hand, are less expensive to use than spiral binders because one does not pay for cardboard covers and a spiral each time notebook paper is purchased. Also, the amount of paper for each course can be regulated in a ring binder by adding it as it is needed. When a desk top is too small to accommodate a ring binder comfortably, remove paper from the binder for note taking.

EXERCISE 2

KEEPING RECORDS IN A NOTEBOOK

Keep records of assignments, tests, instructors, and classmates in a notebook.

1. Records of assignments and tests may be kept in one place for all courses or in different places for each course. Where will you keep records of assignments and tests for your courses?

   _____

2. Summarize the following information on a page in a notebook or on the inside cover of a spiral notebook.
   a. The names, office locations, office telephone numbers, and office hours of your instructors.
   b. The names, addresses, and telephone numbers of two classmates in each course whom you can contact in case you are absent.

Procedures for taking good class notes are explained in Chapter 16.

KEEP UP TO DATE WITH COURSE WORK

College terms start out slowly. They gradually get busier and busier, reaching a peak of activity at final examination time. Students who are not up to date with course work find themselves trying to catch up when they should be completing term papers and preparing for tests. Don't fall behind—keep up to date with the work in all your courses.

It is doubly important to keep up to date in courses for which information or skills learned early in a term are needed to learn other information or skills later in the term. Mathematics, science, technology, and foreign language courses are among those that fit this description. When you study, ask this question: "Do I need to learn this information or skill to learn other information or skills later?" If the answer is yes, learn the information or skill immediately and review it often.

| EXERCISE 3 |

KEEPING UP TO DATE

You are behind in a course if you have not done all reading and other assignments or have not taken all quizzes and tests. If it is early in the term, you are also behind if you have been absent from a class or have not yet purchased required books and other materials. List below the courses in which you are *not* up to date.

_____

_____

If you are behind in a course, catch up now. The farther behind you fall, the harder it will be to catch up.

Chapter 2 explains how to keep up to date with course work by scheduling study time.

DO ASSIGNMENTS ON TIME

Instructors give assignments to provide practice for skills and for other purposes. They expect students to have assignments ready when they are due; many teachers do not accept late assignments and others give lower grades for them.

Some teachers give assignments that they review in class but do not collect and grade. Do them faithfully, as you do the others; their purpose is to help you acquire a skill or to learn other things you need to learn. If you don't do them, you won't know what you're supposed to know— you won't do your best.

EXERCISE 4

DOING ASSIGNMENTS ON TIME

List the reading and other assignments you must complete during the next five school days.

1. _____

2. _____

3. _____

4. _____

5. _____

6. _____

7. _____

8. _____

Which two of these assignments are due first?

1. _____

2. _____

Analyze your assignments in this way to decide which ones to do first, so that you will have all assignments ready on time.

BE PREPARED FOR TESTS

Test grades figure prominently in deciding final course grades for almost all college courses; sometimes test grades are the sole basis for deciding final course grades. Those who receive one low test grade often receive low or failing course grades as a result, and students who are absent from tests are often given test grades of 0 or are required to take difficult make-up tests.

Chapter 2 explains how to schedule study time before tests, and Chapters 16–20 explain methods to use when studying for examinations.

EXERCISE 5

PREPARING FOR TESTS

List the courses you are taking and the days you will take the first test in each of them.

Course   Day of First Test

1. _____

2. _____

3. _____

4. _____

5. _____

6. _____

Will you use the suggestions in Chapter 2 and Chapters 16–20 to do your best when you study for these tests?

ATTEND CLASSES FAITHFULLY

These are some of the strategies used by successful students that have been discussed already in this chapter:

- Know teachers' requirements.
- Keep up to date with course work.
- Do assignments on time.
- Be prepared for tests.

To do these things, it is necessary to attend classes faithfully. Those who are absent do not learn about assignments, and sometimes they are not present when tests are announced. As a result of absence, they also often do not turn in assignments when they are due. And, most important, they miss class notes they need to prepare for tests (see Chapter 16, especially page 252).

College students are 100 percent responsible for everything that happens in classes, even when they are absent. In case you must be absent from a class:

- Deliver due homework to the instructor's mailbox as soon as possible.
- Contact a classmate to learn about assignments or tests announced in your absence.
- Hand copy or photocopy notes taken by a classmate while you were absent.

When you return to class, ask the instructor for suggestions about how you can catch up with the work you missed.

Do not ask an instructor "Did I miss anything?" The answer is yes. Also, do not tell a teacher that an absence is "excused" because of illness or a similar reason. "Excused" absences are noted at high schools but not at most colleges and universities. When a student is absent from a college class, it is assumed that the absence is unavoidable.

If an injury or illness makes it impossible for you to attend classes for an extended period, contact the health services office at your school. Someone in that office will notify your instructors why you are not attending classes. Your teachers may make special arrangements for you to catch up with course work; however, if they do not, you may need to withdraw from your courses (see page 40).

In addition to attending all classes, arrive on time. People who are constantly late tend to be individuals who are self-centered, disorganized, immature, inconsiderate, or hostile. If you are late more than once or twice to a class, your instructor and classmates will assume that you have one of these personality problems.

EXERCISE 6

HEALTH SERVICES OFFICE

Your college has an office that provides health services for students who become ill or are injured while on campus. This is also the office to call in case illness or injury prevents your attending class for an extended period.

1. Where is the health services office located?

   _____

2. What is the telephone number of this office?

   _____

You may need the telephone number in case serious illness or injury prevents you from attending classes.

INCREASE CONCENTRATION

Concentration[1] is the ability to focus thought and attention. Those who can concentrate for long periods learn more in less time and thus do their best in courses. The following suggestions provide help for increasing concentration.

Keep Records of Concentration

When you begin to study, make a note of the time. Then, when you detect that your thought and attention are not focused on studying, record the time again. Compare the two times and make a note of how many minutes you studied before you lost concentration.

Then, spend a few minutes doing something other than studying. You might stand up and stretch, look out the window, or drink some water. When you begin to study the next time, again make notes of how long you concentrate.

Continue in this way until you are satisfied with the length of time you are able to concentrate. Many students report that by keeping these kinds of records their span of concentration doubles or triples very quickly.

EXERCISE 7

KEEPING RECORDS OF CONCENTRATION

Use the procedure just explained for one week to keep records of how long you concentrate when you study.

1. On the average, how many minutes did you concentrate at the beginning of the week?

   _____

2. On the average, how many minutes did you concentrate at the end of the week?

   _____

If you are able to concentrate longer while studying some subjects than others, why do you believe this is so?

---

[1] Boldface terms in this text are defined in the glossary.

Do Routine Tasks First

Use the procedure in Exercise 4 (page 10) to decide which assignments to do first. Then, start a study session by doing what is most routine or easiest. If it is equally important to proofread a draft of a paper for an English course and to study for a chemistry test, proofread the draft first.

Another way to begin a study session is to review things you have studied previously. For instance, before trying to solve a new type of problem for a mathematics course, spend a few minutes solving a kind of problem you already know how to solve. You will provide yourself with review practice you need, and you are also likely to put yourself in the right frame of mind for learning how to solve the new type of problem.

EXERCISE 8

DOING ROUTINE TASKS FIRST

Begin study sessions by doing what is most routine or easiest.

1. In Exercise 4 on page 10 you listed two assignments that are due first. Which of them is the most routine or easiest to do?

    _____

2. For which of your courses might you begin study sessions by reviewing things you studied previously?

    _____

    _____

Do Large Tasks One Small Task at a Time

It is sometimes difficult to concentrate on a task that seems impossible to accomplish. For instance, the thought of reading and learning everything in a 600-page textbook can be overwhelming. However, reading a textbook, like any large task, is accomplished one step at a time. *RSVP* explains how to do the small study tasks that result in accomplishing the large ones. Also, if you use the methods for reading and studying that are explained in *RSVP*, your mind will be so busily engaged in doing what it should be doing that it will be less likely to wander.

Accept Difficult or Unpleasant Tasks

When the mind is focused on the thought that a task is difficult or unpleasant, it cannot concentrate on accomplishing the task. The thought "I don't want to do this difficult task" must be replaced with the thought "To achieve a worthwhile goal, I accept that I must do this and other difficult tasks."

All people who achieve important goals do difficult or unpleasant things they would not do *except* for the fact that they are intent on attaining their objectives. If your goal is to earn a college degree, you may have to do difficult and unpleasant things that you would not do *except* that you are determined to have the benefits of a college education. Each difficult or unpleasant task you accomplish will move you closer to achieving your goal.

EXERCISE 9

ACCEPTING DIFFICULT TASKS

List the most difficult or unpleasant tasks you must do this term.

1. _____

2. _____

3. _____

Is a college education important enough to you that you are willing to accept and do things that you would rather not do?

Reward Yourself for Studying

Concentration can be motivated by arranging a schedule so that study is rewarded by something pleasant to do. Before beginning to study, plan that after an hour or two you will telephone a friend, read a magazine, go jogging, or engage in some other pleasing activity. When studying on a Saturday afternoon, plan that in the evening you will visit with friends, go to a movie, or do something else that entertains you.

Study followed by a reward is usually productive. If you know that you have only three hours to study because you've scheduled some fun for yourself, you may be inspired to make the best use of the three hours that you have set aside for studying.

2. SCHEDULE STUDY TIME

Study in college requires more time than study in high school. In a typical term, college students read five, six, or more textbooks, complete a major project for each course, and take many tests. With a great deal to accomplish in the few weeks of a college term, they find it is essential to schedule time to get everything done. This chapter explains four steps for scheduling study time.

1. Decide how much to study.
2. Determine time available for study.
3. Decide what to study.
4. Decide when to study.

Figure 2.1 is an example of a study schedule. The hours crossed out in it are hours the student cannot study because she is in class, traveling, working, or engaging in other activities. Social activities and important things to do are written in the schedule and "Chem," "Hist," "Eng," and so on indicate the times she will study for specific courses. "Free" indicates the hours that she may use for additional studying or for leisure activities that are not already planned for in her schedule.

DECIDE HOW MUCH TO STUDY

Teachers often advise students that they should spend twice as much time studying outside of class as they spend in class. For instance, instructors of courses that meet for three hours each week frequently advise students to study for six hours each week outside of class. However, you are the only one who can decide how much time you will actually spend studying.

	SUN	MON	TUE	WED	THU	FRI	SAT
8–9	✕	Psych	Hist	Psych	Hist	Psych	Hist
9–10	✕	Chem	Hist	Chem	Hist	Chem	Hist
10–11	Chem	✕	✕	✕	✕	✕	Hist
11–12	Chem	✕	Eng	✕	✕	✕	Hist
12–1	↑	Buy pen, Time, card	✕	✕	✕	✕	✕
1–2	Biking with Ed	Eng	Math	Eng	Math	Eng	Chem
2–3		✕	Math	✕	Math	✕	Chem
3–4	↓	✕	✕	✕	✕	Eng	Chem
4–5	Call Mom and Dad	Math	Psych	Math	Psych	✕	Chem
5–6	↑	✕	(Free)	✕	(Free)	✕	✕
6–7	Laundry ↓	✕	(Free)	✕	(Free)	✕	✕
7–8	✕	✕	✕	✕	✕	✕	(Free)
8–9	Math	(Free)	Hist	↑	Chem	(Free)	(Free)
9–10	Eng	(Free)	Hist	Concert	Chem	(Free)	(Free)
10–11	✕	✕	✕	↓	✕	(Free)	(Free)

FIGURE 2.1

A study schedule

EXERCISE 1

DECIDING HOW MUCH TO STUDY

On the following lines, list the courses you are taking, the grade you want to receive for each course, and the number of hours you will need to study each week in order to earn the grade you want.

	Grade I Want	Weekly Study Hours
Course		

1. _____

2. _____

3. _____

4. _____

5. _____

6. _____

                                        Total weekly study hours _____

Find the total hours you need to study each week by adding the number of hours you need to study for each course.

DETERMINE TIME AVAILABLE FOR STUDY

To determine how much time is available for study, it is necessary to maintain a calendar of social activities and a list of chores and other things that need to be done. The student who prepared the calendar in Figure 2.2 cannot study on Wednesday evening during the week of October 8–14, although Wednesday evening is available for her to study during other weeks. Following is a list of "Things to do" the student prepared on October 8.

Things to do

Call mom and dad

Do the laundry

Buy a pen

Buy *Time* magazine (history)

Buy a birthday card for Ben

The student noted in her study schedule (Figure 2.1) the times she would do the things in this list and her social events for the week of October 8–14.

Maintain a calendar of the type shown in Figure 2.2 and a list of "Things to do" so that you can include your social activities and chores in your study schedules.

FIGURE 2.2

A calendar of social and other activities

OCTOBER

Sun.	Mon.	Tue.	Wed.	Thu.	Fri.	Sat.
1	2	3 Joe and Sara 5PM	4	5	6	7 Dance 9PM
8 Biking with Ed 12–4	9	10	11 Concert 8PM	12	13	14
15	16	17	18 History Paper	19	20	21
22	23	24	25	26 Chem test	27 Movie 7PM	28 Biking with Ed 12–4
29 Dinner with Ed 7PM	30	31				

It is also necessary to plan time for:

- Sleeping
- Eating meals
- Exercising
- Traveling
- Working
- Attending classes
- Dressing and grooming
- Socializing and dating
- Attending meetings
- Fulfilling household responsibilities
- Relaxing (watching television, and so forth)

Allow sufficient time for exercise and relaxation; they are essential for your enjoyment of life and your physical and mental well-being.

EXERCISE 2

DETERMINING TIME AVAILABLE FOR STUDY

Record in a calendar information of the type that is illustrated in Figure 2.2 and prepare a list of "Things to do." Then, do the following for the *next* school week.

1. Write in Figure 2.3 the times you will do things in your calendar or accomplish activities on your list of "Things to do."

2. Cross out in Figure 2.3 the times next week you cannot study because you are attending class, eating, sleeping, working, and so forth.

3. Count the hours that have nothing written in them and that are not crossed out—they are hours you can study. Write the number on the following line.

_____

4. Do you have available next week more or fewer hours than you decided you need for studying in Exercise 1?

_____

If you have fewer hours than you need for studying, figure out how you can make more time available or consider whether you overestimated the number of hours you need for studying when you did Exercise 1.

	SUN	MON	TUE	WED	THU	FRI	SAT
8–9							
9–10							
10–11							
11–12							
12–1							
1–2							
2–3							
3–4							
4–5							
5–6							
6–7							
7–8							
8–9							
9–10							
10–11							

FIGURE 2.3

A form for a study
schedule

DECIDE WHAT TO STUDY

When you know the hours that are available for studying, prepare a list of assignments and tests. Analyze your list to decide what to study first. The following list was prepared by the student who is used as an example in this chapter.

October 8-14

History paper due October 18

Chemistry test October 26

Read history chapters 11-12

Chemistry assignments (Mon, Wed, Fri)

Read psychology chapters 7-8

English assignments (Mon and Fri)

Math assignments (Mon, Tue, Wed, Thu)

When the student analyzed this list, she decided the assignments due Monday for her chemistry, English, and mathematics courses should be done first. She also scheduled in Figure 2.1 time for reading in history and psychology; working on her history paper, due October 18; and studying for a chemistry test scheduled for October 26.

EXERCISE 3

DECIDING WHAT TO STUDY

On a sheet of notebook paper, list the assignments you must do next week and papers you must write or tests you must take during the next three weeks. Analyze the list to arrange the items on the lines below in the order in which they need to be done.

© 1984 by Houghton Mifflin Company

Assignment   Date Due

1. _____

2. _____

3. _____

4. _____

5. _____

6. _____

7. _____

8. _____

Use this method to help in deciding the days and times you will study for each course.

DECIDE WHEN TO STUDY

The hours not already used in Figure 2.3 are hours you can study next week. Refer to the list you wrote in Exercise 3 and consider the following suggestions to decide when you will study for each of your courses.

- A free period immediately before a class is the best time to study about the lecture topic for the class (see Chapter 16, especially page 249).
- A free period immediately after a class is the best time to review notes taken during the class (see Chapter 16, especially page 254).
- A brief period of less than an hour is good for reciting or reviewing information (see Chapter 20, especially pages 286–289).
- A long period of an hour or more is good for doing challenging activities such as learning to solve a new type of chemical equation or writing the draft of a paper.
- Free periods just before sleep are good times for learning information; there is evidence that information learned just before sleep is remembered longer than information learned at other times.
- Schedule something enjoyable to do following study sessions (see page 15).

It is necessary to revise study schedules often to accommodate changing school, social, and other obligations. Also, some weeks have holidays that afford uninterrupted periods of time for working on major projects and preparing for examinations.

EXERCISE 4

DECIDING WHEN TO STUDY

Referring to the list you prepared when you did Exercise 3 and the suggestions in this section, enter in Figure 2.3 the times you will study for each of your courses next week.

1. For which course will you spend the most time studying?

   _____

2. For which course will you spend the least time studying?

   _____

Additional forms for study schedules are provided at the back of the book.

PLAN AHEAD FOR TESTS

Advanced planning is necessary to be properly prepared for tests. Before mid-term and final examinations, make a two- or three-week study schedule rather than a one-week schedule.

In scheduling time to study for tests, keep in mind that information learned just before sleep is likely to be remembered longer than information learned at other times. Also, schedule time for sufficient exercise, relaxation, and sleep; you will learn more efficiently and do better when you take tests if you are in good physical condition.

EXERCISE 5

PLANNING AHEAD FOR TESTS

Make a form of the type illustrated in Figure 2.4 and use the suggestions in this chapter to schedule study time during the three weeks before mid-term or final examinations.

A form of the type shown in Figure 2.4 may be made on a page that measures 11 by 17 inches, created by joining two pieces of 8½-by-11-inch paper with tape along their 11-inch edges. Make the vertical columns for days ¾ inch wide and draw the horizontal lines for hours ½ inch apart.

FIGURE 2.4

Format for a three-week
study schedule

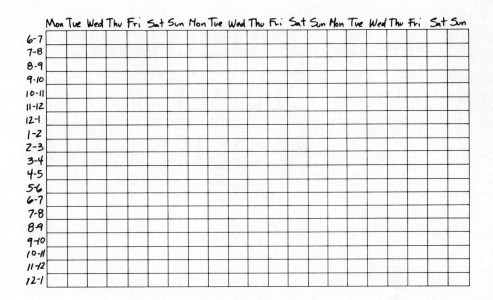

If you schedule your time using the suggestions in this chapter, you
will be better prepared when you take tests and you will enjoy life more
because you will plan for pleasurable activities in your life rather than
simply hoping that they will happen by chance.

3. UNDERSTAND
DEGREE
REQUIREMENTS

This chapter explains how to learn about the degree requirements and grading practices at your college or university.

DEGREES AND CURRICULUMS

Degrees are ranks awarded by colleges for the successful completion of specified requirements. The most common degrees are the associate degree and the bachelor's degree. **Associate degrees** are usually offered by two-year and community colleges. They are most commonly the A.A. (Associate of Arts), the A.S. (Associate of Science), and the A.A.S. (Associate of Applied Science). **Bachelor's degrees** are offered by four-year colleges and universities. They are usually the B.A. (Bachelor of Arts) and the B.S. (Bachelor of Science). Some colleges and universities also offer **master's degrees** and **doctoral degrees** for advanced study.

Degrees are awarded for the satisfactory completion of courses and other requirements of a **curriculum**, or program of study. Following is the program for the first semester of a premedical curriculum:

	Credits
English Composition I (EN-101)	3
Mathematics (MA-441)	4
General Biology (BI-201)	4
General Chemistry (CH-151)	4
Physical Education *or* Dance	1
	16

Information about curriculums is usually printed in **catalogues**—booklets in which colleges publish admission requirements, course descriptions, and other important information.

EXERCISE 1

YOUR CURRICULUM

Study your catalogue for the answers to the following questions. Information about curriculums may be listed under a heading such as "Curriculums," "Programs of Study," or "Degree Programs."

1. For what degree are you now studying?

_____

2. In what curriculum, or program of study, are you now enrolled?

_____

3. On what pages in the catalogue are the requirements of your curriculum stated?

_____

If your curriculum is not in the catalogue, secure it from a counselor or adviser. It is essential for you to know the requirements of your degree program.

PREREQUISITES

A **prerequisite** is a requirement that must be completed satisfactorily before enrolling in a course. For instance, the prerequisite for Intermediate Algebra may be Beginning Algebra or one year of algebra study in a high school. It is essential for you to know the prerequisites for courses in your curriculum so that you will take courses in the correct sequence and not be delayed in graduating from college.

Students are usually required to drop courses for which they enroll without having satisfied prerequisites. In dropping a course, the total number of credits in a program is sometimes reduced to fewer than is needed for full-time student status. In losing full-time status, students also often lose important benefits such as financial aid or the privilege of playing varsity athletics. It is unwise to enroll in a course without having first completed the prerequisites for it.

EXERCISE 2

YOUR PREREQUISITES

Answer the following questions by studying in your catalogue the prerequisites for courses in your curriculum.

1. List the courses you are taking this term that are prerequisites for courses you will take in the future.

_____

_____

_____

2. List two courses you could take next term that are prerequisites for courses you will take in the future.

_____

_____

CREDITS AND HOURS

Credits and hours are assigned to most college courses. **Credits** are units given for the satisfactory completion of study that applies toward a degree. **Hours** are units that designate time spent in classrooms, laboratories, or conferences—they may be shorter or longer than sixty minutes. For example, upon satisfactorily completing a three-credit, four-hour English composition course students earn three credits toward their degrees. However, it is a _four_-hour course because each week they spend _three_ hours in class and _one_ hour in conference with their composition teachers.

EXERCISE 3

ACADEMIC CREDITS

The answers to the first three questions should be in your catalogue.

1. How many credits are required in your curriculum?

_____

2. What is the minimum number of credits for which you must register to be classified as a full-time student?

_____

3. What is the maximum number of credits for which you may register during a term without receiving special permission?

_____

4. How many credits are you attempting to complete this term?

_____

LETTER AND NUMBER GRADES

Instructors evaluate papers, tests, and other student work using letter or number grades. Figure 3.1 shows the correspondences between letter grades and number grades used at many schools. Notice, for example, in Figure 3.1 that the **letter grade** of B+ corresponds to a **number grade** of 87, 88, or 89. Study your catalogue to learn the correspondences between letter grades and number grades at your school. There are sometimes

FIGURE 3.1

The usual correspondences between number grades and letter grades

Letter Grades	Meanings	Number Grades
A	Excellent	96–100
A–		90–95
B+		87–89
B	Good	84–86
B–		80–83
C+		77–79
C	Satisfactory	74–76
C–		70–73
D+		67–69
D		64–66
D–	Passing	60–63
F	Failing	0–59

important differences among colleges. For instance, some schools offer the letter grade of A+ and do not offer D−.

Knowledge of how letter grades correspond to number grades can be used to estimate final course grades. For example, a student who receives the number grades of 82, 86, and 72 in a course may estimate a final course grade of B− because the average of these numbers is 80 (see Figure 3.1). However, teachers often double the value of final examination grades. For example, if a student has grades of 82 and 86 and a final examination grade of 72, the 72 is doubled (144) and added to the 82 and 86. The resulting sum (312) is then divided by 4 (rather than 3) to find the average. In this case, the average is 78, not 80, and the course grade is C+, not B− (see Figure 3.1).

EXERCISE 4

LETTER AND NUMBER GRADES

Study your catalogue to learn the correspondences between letter grades and number grades at your school. Then, write the letter grades that correspond to the following number grades.

1. 86 _____   2. 70 _____

3. 77 _____   4. 63 _____

5. 74 _____   6. 59 _____

7. 66 _____   8. 84 _____

9. 90 _____   10. 79 _____

11. 83 _____   12. 64 _____

13. 67 _____   14. 80 _____

15. 89 _____   16. 76 _____

17. 73 _____   18. 69 _____

19. 60 _____   20. 87 _____

MINIMUM GRADE REQUIREMENTS

Most colleges compute students' average grades using the **grade point average,** or **GPA,** which is a number that ranges from 0.00 to 4.00.

Following final examinations, instructors submit letter grades to the **registrar** who enters them on students' **transcripts** and assigns numerical values to them for the purpose of computing GPAs.

Figure 3.2 shows two widely used methods for assigning **GPA values** to letter grades. Notice in Figure 3.2 that when System 1 is used, letter grades have the same value whether they are accompanied by a plus or a minus (for example, C+, C, and C− all have a value of 2.00). But when System 2 is used, letter grades have larger values when they are accompanied by a plus and smaller values when they are accompanied by a minus (for example, C has a value of 2.00, but C+ has a value of 2.30 and C− has a value of 1.70).

Some first-year college students believe incorrectly that they do well when they receive passing grades for courses. However, since most colleges require a minimum GPA of 2.00 for graduation, students who have many passing grades of D (1.00) usually do not have GPAs high enough to earn a degree.

FIGURE 3.2

Two systems for assigning GPA values to letter grades

| | | GPA Values | |
Letter Grades	Meanings	System 1	System 2
A	Excellent	4.00	4.00
A−		4.00	3.70
B+		3.00	3.30
B	Good	3.00	3.00
B−		3.00	2.70
C+		2.00	2.30
C	Satisfactory	2.00	2.00
C−		2.00	1.70
D+		1.00	1.30
D		1.00	1.00
D−	Passing	1.00	0.70
F	Failing	0.00	0.00

EXERCISE 5

THE GRADING SYSTEM

Study your catalogue to find the answers to the following questions.

1. Write the GPA values for the following letter grades.

   a. C _____   b. D   _____

   c. B+ _____   d. D+ _____

   e. A _____   f. C− _____

   g. C+ _____   h. F   _____

   i. D− _____   j. A− _____

   k. B− _____   l. B   _____

2. What is the minimum GPA required for graduation?

   _____

3. A college may have minimum requirements for specified courses. For instance, many schools require students to earn grades of at least C (2.00) for courses in their major subjects. If your school has minimum grade requirements for specified courses, state them below.

   _____

   _____

4. Most schools have a lower GPA requirement for the first term or two of study and a higher one for subsequent terms. For instance, students may be required to have GPAs of at least 1.75 until they complete 18 credits but GPAs of at least 2.00 thereafter. If your school has such a policy, describe it below.

   _____

   _____

   _____

   _____

5. Is there any grade other than F that has a value of 0.00 for the purpose of computing the GPA? If so, what is the grade?

_____

The answers to these questions summarize very important information. Many students are forced to drop out of college because they do not know the answers to these questions or understand their importance.

COMPUTATION OF THE GPA

Figure 3.3 illustrates the procedures for computing a grade point average.

1. Assign GPA values to letter grades.
2. Multiply GPA values by credits.
3. Add credits and add grade points to find totals.
4. Divide total grade points by total credits.

FIGURE 3.3

Computation of the GPA using System 1 and System 2

				System 1			
Letter Grades		Credits			GPA Values		Grade Points
A		3	×		4.00	=	12.00
B−		6	×		3.00	=	18.00
C−		6	×		2.00	=	12.00
		15					42.00

$$\frac{42.00}{15} = 2.80 \text{ GPA}$$

				System 2			
Letter Grades		Credits			GPA Values		GPA Points
A		3	×		4.00	=	12.00
B−		6	×		2.70	=	16.20
C−		6	×		1.70	=	10.20
		15					38.40

$$\frac{38.40}{15} = 2.56 \text{ GPA}$$

Notice in Figure 3.3 that the GPA is 2.80 when System 1 is used, but it is 2.56 when System 2 is used. System 2 renders a lower GPA because under this system minus grades have lower values (see Figure 3.2).

The GPA works to the advantage of students who earn good grades and to the disadvantage of those who earn poor grades. Students who have GPAs in the 2.50–3.50 range can receive a D, D+, or C− in one or two courses and still have good averages. On the other hand, students who have GPAs less than 2.00, usually find it extremely difficult to raise their averages. For instance, students who complete fifteen credits in their first terms with GPAs of 1.65 must have GPAs of at least 2.35 for fifteen credits in their second terms to bring the GPAs up to 2.00. Unfortunately, students who have D+ averages in their first terms seldom have C+ averages in their second terms.

Credits students earn for courses have no value toward earning a degree unless their grade point averages satisfy minimum requirements.

EXERCISE 6

COMPUTING THE GPA

Study your catalogue to learn how GPAs are computed at your school and use the method to compute GPAs for the following problems. If you own a calculator, use it.

1.

Letter Grades	Credits		GPA Values		Grade Points
A	12	×		=	
B	8	×		=	
C	15	×		=	

GPA = _____

2.

Letter Grades	Credits		GPA Values		Grade Points
B	10	×		=	
C	6	×		=	
D	2	×		=	

GPA = _____

3.

Letter Grades	Credits		GPA Values		Grade Points
B	6	×		=	
C	6	×		=	
D	6	×		=	
F	3	×		=	

GPA = _____

4.

Letter Grades	Credits		GPA Values		Grade Points
B	6	×		=	
C	7	×		=	
D	4	×		=	_____

GPA = _____

5.

Letter Grades	Credits		GPA Values		Grade Points
B+	5	×		=	
C	4	×		=	
C−	6	×		=	_____

GPA = _____

4. FIND
HELP
FOR
PROBLEMS

Most students have difficulty with a course at some time during their college careers. This chapter explains sources of help when academic problems arise.

USE *RSVP*

If you have a problem with a course, first determine whether there are suggestions in *RSVP* that may help you solve it. The table of contents provides an overview of the topics in this book and the index is a complete listing of the page numbers on which specific topics are discussed.

EXERCISE 1

USING *RSVP*

Consult the table of contents at the beginning of the book to answer the following questions.

1. What chapters explain how to read textbooks with better understanding?

_____

2. What chapter explains how to take class notes?

_____

3. What chapter explains how to decide what to study for tests?

_____

4. What chapter explains how to recite and learn information for tests?

_____

5. What chapter explains how to answer multiple-choice questions?

_____

6. What chapter explains how to answer essay test questions?

_____

The method for writing research papers is explained in English handbooks; they are available in libraries and bookstores in case you do not own one.

TALK WITH HELPFUL PERSONS

Teachers, counselors, advisers, and other students are sources of help when academic difficulties arise.

Teachers can sometimes offer solutions that do not occur to students. A young woman who lived off campus with her family was unable to concentrate during her nine o'clock class because she argued with her mother each morning at breakfast—she was failing the course. When she explained the problem to her instructor, he invited her to attend another **section** of the same course he taught later in the day. With the change of class hour, she did well in the course.

Teachers, counselors, and advisers also usually know if there are study groups, **tutors,** or other sources of help available. If they do not, they can suggest where to look further for help. They may advise visiting the office of the department that offers the problem course. Or they may suggest visiting an office of academic skills, a learning center, a tutorial service, or some other department or service on campus.

Also, and very important, students who have already taken a course in which you are having difficulty may sometimes be your best source of help—they have already solved problems you are having. Make friends with second-, third-, and fourth-year students who are enrolled in your curriculum and who will give you suggestions on how to study for courses they have already taken.

EXERCISE 2

TALKING WITH HELPFUL PERSONS

Seek the help of faculty, staff, and other students in case you have academic problems.

1. How many courses are you taking?

   _____

2. Of these courses, how many have teachers with whom you would talk if you have difficulty in their course?

   _____

3. List the names of two counselors or advisers with whom you would talk if you have difficulty with a course.

   _____   _____

4. List the names of four second-, third-, or fourth-year students enrolled in your curriculum from whom you would seek help if you have difficulty with a course.

   _____   _____

   _____   _____

USE COURSE GUIDES OR OUTLINES

When a textbook is difficult to understand, it is sometimes necessary to locate another book on the same subject that is easier to read. The book is likely to be a course guide or course outline.

Course guides and **course outlines** are paperback books that summarize the information taught in college courses. There are at least two or three course guides or outlines available in bookstores for most popular college subjects.

Select a guide or outline by comparing its table of contents to the table of contents of the textbook you are using—they will not be identical, but they should be similar. Then, read a portion of it that corresponds to information you find difficult to understand in the textbook. After examining the available guides and outlines in this way, purchase the one that is most understandable and useful.

Some teachers object when students use guides or outlines; however, there is no good reason for a teacher to object when students make an effort to learn things they want or need to know.

EXERCISE 3

FINDING COURSE GUIDES AND OUTLINES

Visit a bookstore to find a course guide or outline for two courses you are taking. Write their titles on the following lines.

1. _____

2. _____

IMPROVE LEARNING SKILLS

Very few people read, write, and solve mathematical problems as well as they are able. As a result, colleges test students to decide whether they should receive special reading, writing, or mathematics instruction. Take full advantage of learning skills instruction that is offered to you— it is provided to help you earn good grades and a degree.

EXERCISE 4

IMPROVING LEARNING SKILLS

List any types of learning skills instruction that you have been advised or required to receive.

1. _____

2. _____

3. _____

Are you receiving, or will you receive, this instruction at the times you are advised or required to receive it?

_____

If your answer to this question is no, you may encounter problems. Many of the students who have academic difficulties are the ones who do not receive learning skills instruction at the times they are supposed to.

USE W OR INC GRADES

When an academic problem cannot be solved in any other way, it may be necessary to request a withdrawal grade or an incomplete grade.

The **withdrawal grade,** or **W,** is for students who must leave school or who must drop a course that is giving them serious difficulty. It is usually not used to compute grade point averages; thus, it usually does not raise or lower GPAs. However, there are strict limitations on the time period during which a W grade may be requested.

It is advisable to request a W grade when a final course grade is likely to be F. Also, it is usually wiser to request a W than to accept a low grade, such as D. A grade of D is acceptable only for an extremely difficult course that is not in your major.

The **incomplete grade,** or **INC,** is for students who did satisfactory work in a course but who have not completed a term paper or other important project. For instance, when a student has done satisfactorily on all tests for a course but has not written a required report, a teacher may give an INC rather than a grade such as C or D. When the report is completed, the INC grade is changed to a B, C, D, or some other letter grade.

However, there are deadlines after which past-due work is not accepted. At most schools, when work is not turned in by deadlines, INC grades are automatically changed to Fs. It is much better to keep up to date with course work than to request an INC grade and run the risk of having it changed to an F.

EXERCISE 5

USING W OR INC GRADES

Find the answers to the following questions in your catalogue.

1. What is the last day this term to request a W grade?

   _____

2. What is the deadline for completing past-due work for INC grades students receive at the end of this term?

   _____

3. What will happen to INC grades when past-due work is not completed by the deadline?

_____

_____

II. IMPROVE VOCABULARY

There are more than 500,000 English words, but it is estimated that average well-educated Americans make practical use of fewer than 30,000 of them. Thus, as you pursue college study, you may expect that any one of more than 470,000 words that are unfamiliar to you may suddenly appear in books, articles, and other materials you read. You must be able to identify quickly and accurately the meanings of most of these words so that you can understand fully what you read.

This part of *RSVP* explains three methods for determining the meanings of unfamiliar words. Chapter 5 explains how to find, or figure out, word meanings by studying other words printed in the sentences or paragraphs that contain unfamiliar words. In Chapter 6 you will learn how to determine word meanings by analyzing them to locate familiar base words, prefixes, and other word elements. Methods for locating definitions and other information about words in standard desk dictionaries are explained in Chapter 7.

You will also learn when you read Chapter 8 how to undertake a systematic program for increasing the words in your vocabulary.

5. STUDY CONTEXT

A **context** is a sentence, paragraph, or longer unit of writing that surrounds a word and determines its meaning. For example, *depression* sometimes refers to sadness and dejection, but the context of the following sentence determines another meaning for the word.

Unemployment was very high during the *depression* of the 1930s.

This context determines that *depression* refers to a period of economic decline.

Words unfamiliar to you may often have meanings stated in or suggested by context. This chapter explains how to use context to locate or infer word meanings, so that you will have less need to use a dictionary when you read.

STATED WORD MEANINGS

When the meaning of a word is stated in context, it can be located and underlined. Underline the meaning of the italicized term that is stated in the following sentence.

Your *receptive vocabulary* is the words you know when you read or listen.

You should have drawn a line under the last eight words in the sentence.

Word meanings are often set off in sentences using punctuation such as parentheses, commas, or dashes. Underline the meanings of *progeny*, *tactile sense*, and *plagiarize* that are set off by punctuation in the following sentences.

The *progeny* (offspring) of one insect can number in the thousands, but most of them do not survive for long.

The masterpieces of great painters stimulate the *tactile sense*, or sense of touch; they may appear to be rough, slippery, or soft.

When you write papers for your college courses, take care that you do not *plagiarize*—present the words or ideas of others as though they are your own.

You should have underlined "offspring," "sense of touch," and "present the words or ideas of others as though they are your own." They are the meanings of *progeny*, *tactile sense*, and *plagiarize*, respectively.

EXERCISE 1

STATED MEANINGS

Underline the meanings of the boldface words stated in the contexts of the following sentences.

1. Some people are **gullible**—easily cheated or tricked because they believe everything that others say.

2. Erika does many things well; she is an extremely **versatile** young woman.

3. Those who want careers as actors must be **tenacious**—persistent and stubbornly determined to succeed.

4. Study for tests by reciting to yourself; it is **futile** (useless or ineffective) to try to learn information by reading it over and over.

5. Some shoppers forgive, or overlook, poor service in stores, but others do not **condone** it.

6. When the going gets tough, the tough get going; they continue in spite of difficulty—they **persevere.**

7. I **perceive** that you are displeased with me; I am very much aware that I have made you unhappy for some reason.

8. The notion that it is sophisticated to smoke is **passé**—it's as old-fashioned and out-of-date as greasy hair.

9. He is confident that his rudeness will not **impede** (hinder) his success at work.

10. Please **obliterate,** or erase, from your mind all worry that you may fail.

11. If I say, "Please call me Jim," it is **explicit** (or clearly stated) that I want you to call me Jim.

12. However, if I introduce myself to you as "Jim," it is **implicit**—suggested, though not directly stated—that I want you to call me "Jim."

13. Standard desk dictionaries are **comprehensive,** or all inclusive, lists of commonly used words and their meanings.

14. Our thoughts are **covert**—concealed, or hidden from others—until we share them.

15. Those who have **contempt** for others often have a total lack of respect for themselves as well.

16. The doctor's **prognosis** (prediction about recovery) is that Luis will be strong enough to return to work in two weeks.

EXERCISE 2

STATED MEANINGS

Underline the meanings of the boldface words that are stated in the following excerpts from English, business, and sociology textbooks.

1. The most familiar use of words is to name things—trees, cars, games, people, stars, oceans. When words are used in this way, the things they refer to are called their **denotations.** The word *chair* most commonly denotes a piece of furniture for sitting on. The denotation of *Detroit* is the city of that name.

2. But words acquire **connotations** as well as denotations. Connotations are attitudes that we associate with particular words. When we call an action "courageous" or "foolhardy," we are not only describing it; we are expressing, and inviting a reader to share, an attitude toward it.

3. The writing is almost completely **subjective**—that is, it deals chiefly with how the writer *feels* about the movie.

4. A **fallacy** is an error in the reasoning process that makes an argument unreliable.

5. In hunting, a strongly scented object drawn across a trail will distract hounds and cause them to follow the new scent. In rhetoric, a **red herring** is a false issue used to lead attention away from the real one.

6. A **stereotype** is a standardized mental image that pays too much attention to characteristics supposedly common to a group and not enough to individual differences.

7. The basic use of an **ellipsis** (. . .) is to mark the omission of one or more words from a quotation.

8. There are two different categories of rewards. **Extrinsic** rewards are payoffs granted to the individual by other people. Examples include money, fringe benefits, promotions, recognition, status symbols, and praise.

9. The second category is called **intrinsic** rewards, which are self-granted and internally experienced payoffs. Among intrinsic rewards are a sense of accomplishment and feelings of achievement, self-esteem, and self-actualization.

10. One of the fundamental principles of good listening is listening with **empathy,** that is, understanding what is being said from the speaker's point of view.

11. As children grow older they spend more and more time in the company of their **peers**—equals of roughly the same age, background, and interests.

12. The reason for these and countless other patterns of social behavior is that they are controlled by social **norms**—shared rules or guidelines which prescribe the behavior that is appropriate in a given situation.

13. The word "alienation" has come into popular usage as a catch-all term for a variety of psychological ills, so we must define its sociological meaning closely. Essentially, **alienation** refers to the sense of powerlessness, isolation, and meaninglessness experienced by human beings when they are confronted with social institutions and conditions that they cannot control and consider oppressive.

14. Mead emphasized that the mind is a social product; and, indeed, one of the most important achievements of socialization is the development of **cognitive** abilities—intellectual capacities such as perceiving, remembering, reasoning, calculating, believing.

15. Every known society has had an **incest** taboo that prohibits sexual relations between specific categories of relatives. The taboo almost always applies to relations between parent and child and between brother and sister, and it always applies to other classes of relatives as well, although different societies have different rules in this regard.

16. All norms, whether they are codified in law or not, are supported by **sanctions,** rewards for conformity and punishments for nonconformity. The positive sanctions may range from an approving nod to a ceremony of public acclaim; the negative sanctions may range from mild disapproval to imprisonment or even execution.

EXERCISE 3

STATED MEANINGS

Underline the meanings of the boldface words that are stated in the following excerpts from science textbooks.

1. Two disciplines in biology—**nomenclature,** the system of names in
2. a field of knowledge, and **taxonomy,** the study of the classification of properly named organisms—are interdependent.

3. Thus, enzymes are organic **catalysts.** (A catalyst is a substance that hastens the rate of a chemical reaction without being used up in that reaction.)

4. Some of the adverse side effects in this type of therapy are **phlebitis**—
5. vein inflamation—and certain types of **anemia,** or reduction in numbers of blood cells.

6. Both Pasteur and Koch, working independently, discovered that pathogens that had been either killed or **attenuated** (rendered less capable of causing a disease) could sometimes be used to produce some
7. degree of **immunity** (resistance) to that disease.

8. **Lymphoid tissues** are aggregations of specialized connective tissue cells that function mainly to remove foreign substances from the lymph, or tissue of the body.

9. Symptoms of an allergic reaction to poison oak include localized redness and watery blistering of the skin, a condition known as **eczema.**

10. It is somewhat difficult to distinguish between **rubella** (German measles) and rubeola.

11. The **cochlea,** which is the organ of hearing, occupies the innermost portion of the inner ear.

12. The entire living world is a complex interwoven pattern of relationships in which organisms affect each other and in which each organism is affected by the chemical and physical components of its environment. The study of these complex interrelationships is called **ecology.**

13. Both chemical and physical components constitute the "ground" factors that enable the **biotic** components, or living organisms, to grow.

14. **Carriers** are people who harbor disease organisms in their bodies, sometimes permanently, but have not had the actual disease.

15. This creates a molecule that is **bipolar** (that is, it has two poles, one positive and the other negative).

16. Many of the pollutants emitted by automobile exhaust and industrial processes are **carcinogenic** (cancer-producing).

IMPLIED WORD MEANINGS

When the meaning of a word is not stated in context, it may be **implied**—that is, suggested or hinted. When a word meaning is implied, it may be inferred. To **infer** is to use reasoning for the purpose of arriving at a conclusion or decision.

A word meaning may be implied by the general sense of a context, as is the meaning of *incarcerated* in the following sentence.

Murderers are usually *incarcerated* for longer periods of time than robbers.

The meaning of *incarcerated* may be inferred by asking the following question:

What usually happens to those found guilty of murder and robbery?

Write your answer on the following line:

_____

If you wrote words to the effect that they are locked up in a jail, prison, or penitentiary, you inferred the meaning of *incarcerated*.

In the following sentence, the meaning of *gregarious* is suggested by examples:

Those who enjoy belonging to clubs, going to parties, and inviting friends to their homes for dinner are *gregarious*.

The meaning of *gregarious* may be inferred by answering the following question:

What word or words describe people who enjoy belonging to clubs, going to parties, and inviting friends to their homes for dinner?

Write your answer on the following line:

_____

If you wrote "social" or words such as "people who enjoy the company of others," you inferred the meaning of *gregarious*.

A contrast in the following sentence implies the meaning of *credence*.

Dad gave *credence* to my story, but Mom's reaction was one of total disbelief.

The meaning of *credence* may be inferred by answering the following question:

If Mom's reaction was disbelief but Dad's reaction was very different from Mom's, what was Dad's reaction?

Write your answer on the following line:

_____

If you wrote words to the effect that Dad believed the story, you inferred the meaning of *credence*; it means the opposite of disbelief—belief.

EXERCISE 4

IMPLIED MEANINGS

First, test your knowledge of the words in the sixteen multiple-choice questions by circling the letter in front of the correct meaning of each word. Second, infer the meanings of the words you do not know by studying the sentences that follow the questions. Third, write the correct answers on the lines provided.

_____ 1. zenith
    a. trust
    b. peak
    c. perfection
    d. excellence

_____ 2. procrastinate
    a. compute
    b. complain
    c. delay
    d. question

_____ 3. divulge
   a. vomit
   b. squeeze
   c. tell
   d. reply

_____ 4. negligible
   a. small
   b. alluring
   c. complicated
   d. undisputed

_____ 5. infamous
   a. unfamiliar
   b. insightful
   c. detestable
   d. lackluster

_____ 6. convene
   a. break up
   b. get together
   c. proceed
   d. retreat

_____ 7. deterrent
   a. prevention
   b. extermination
   c. duplication
   d. intervention

_____ 8. inadvertent
   a. cowardly
   b. effective
   c. unadvertised
   d. unintentional

_____ 9. deteriorating
   a. persistent
   b. worsening
   c. unhealthful
   d. unessential

_____ 10. curtail
   a. erase
   b. engage
   c. discontinue
   d. decrease

_____ 11. gist
   a. trust
   b. heart
   c. comfort
   d. equality

_____ 12. obligatory
   a. required
   b. disclosed
   c. effective
   d. fashionable

_____ 13. ostentatious
   a. many-sided
   b. ornamented
   c. showy
   d. influential

_____ 14. mortified
   a. concise
   b. mistaken
   c. frightened
   d. embarrassed

_____ 15. fiasco
   a. failure
   b. paradox
   c. fashion
   d. contradiction

_____ 16. fallible
   a. believing
   b. disbelieving
   c. may be correct
   d. may be mistaken

1. At the **zenith** of her career, she was starring in four motion pictures each year.

2. If there is something you must do that you can do today, do it today— don't **procrastinate.**

3. It is usually best not to **divulge** the unhappy moments of one's childhood to acquaintances at work.

4. His work gives him great satisfaction, but the financial rewards he receives are **negligible.**

5. In all of history there is no name more **infamous** than that of Adolf Hitler.

6. Our next student council meeting will **convene** two weeks from today, on November 18 at two o'clock.

7. Audits by the Internal Revenue Service are a **deterrent** to cheating when reporting taxable income.

8. The error was **inadvertent**; they did not intend to overcharge us.

9. The subway system in New York City is **deteriorating**; it is dirtier, less reliable, and more crime-ridden than ever before.

10. Eating in restaurants became so expensive that we had to **curtail** dining out from once a week to once a month.

11. The **gist** of etiquette is "Treat others kindly—make them feel comfortable."

12. He doesn't need to study chemistry, but it is **obligatory** for him to take a natural science to earn a degree.

13. Jack and Jill are incredibly **ostentatious**—they used fine silver, china, and crystal at a picnic on the beach.

14. Bart was **mortified** when his friends learned that he was failing most of his college courses.

15. Only a few of the many new businesses started each year are successes—most are **fiascos.**

16. Some of us expect physicians to be always correct, forgetting that they, like us, are **fallible.**

EXERCISE 5

IMPLIED MEANINGS

First, test your knowledge of the words in the sixteen multiple-choice questions by circling the letter in front of the correct meaning of each word. Second, infer the meanings of the words you do not know by studying the excerpts from an English and business textbook that follow the questions. Third, write the correct answers on the lines provided.

_____ 1. virtue
  a. merit
  b. truth
  c. reality
  d. existence

_____ 2. allusion
  a. prediction
  b. contradiction
  c. indirect mention
  d. invisible object

_____ 3. conception
  a. plan for change
  b. start of pregnancy
  c. fact clarification
  d. deceptive action

_____ 4. pertinent
  a. relevant
  b. irrelevant
  c. respectful
  d. disrespectful

_____ 5. superficial
  a. unrelated
  b. exaggerated
  c. powerless
  d. shallow

_____ 6. suppress
  a. push up
  b. hold back
  c. make bad
  d. turn down

_____ 7. delete
  a. stymie
  b. censure
  c. eliminate
  d. excuse

_____ 8. devastating
  a. confusing
  b. repulsive
  c. embarrassing
  d. destructive

_____ 9. amass
  a. accomplish
  b. accumulate
  c. accustom
  d. accredit

_____ 10. competence
  a. confidence
  b. ability
  c. competition
  d. dependability

_____ 11. disclosure
  a. reporting
  b. insertion
  c. reversal
  d. withdrawal

_____ 12. desist
  a. state
  b. help
  c. free
  d. halt

_____ 13. rescind
     a. entwine
     b. flourish
     c. combine
     d. abolish

_____ 14. allocate
     a. change
     b. return
     c. assign
     d. repeat

_____ 15. alternative
     a. specialty
     b. change
     c. choice
     d. observation

_____ 16. expressly
     a. especially
     b. quickly
     c. thoughtfully
     d. smoothly

1. Unfortunately, some students have the mistaken idea that in an English class formality is a **virtue** and that big, fancy words are preferred to short, common ones.

2. Therefore the writer must be reasonably sure that the **allusion** is suited to the audience. Likening an uncomfortable cot to the bed of Procrustes will be received as humorous exaggeration only by readers who know that Procrustes used to stretch or shorten his guests to fit the bed. If the allusion is not likely to be understood, what is the point of using it?

3. A reader who believes that creation is an act of God and that a child is created at the moment of **conception** must view deliberate abortion as murder and cannot give up that image without denying a basic article of faith.

4. A student who has carefully studied a subject and shows familiarity with the **pertinent** facts will be considered more knowledgeable than
5. another who has only a **superficial** grasp of the subject and is often wrong on significant details.

6. Slanting is the practice of selecting facts favorable to one's opinion and **suppressing** those against it. . . . For example, a writer who says there can be no real poverty in a country where the average annual income is more than $10,000 ignores two facts: that this average includes incomes of a million dollars or more, and that great numbers of people do not have anywhere near the average income.

7. You probably know that by **deleting** certain parts of a taped speech and then recording the edited tape, one can greatly distort the original speech.

8. Although the Industrial Revolution and the rapid growth in business enterprises may have had some long-run beneficial effects on society, these changes often had **devastating** effects on individuals. Masses of workers toiled long, hard hours for little money under bad working
9. conditions. Yet a few industrialists continued to **amass** large amounts of wealth.

10. Increased interest in consumer protection has occurred for several reasons. Consumers do not have the time or **competence** to evaluate all products that they purchase. Because of inadequate product stan-
11. dards, poor information **disclosure** and deceptive marketing techniques in some cases, laws to protect consumers have become popular.

12. If the company continues the questionable practice, the FTC can issue a cease and **desist** order, which is simply an order for the business to stop doing whatever caused the complaint in the first place. The firm can appeal to the federal courts to have the FTC
13. order **rescinded.**

14. Although the FTC helps to regulate a variety of business practices, it **allocates** a large portion of its resources to curbing false advertising, misleading pricing, and deceptive packaging and labeling.

15. When a marketer wishes to add products to the firm's product mix, one **alternative** is to merge with another business that already produces the desired product.

16. At the federal level few agencies exist solely to protect consumers. One federal agency, however, the Consumer Product Safety Commission, has been created **expressly** for this purpose.

EXERCISE 6

IMPLIED MEANINGS

First, test your knowledge of the words in the sixteen multiple-choice questions by circling the letter in front of the correct meaning of each word. Second, infer the meanings of the words you do not know by studying the excerpts from a history and health education textbook that follow the questions. Third, write the correct answers on the lines provided.

_____ 1. solvent
    a. spiritually clean
    b. financially able
    c. physically weak
    d. mentally alert

_____ 2. mortality
    a. death
    b. life
    c. burial
    d. birth

_____ 3. influx
    a. odor
    b. copy
    c. slight bend
    d. great flow

_____ 4. compounded
    a. devised
    b. improved
    c. increased
    d. excluded

_____ 5. opulent
    a. ornamented
    b. luxurious
    c. increasing
    d. out-dated

_____ 6. gravitate
    a. send
    b. move
    c. rise
    d. flow

_____ 7. means
    a. equal
    b. cause
    c. wealth
    d. center

_____ 8. astute
    a. clever
    b. crooked
    c. cranky
    d. humble

_____ 9. squander
    a. waste
    b. drown
    c. wonder
    d. crush

_____ 10. enhance
    a. improve
    b. erase
    c. confine
    d. bewilder

_____ 11. optimum
    a. superb
    b. chosen
    c. silent
    d. mindful

_____ 12. facilitate
    a. commingle
    b. manufacture
    c. make cleaner
    d. make easier

_____ 13. abstain
    a. tie or bind
    b. free or unfetter
    c. withhold from
    d. remove from

_____ 14. criteria
    a. facts
    b. standards
    c. research
    d. opinions

_____ 15. proliferating
    a. hastening
    b. aggravating
    c. complicating
    d. multiplying

_____ 16. ingestion
    a. answering
    b. questioning
    c. swallowing
    d. chewing

1. Abigail Adams managed to keep her family **solvent** during the war primarily by selling small luxury items her husband John sent at her request from his diplomatic posts in Europe.

2. Infant **mortality** in the first year of life exceeded 10 percent. In the South in 1860 almost five out of ten children died before age five, and among all South Carolinians younger than twenty, fewer than four in ten survived to reach the 20-to-60-year-old category.

3. And the **influx** of immigrants to the cities **compounded** social ten-
4. sions by pitting people of different backgrounds against each other

in the contest for jobs and housing. Ironically, in the midst of the dirt, the noise, the crime, and the conflict, as if to tempt those who
5. struggled to survive, rose the **opulent** residences of the very rich.

6. Most immigrants **gravitated** toward the cities, since only a minority
7. had farming experience or the **means** to purchase lands and equipment.

8. Marshall was an **astute** lawyer who was always to be found on the winning side.

9. Don't **squander** money on products that are supposed to open or
10. close pores, prevent or erase wrinkles, **enhance** skin beauty, stimulate hair follicles, grow hair, or alter secretions of the sebaceous glands.

11. It is true that protein is essential for **optimum** growth and well-being, but protein is utilized in conjunction with other nutrients in the complex process of metabolism, rather like parts of an extremely sophisticated biochemical factory.

12. In an indirect way, vitamin C helps to **facilitate** wound healing, prevent bleeding gums, and enhance a person's resistance to infections.

13. By definition, a vegetarian is a person who **abstains** from eating meat as a food, and this abstention may or may not include dairy products and eggs.

14. It might be worthwhile to self-examine the **criteria** you use to make decisions about things that influence the quality of your life. Is the information you use to make such decisions founded upon scientific data or is it a product of hearsay, your friends' opinions, and the influence of mass media?

15. Perhaps no other health issue warrants as much attention as the **proliferating** use and misuse of nonprescription drugs, commonly called proprietary drugs, that are sold over the counter.

16. As for breath odor caused by the **ingestion** of certain foods, such as onions, garlic, or alcohol, it is important to understand that most of the odor is from the lungs and not the mouth.

6. ANALYZE WORD STRUCTURE

When a context does not state or imply a word meaning, it may sometimes be determined by studying the base and prefix or suffix in the word. This chapter explains how to determine word meanings by analyzing their parts so you will have less need to use a dictionary when you read.

SUFFIXES

A **suffix** is a letter or group of letters that is added to the end of base words; in *truthful, truth* is a base word and *-ful* is a suffix. Words that are unfamiliar to you may sometimes consist of a base word you know and an added suffix. For instance,

How many years was her *mayoralty*?

Mayoralty does not appear very often in print—it may be unfamiliar to you. However, by locating the base word in *mayoralty* you can easily understand that the question is "How many years was she mayor?"

Words you know may be the base words for five, ten, fifteen, or more other words that you do not read often. For example,

*adapt*able	*adapt*ationally
*adapt*ableness	*adapt*edness
*adapt*ability	*adapt*er
*adapt*ation	*adapt*ive
*adapt*ational	*adapt*iveness

If you know that *adapt* means "to make suitable," you know the essential meaning of these ten words even if you have never seen some of them in print before.

A suffix usually identifies a word's part of speech without giving important information about its meaning. For instance, *adapt* is a verb, but *adaptable* is an adjective and *adaptation* is a noun. *Adapt, adaptable,* and *adaptation* represent different parts of speech but they have similar meanings. Since they are different parts of speech, they cannot be used correctly in identical grammatical constructions.

> She can *adapt* to difficult situations.
> She is *adaptable* to difficult situations.
> She can make *adaptations* to difficult situations.

Figure 6.1 lists the parts of speech indicated by some common suffixes.

When a suffix is added to a base word, final *e* may be dropped (mature + -ity = maturity), final *y* may be changed to *i* (harmony + -ous = harmonious), or a base word may undergo some other spelling change (reclaim + -ation = reclamation). Keep these facts in mind as you do the exercises in this chapter.

EXERCISE 1

SUFFIXES

Answer the following twenty questions by writing the base words in the boldface terms. The first question is answered to illustrate what you are to do.

Alexandria has **prophetic** powers.

She has the powers of a ____prophet____ .

1. The flood was a **calamitous** event.

   The flood was a _____ .

2. The stages of life are **cyclical**.

   The stages of life occur in a _____ .

3. We had **comparative** good luck.

   If you _____ our luck to their luck, ours was good.

4. Please make a **compilation** of the facts.

   Please _____ the facts.

FIGURE 6.1

Some common suffixes

Noun Suffixes	Examples
-ance	appearance, assurance, defiance
-ancy	pregnancy, vacancy, malignancy
-ence	preference, difference, independence
-ion	depression, confusion, transfusion
-ity	acidity, liquidity, captivity
-ive	detective, directive, relative
-ment	government, management, requirement
-ness	happiness, kindness, bitterness
-ure	displeasure, exposure, departure

Adjective Suffixes	
-able	touchable, comfortable, lovable
-ful	peaceful, wasteful, plentiful
-ible	reversible, reducible, perfectible
-ical	spherical, theatrical, quizzical
-ious	prestigious, infectious, spacious
-ive	reflective, speculative, enhancive
-y	thrifty, cloudy, syrupy

Verb Suffixes	
-ify	simplify, glorify, falsify
-ize	personalize, categorize, popularize

Adverb Suffixes	
-ly	quickly, slowly, beautifully
-ward	homeward, backward, afterward

5. We insist on his **compliance** with the rules.

   We insist that he _____ with the rules.

6. Who were the **disputants**?

   Who engaged in the _____ ?

7. We selected clothing for its **durability**.

   We chose _____ clothing.

8. We find his pleasant disposition **enviable**.

   We _____ his pleasant disposition.

9. Amy has **expertise** in mathematics.

   She is an _____ in mathematics.

10. Tom had some **familial** difficulties.

    He had difficulties with his _____ .

11. An arm injury is a **hindrance** to ball pitching.

    An arm injury will _____ ball pitching.

12. This machine has a **multiplicity** of tiny parts.

    The machine has _____ tiny parts.

13. Its **porosity** makes this cloth cool to wear.

    The _____ s make the cloth cool to wear.

14. There is no **quantitative** difference in their weights.

    Their weights do not differ in _____ .

15. The problem is **remediable**.

    There is a _____ for the problem.

16. They have **servile** attitudes.

    They have attitudes of those who _____ .

17. Drive only in a state of **sobriety**.

    Drive only when _____ .

18. He had a **torturous** childhood.

    His childhood was _____ .

19. Make a **transposition** of the letters in *ache* to spell *each*.

    _____ the letters in *ache* to spell *each*.

20. The murder trial records are **voluminous**.

There is a great _____ of records for the trial.

PREFIXES

A **prefix** is a letter or group of letters that is added to the beginning of a base word; in *miscalculate, mis-* is a prefix and *calculate* is a base word. Words that are unfamiliar to you may sometimes be base words you know with a prefix added. For example,

We were shocked to learn of the *illimitability* of the dictator's power.

Illimitability may be unfamiliar to you, but you know its base word *limit* means "to restrict." If you also know that the prefix *il-* (as in *illegal*) means "not or no," you can determine that *illimitability* refers to that which has no limits, or restrictions. The sentence means: "We were shocked to learn that there is no limit to the dictator's power."

The preceding discussion of suffixes included a list of ten words in which *adapt* is the base word. Following are additional words in which *adapt* is the base word:

mal*adapt*ation	non*adapt*er	re*adapt*ation
mal*adapt*ed	non*adapt*ing	re*adapt*ive
mal*adapt*ive	non*adapt*ive	re*adapt*iveness
mis*adapt*ation	pre*adapt*	un*adapt*able
non*adapt*ability	pre*adapt*able	un*adapt*ableness
non*adapt*able	pre*adapt*ation	un*adapt*ive
non*adapt*ation	re*adapt*ability	un*adapt*ively
non*adapt*ational	re*adapt*able	un*adapt*iveness

If you know that *adapt* means "to make suitable" and also know the meanings of the prefixes *mal-, mis-, non-, pre-, re-,* and *un-,* you know the essential meanings of these twenty-four words even if you have not seen some of them in print before.

Do Exercise 2 before you read farther in this chapter.

EXERCISE 2

PREFIX QUIZ

To determine the meaning of a word that has a prefix, you must know the meaning of the prefix. Take this quiz to determine whether you already know the meanings of most of the common prefixes. *You are to write the meanings of prefixes,* not the meanings of words. The first one is completed to illustrate what you are to do.

What is the meaning of *un-*, as in *unhappy?*

_____ not _____

1. What is the meaning of *anti-*, as in *antilabor?*

   _____

2. What is the meaning of *ir-*, as in *irregular?*

   _____

3. What is the meaning of *im-*, as in *immoderate?*

   _____

4. What is the meaning of *inter-*, as in *interstate?*

   _____

5. What is the meaning of *pseudo-*, as in *pseudoscience?*

   _____

6. What is the meaning of *mal-*, as in *malformed?*

   _____

7. What is the meaning of *mis-*, as in *miscalculate?*

   _____

8. What is the meaning of *pro-*, as in *prodemocratic?*

   _____

9. What is the meaning of *semi-*, as in *semipublic*?

_____

10. What is the meaning of *post-*, as in *postwar*?

_____

Check your answers by referring to Figure 6.2.

If, in Exercise 2, you wrote meanings for prefixes that are different from ones in Figure 6.2, learn the meanings of prefixes that are listed in Figure 6.2; they are useful meanings of prefixes to learn and remember. For instance, if you think of *semi* as meaning "half," it would benefit you to also think of it as meaning "partly" or "partially." *Semi-* indicates "half" in a few common words, such as *semicircle*, as well as in some highly technical words. However, it usually indicates "partly" or "partially," as in *semiarid, semisoft, semiopen,* and *semipublic*.

FIGURE 6.2

Meanings of common prefixes

Prefix	Meaning	Example
1. un-	not; no	*un*happy means *not* happy
2. non-	not; no	*non*living means *not* living
3. dis-	not; no	to *dis*trust is to *not* trust
4. in-	not; no	*in*direct means *not* direct
5. im-	not; no	*im*perfect means *not* perfect
6. ir-	not; no	*ir*rational means *not* rational
7. il-	not; no	*il*legal means *not* legal
8. pre-	before; beforehand	*pre*war means *before* a war
9. post-	after	*post*war means *after* a war
10. pro-	favor(ing)	*pro*war means *favoring* a war
11. anti-	oppos(ing)	*anti*war means *opposing* war
12. hyper-	excessive(ly)	*hyper*active means *excessively* active
13. inter-	between	*inter*state means *between* states
14. mal-	bad(ly)	*mal*nutrition is *bad* nutrition
15. mis-	incorrect(ly)	to *mis*spell is to spell *incorrectly*
16. pseudo-	false(ly)	a *pseudo*science is a false science
17. semi-	partly; partially	*semi*public means *partly* public
18. re-	again	to *re*write is to write *again*

Figure 6.2 lists only the most common prefixes. Other prefixes that occur from time to time include *ante-, circum-, co-, contra-, counter-, de-, extra-, intra-, retro-, sub-, super-, trans-,* and *ultra-.* The meanings of all prefixes are explained in desk dictionaries. For instance,

> **trans-** *pref.* **1.** Across; on the other side; beyond: *transpolar.* **2.** Through: *trans-cutaneous.* **3.** Change; transfer: *transliterate.* [< Lat. *trans.* beyond, through.]

Desk dictionaries are described in Chapter 7.

EXERCISE 3

PREFIXES

Answer the following twenty questions by writing the base word and the meanings of prefixes in boldface terms. Meanings of prefixes are listed in Figure 6.2. The first question is answered to illustrate what you are to do.

His work is **unprofessional.**

It does _____ not _____ meet the standards of his _____ profession _____.

1. They found the desert heat **unendurable.**

   They could _____ the heat.

2. What was your **presupposition**?

   What did you _____ ?

3. Will you do **postgraduate** study?

   Will you study _____ you _____ ?

4. He wants to be a **nonconformist.**

   He does _____ want to _____ .

5. They are **procensorship.**

   They _____ those who _____ .

6. They are **anti-intellectual**.

They _____ activity of the _____ .

7. Do you see their **dissimilarity**?

Do you see how they are _____ ?

8. The child's **hyperactivity** is alarming.

The child is _____ .

9. They took an **intercontinental** flight.

They took a flight _____ s.

10. The difference is **indistinguishable**.

One can _____ the difference.

11. The garbage is **malodorous**.

The garbage has a _____ .

12. Her love for him is **immeasurable**.

One can _____ her love for him.

13. Is the statement a **misrepresentation** of the truth?

Does it _____ the truth _____ ?

14. The painting is done **pseudoartistically**.

It is _____ .

15. The machine is **semiautomatic**.

The machine is _____ .

16. Our differences are **irreconcilable**.

We can _____ our differences.

17. Is its **remodification** possible?

Is it possible to _____ it _____ ?

18. Did he **misappropriate** the money?

Did he _____ it _____ ?

19. His point of view is **illiberal**.

His point of view is _____ .

20. The rule is **nonapplicable** here.

The rule does _____ here.

COMBINING FORMS

Combining forms are Greek and Latin word parts that are joined to base words or other combining forms to create words. For instance, *micro-*, which indicates "small," is a combining form in *microfilm*—film on which printed or drawn material is greatly reduced in size. Also, *-logy*, which indicates "science" or "study of," is a combining form in *Egyptology*—the study of the civilization of ancient Egypt.

Prefixes and suffixes are not joined, or combined, to create words, but combining forms are. For instance, *biblio-* and *-phile* are joined to create the word *bibliophile*. Read the following dictionary entries for *biblio-*, *-phile*, and *bibliophile*.

> **biblio-** *pref.* Book: *bibliophile.* [< Gk. *biblion,* book. —see BIBLE.]
> **-phile** or **-phil** *suff.* **1.** One that loves or has a strong affinity or preference for: *audiophile.* **2.** Loving; having a strong affinity or preference for: *Francophile.* [Partly < Fr. *-phile,* and partly < NLat. *-philus* (< Lat.), both < Gk. *-philos* < *philos,* beloved, dear.]
> **bib·li·o·phile** (bĭb′lē-ə-fīl′) also **bib·li·o·phil** (-fĭl′) or **bib·li·oph·i·list** (bĭb′lē-ŏf′ə-lĭst) *n.* **1.** One who loves books. **2.** A book collector —**bib·li·oph·i·lism** *n.* — **bib′li·oph′i·lis′tic** *adj.*

Notice that the meanings of *biblio-* and *-phile* are very closely related to the meaning of *bibliophile*.

Figure 6.3 lists the meanings of some combining forms. Knowledge of combining forms is usually essential for the study of a natural science. For example, it is important for students of biology to know the meanings

FIGURE 6.3

Some combining forms

Combining Form	Meaning	Example
anthropo-	human	*anthropo*logy
biblio-	books	*biblio*graphy
-cracy	government	demo*cracy*
deca-, dec-	ten	*dec*ade
-graph	write, written	tele*graph*
gyneco-, gyn-	women	*gyneco*logy
-mania	abnormal craving	klepto*mania*
miso-	hatred	*miso*gynist
necro-	death	*necro*logy
neo-	new	*neo*classical
octo-	eight	*octo*pus
-phile	love	biblio*phile*
-phobia	abnormal fear	claustro*phobia*
pyro-	fire	*pyro*lysis
seismo-	earthquake	*seismo*logy
sept-	seven	*sept*et
sex-	six	*sex*tet
somato-	body	psycho*somatic*
uni-	one	*uni*form

of *amph-* (both), *capilli-* (hair), *cocco-* (berry), *derma-* (skin), *entero-* (intestine), *macro-* (large), *nephr-* (kidney), and many other combining forms. If you study biology, chemistry, or other natural sciences, you may find a list of combining forms or Greek and Latin roots in your textbook. If so, learn their meanings.

EXERCISE 4

COMBINING FORMS

Use the meanings of combining forms in Figure 6.3 to write the answers to the following questions.

1. *Anthropoids* resemble _____ .

2. *Bibliophobia* is the fear of _____ .

3. There are _____ events in the *decathlon*.

4. To *decimate* an army is to kill every _____ man.

5. A *seismograph* records _____ .

6. *September* was the _____ month of the Roman calendar.

7. *October* was the _____ month of the Roman calendar.

8. *December* was the _____ month of the Roman calendar.

9. *Sexagenarians* are people _____ to _____ years old.

10. *Septuagenarians* are people _____ to _____ years old.

11. *Octogenarians* are people _____ to _____ years old.

12. In a *gynecocracy*, _____ rule.

13. A *misanthrope* hates _____ .

14. A *misogynist* hates _____ .

15. A *somatic* illness is an illness of the _____ .

16. July 4th *pyrotechnics* are _____ .

17. If a thing is *unique,* it is the only _____ like it.

18. *Pyromaniacs* are insanely attracted to _____ .

19. *Necrophobia* is the fear of _____ .

20. A *neophyte* parent is a _____ parent.

ANALYZING WORD STRUCTURE

The following exercises provide additional practice in analyzing word structure. Exercise 5 is practice for base words, prefixes, and suffixes; Exercises 6–9 are practice for learning the meanings of some combining forms.

EXERCISE 5

PREFIXES AND SUFFIXES

Answer the following questions by writing the base words in the boldface terms and the meanings of prefixes for boldface terms that contain prefixes (see Figure 6.2). The first two questions are answered to illustrate what you are to do.

He renewed his license just before its **expiration**.

It was about to _____*expire*_____ when he renewed it.

She used a **dispassionate** appeal to reason rather than emotion.

Her appeal was _____*not*_____ marked by _____*passion*_____ .

1. Proper exercise can correct **postural** problems.

   Exercise can correct problems with _____ .

2. **Immobilization** of a body joint is a symptom of loss of suppleness, or flexibility.

   If a joint is _____ , suppleness, or flexibility, has been lost.

3. Air **deprivation,** even for a short time, can cause death.

   To _____ a person of air, even for a short time, can cause death.

4. Patients often remain in the hospital for **postsurgical** care.

   Patients often remain for care _____ .

5. It is not uncommon for **devotees** of strict vegetarian diets to contract diseases such as rickets and scurvy.

   Those who _____ themselves to strict vegetarian diets may contract some diseases.

6. Food faddists sometimes claim that a specific food is a **curative** or preventive for disease.

   They claim a food is a _____ for a disease.

7. Medical specialists, such as radiologists, are more **knowledgeable** about their specialties than other physicians.

   Medical specialists have specific _____ that other physicians do not have.

8. Acupuncturists are **practitioners** of an ancient medical art.

   They _____ an ancient medical art.

9. In the past decade there have been great **fluctuations** in the price of gold.

   The price of gold has tended to _____ during the past ten years.

10. Advertisers argue that most criticisms of advertising are **unjustifiable**.

    They claim one can _____ most criticisms of advertising.

11. **Inconsistencies** of fact are often found in student writing.

    Facts are often _____ in student writing.

12. In the late 1700s, whites and blacks of the United States realized that they must move toward an **accommodation** to their new circumstances.

    They realized that they must _____ to their new circumstances.

13. Laws are **ineffectual** unless most citizens approve and heed them.

    Laws have _____ unless most citizens approve and heed them.

14. Diplomacy often requires that those who negotiate be **noncommittal** for long periods of time.

    Those who negotiate often can _____ themselves for long periods of time.

15. After the Watergate scandal, President Nixon fell into **disesteem.**

    Many did _____ President Nixon after the Watergate scandal.

EXERCISE 6

COMBINING FORMS

Referring to the meanings of combining forms listed below, match the words on the left with their definitions on the right.

astro-, astr-   star or outer space
bio-   life or living organisms
chrono-, chron-   time
-cide   killer or killing
omni-   all

_____ 1. **asterisk**

_____ 2. **astral**

_____ 3. **biocide**

_____ 4. **biotic**

_____ 5. **chronic**

_____ 6. **chronological**

_____ 7. **infanticide**

_____ 8. **omnipotent**

_____ 9. **omnipresent**

_____ 10. **omnivorous**

a. pertaining to living things

b. the killing of an infant

c. being everywhere at the same time

d. life-destroying substance

e. taking in everything mentally

f. pertaining to the stars

g. a star-shaped symbol (*)

h. arranged in time sequence

i. continuing for a long time

j. having unlimited power

EXERCISE 7

COMBINING FORMS

Referring to the meanings of combining forms listed below, match the words on the left with their definitions on the right.

archaeo-   ancient times
audio-   sound or hearing
patho-   disease or suffering
psycho-   mind or mental processes
theo-   God or gods
-logy   study or science

_____ 1. **archaeology**

_____ 2. **archaic**

_____ 3. **audiology**

_____ 4. **auditory**

_____ 5. **pathology**

_____ 6. **psychopath**

_____ 7. **psychopathology**

_____ 8. **psychic**

_____ 9. **theology**

_____ 10. **atheism**

a. the scientific study of disease

b. disbelief or denial of God

c. a highly antisocial person

d. the study of mental diseases

e. having extraordinary mental abilities

f. belonging to ancient times

g. study of cultures from the distant past

h. the study of the nature of God

i. pertaining to hearing

j. the study of hearing defects

EXERCISE 8

COMBINING FORMS

Referring to the meanings of combining forms listed below, match the words on the left with their definitions on the right.

mono-   one, single, alone
poly-   more than one, many
chrom-   color or colors
hetero-   different or other
homo-   same or like
gamo-   marriage or sexual union

_____ 1. **monochromatic**

_____ 2. **monogamous**

_____ 3. **monologue**

_____ 4. **polygamous**

_____ 5. **polychromatic**

_____ 6. **chromatic**

_____ 7. **heterosexual**

_____ 8. **heterogeneous**

_____ 9. **homogamous**

_____ 10. **homogeneous**

a. a long talk by one person

b. having many colors

c. having similar elements or parts

d. pertaining to color or colors

e. attracted to the opposite sex

f. marrying one with similar characteristics

g. having one marriage partner

h. having one color

i. having dissimilar elements or parts

j. having more than one spouse

EXERCISE 9

COMBINING FORMS

Referring to the meanings of combining forms listed below and in Exercises 6–8, match the words on the left with their definitions on the right.

bene-   good or well
mal-   bad or badly

_____ 1. **benevolence**

_____ 2. **benevolent**

_____ 3. **benign**

_____ 4. **malevolent**

_____ 5. **malice**

_____ 6. **malignant**

_____ 7. **polytheism**

_____ 8. **monotheism**

_____ 9. **omniscient**

_____ 10. **audiophile**

a. lover of high-fidelity sound

b. harmful, not benign

c. the belief in more than one god

d. the desire to harm others

e. good or kindly

f. inclination to kindness

g. having knowledge of everything

h. the belief in one God

i. mild, not malignant

j. wishing or doing harm

7. USE
A
DICTIONARY

It is necessary to use a dictionary when a word meaning cannot be determined by studying context, analyzing word structure, or referring to a glossary (see page 106).

This chapter explains some of the features of desk dictionaries, which are hardcover books that list the meanings from 150,000 to 200,000 words and that include a great deal of other information as well. Figure 7.1 on page 78 shows the entries for *costly* through *cote* in the desk and paperback editions of *The American Heritage Dictionary*. Notice that seventeen entries are listed in the desk edition in contrast to only six in the paperback edition. When desk dictionaries are condensed to paperback books, more than 100,000 words are omitted and many definitions in desk dictionaries are not included in paperback editions.

College students need paperback dictionaries to carry to classes and desk dictionaries to use at their study places.

Of the several excellent desk dictionaries, I especially recommend the following:

The American Heritage Dictionary of the English Language
Webster's New World Dictionary of the American Language
The Random House Dictionary of the English Language

Compare definitions in dictionaries to select one with definitions that you find easiest to understand; it is essential to own a dictionary with clearly written and easy-to-understand definitions.

WORD MEANINGS

Desk dictionaries explain the meanings of words using definitions, synonyms, and examples. **Definitions** are statements of the meanings of words; **synonyms** are words that have the same or nearly the same meaning; and **examples,** in dictionary entries, are phrases or sentences

FIGURE 7.1

The entries for *costly* through *cote* in the desk and paperback editions of *The American Heritage Dictionary*

Desk edition

cost·ly (kôst′lē) *adj.* **-li·er, -li·est. 1.** Of high price or value; expensive: *costly jewelry.* **2.** Entailing loss or sacrifice: *a costly war.* **—cost′li·ness** *n.*
 Synonyms: *costly, expensive, dear, valuable, precious, invaluable, priceless.* These adjectives apply to the measure of worth or value of things or, less often, of persons. *Costly, expensive,* and *dear* refer principally to the high price of things on sale. *Costly,* thus used, implies especially high quality or rarity of an object. *Valuable* stresses the quality and importance of the object without specifying the price. *Precious* implies uniqueness and irreplaceability. *Invaluable* and *priceless* describe worth beyond a person's power to estimate.
cost·mar·y (kôst′mâr′ē, kôst′-) *n.* An herb, *Chrysanthemum balsamita,* native to Asia, having aromatic foliage sometimes used as seasoning. [ME *costmarie* : *cost,* costmary (< OE < Lat. *costum* < Gk. *kostos* < Skt. *kúṣṭhaḥ*) + *marie,* Mary, the mother of Jesus.]
cost of living *n.* **1.** The average cost of the basic necessities of life, such as food, shelter, and clothing. **2.** The cost of basic necessities as defined by an accepted standard.
cost-of-liv·ing adjustment (kôst′əv-lĭv′ĭng) *n.* An adjustment made in wages that corresponds with a change in the cost of living.
cost-of-living index *n.* The consumer price index.
cost-plus (kôst′plŭs′, kôst′-) *n.* The cost of production plus a fixed rate of profit. **—adj.** Paid or negotiated on the basis of cost-plus: *a cost-plus contract.*
cost-push (kôst′pŏosh′, kôst′-) *adj.* Designating a type of inflation in which increased production costs, as from higher wages, tend to drive prices up.
cos·trel (kŏs′trəl) *n.* A flat, pear-shaped drinking vessel with loops for attachment to the belt of the user. [ME < OFr. *costerel,* prob. < *costier,* at the side < *coste,* rib < Lat. *costa.*]
cos·tume (kŏs′tōom′, -tyōom′) *n.* **1.** A prevalent fashion of dress, including garments, accessories, and hair style. **2.** A style of dress characteristic of a particular country, period, or people, often worn in a play or at a masquerade. **3.** A set of clothes appropriate for a particular occasion or season. **—modifier:** *a costume ball; a costume play.* **—tr.v.** (kŏ-stōom′, -styōom′, kŏs′tōom′, -tyōom′) **-tumed, -tum·ing, -tumes. 1.** To put a costume on; dress. **2.** To design or furnish costumes for. [Fr. < Ital. < Lat. *consuetudo,* custom.—see CUSTOM.]
cos·tum·er (kŏs′tōo′mər, -tyōo′-, kŏ-stōo′mər, -styōo′-) also **cos·tum·i·er** (kŏ-stōom′yər, -styōom′-) *n.* A person who makes or supplies costumes, as for plays or masquerades.
co·sy (kō′zē) *adj. & n.* Variant of **cozy.**
cot¹ (kŏt) *n.* A narrow bed, esp. one made of canvas stretched on a collapsible frame. [Hindi *khāṭ,* couch < Skt. *khaṭvā,* of Dravidian orig.]
cot² (kŏt) *n.* **1. a.** A small house; cottage. **b.** A small shelter. **2.** A protective covering. [ME < OE.]
co·tan·gent (kō-tăn′jənt) *n. Math.* The tangent of the complement of a directed angle or arc. **—co′tan·gen′tial** (-jĕn′-shəl) *adj.*
cot death *n. Chiefly Brit.* Sudden infant death syndrome.
cote¹ (kōt) *n.* **1.** A small shed or shelter for sheep or birds. **2.** *Regional.* A cottage; hut. [ME < OE.]
cote² (kōt) *tr.v.* **cot·ed, cot·ing, cotes.** *Archaic.* To go around by the side of; pass. [Orig. unknown.]

Paperback edition

cost·ly (kôst′lē) *adj.* **-lier, -liest. 1.** Of high price or value; expensive. **2.** Entailing loss or sacrifice. **—cost′li·ness** *n.*
cost-plus (kôst′plŭs′, kôst′-) *n.* Cost of production plus a fixed rate of profit. Often used as a basis for government contracts.
cos·tume (kŏs′t/y/ōom, kŏs-t/y/ōom′) *n.* **1.** A style of dress, esp. one characteristic of a particular country or period. **2.** A set of clothes for a particular occasion or season. [< L *consuētūdō,* CUSTOM.]
co·sy. Variant of **cozy.**
cot (kŏt) *n.* A narrow bed, esp. one made of canvas stretched on a collapsible frame. [Hindi *khāṭ,* bedstead, couch.]
cote (kōt) *n.* A small shed or shelter for sheep or birds. [< OE.]

that illustrate the ways in which words are used. Locate the definitions, synonyms, and examples in the following entry.

> **ex·tem·po·ra·ne·ous** (ĭk-stĕm′pə-rā′nē-əs) *adj.* **1.** Done with little or no preparation or practice; impromptu: *an extemporaneous recital.* **2.** Prepared in advance but delivered without notes or text: *an extemporaneous sermon.* **3.** Skilled at or given to unrehearsed speech or performance. **4.** Provided, made, or adapted as an expedient; makeshift. [LLat. *extemporaneous* < Lat. *ex tempore,* of the time.] **—ex·tem′po·ra′ne·ous·ly** *adv.* **—ex·tem′po·ra′ne·ous·ness** *n.*

Answer the following questions about this entry:

1. What is the third definition of *extemporaneous*?

_____

2. What synonym is given for the fourth definition of *extemporaneous*?

_____

3. What example is given for the second definition of *extemporaneous*?

_____

The answers to the questions are "skilled at or given to unrehearsed speech or performance," "makeshift," and "an extemporaneous sermon," respectively.

MULTIPLE MEANINGS

Since most words have more than one meaning, it is often necessary to read several definitions to locate the one that is wanted. Read the following definitions for *personification*.

> **per·son·i·fi·ca·tion** (pər-sŏn'ə-fĭ-kā'shən) *n.*
> **1.** The act of personifying. **2.** A person or thing typifying a certain quality or idea that is outstanding; an embodiment; exemplification: *"He's invisible, a walking personification of the Negative"* (Ralph Ellison). **3.** A rhetorical figure of speech in which inanimate objects or abstractions are endowed with human qualities or are represented as possessing human form, as in *Hunger sat shivering on the road* or *Flowers danced about the lawn.* **4.** The artistic representation of an abstract quality or idea as a person.

Answer the following questions about this entry:

1. What does it mean to say "Albert Einstein is the *personification* of brains"?

_____

_____

2. "'The waves licked the shore' is an example of *personification*." What is the meaning of personification in this sentence?

_____

_____

To say that Albert Einstein is the personification of brains is to say that he "typifies brains," "possesses brains to an outstanding degree," or "embodies the concept of braininess." In the second question, *personification* refers to a figure of speech in which inanimate objects (waves) are given a human characteristic (the ability to lick).

SUBJECT LABELS

Desk dictionaries provide subject labels to help in locating definitions. **Subject labels** are terms printed in italics to indicate the fields of knowledge to which definitions apply. The following entry for *depression* includes four subject labels—the italicized abbreviations *Meteorol*[ogy], *Astron*[omy], *Psychiat*[ry], and *Econ*[omics].

> **de·pres·sion** (dĭ-prĕsh'ən) *n.* **1. a.** The act of depressing. **b.** The condition of being depressed. **2.** An area that is sunk below its surroundings; hollow. **3.** *Meteorol.* A region of low barometric pressure. **4.** The angular distance below the horizontal plane through the point of observation. **5.** *Astron.* The angular distance of a celestial body below the horizon. **6.** A reduction in activity or force. **7.** The condition of feeling sad or melancholy. **8.** *Psychiat.* A psychotic or neurotic condition characterized by an inability to concentrate, insomnia, and feelings of dejection and guilt. **9.** *Econ.* A period of drastic decline in the national economy, characterized by decreasing business activity, falling prices, and unemployment.

Answer the following questions about this entry:

1. What is the meaning of *depression* in the study of meteorology?

_____

2. What is the meaning of *depression* in the study of psychiatry?

_____

_____

For the first question you should have stated information in the third definition, and for the second question you should have stated information in the eighth definition.

SYNONYMS

Desk dictionaries are excellent sources of information about **synonyms**—words that have the same or nearly the same meaning. The following entry for *costly* is accompanied by explanations of the synonyms *expensive, dear, valuable, precious, invaluable,* and *priceless.*

> **cost·ly** (kôst'lē) *adj.* **-li·er, -li·est. 1.** Of high price or value; expensive: *costly jewelry.* **2.** Entailing loss or sacrifice: *a costly war.* **—cost'li·ness** *n.*
>   **Synonyms:** *costly, expensive, dear, valuable, precious, invaluable, priceless.* These adjectives apply to the measure of worth or value of things or, less often, of persons. *Costly, expensive,* and *dear* refer principally to the high price of things on sale. *Costly,* thus used, implies especially high quality or rarity of an object. *Valuable* stresses the quality and importance of the object without specifying the price. *Precious* implies uniqueness and irreplaceability. *Invaluable* and *priceless* describe worth beyond a person's power to estimate.

Refer to the discussion of synonyms to complete the following sentences using the words *dear, valuable,* and *precious.*

1. A large vocabulary is _____ to have.

2. The love of a child is _____ .

3. Rolls Royce automobiles are _____ .

If you wrote "valuable," "precious," and "dear," respectively, you are correct.

Use discussions of synonyms to better understand differences among the meanings of words that have similar meanings.

ETYMOLOGIES

The **etymology** of a word is information about how it became an English word; it is enclosed in brackets, as at the end of the following entry for *serendipity*.

> **ser·en·dip·i·ty** (sĕr'ən-dĭp'ĭ-tē); *n.* The faculty of making fortunate and unexpected discoveries by accident. [From its possession by the characters in the Persian fairy tale *The Three Princes of Serendip.*] — **ser'en·dip'i·tous** *adj.*

Answer the following questions about this entry.

1. What is *serendipity*?

   _____

   _____

2. How did *serendipity* become an English word?

   _____

   _____

For the first question you should have copied, restated, or summarized the definition in the entry. *Serendipity* was first used to describe a quality of characters in a fairy tale, *The Three Princes of Serendip*—and that's how it became an English word.

USING A DICTIONARY

Desk dictionaries contain many types of information in addition to those explained in this chapter. They include the correct spellings of words and basic facts about well-known persons, places, religions, philosophies, events, and many other topics. The first of the following exercises is a guided tour of some of the types of information in desk dictionaries that are not explained in this chapter.

EXERCISE 1

STUDYING A DESK DICTIONARY

Do this exercise using a desk dictionary that your instructor recommends. If you do not own a desk dictionary, you may find one in the reference section of a library. Write the name of the dictionary you use for this exercise on the following line:

_____

Answer the questions by studying what is stated in the dictionary about the italicized words in the questions.

1. When was *John F. Kennedy* born, and in what year was he assassinated?

_____

2. During what years was *World War II* fought?

_____

3. On what continent is the *Nile* river located and approximately how many miles long is it?

_____

4. What is the principal belief of *Hinduism*?

_____

5. What is the meaning of the prefix *contra-*?

_____

6. What is the meaning of the suffix *-ist*?

_____

7. What is the meaning of the combining form *helio-*?

_____

8. What is a *homograph*?

_____

9. What is indicated by the raised numbers following *banker*[1], *banker*[2], and *banker*[3]?

_____

10. What is an *idiom*?

_____

11. What is meant by the expression "with a high *hand*"?

_____

12. What is indicated by the word *informal,* or *colloquial,* printed in italics before a definition in a dictionary?

_____

13. What is indicated by the word *slang* printed in italics before a definition in a dictionary?

_____

14. Where is the spelling of *dependability* located in the dictionary?

_____

15. Which is correct, "the *data* is" or "the data are"?

_____

16. Which of the following spellings for variations of *commit* are correct: commited, committed, commiting, committing, commitment, and committment?

_____

17. Which of the following is the correct plural spelling of *monkey*: monkies, monkeys, monkeyes?

_____

18. Which of the following is the correct superlative spelling of *tiny*: tiniest, tinyest, or tinniest?

_____

EXERCISE 2

USING A DESK DICTIONARY

Answer the questions by referring to the dictionary entries that follow the questions.

1. What does it mean "to **rectify** an error"?

   _____

   Complete sentences 2–4 using the words **admonished, rebuked,** and **reprimanded.**

2. An army officer was _____ for inattention to duty, and a report of his negligence was placed in his personnel file.

3. The child's mother _____ him to wait for the green light before crossing the street.

4. Jesus _____ shopkeepers in the temple of worship.

5. Who is the author of a poem signed "**anon.**"?

   _____

6. How many donuts are there in a **baker's dozen**?

   _____

7. What is the etymological source of **baker's dozen**?

   _____

8. What is a "**caustic** remark"?

   _____

9. What does it mean to "**conceive** a plan"?

   _____

10. What is meant by the **spoonerism** "they hissed my mystery lectures"?

    _____

11. What is the etymological source of **spoonerism**?

_____

12. What does **rectify** mean in the study of chemistry?

_____

ad·mon·ish (ăd-mŏn'ĭsh) _tr.v._ **-ished, -ish·ing, -ish·es. 1.** To reprove mildly or kindly but seriously. **2.** To counsel against something; caution. **3.** To point out something forgotten or disregarded, by means of a warning, reproof, or exhortation. [ME _admonishen,_ alteration of _amonesten_ < OFr. _amonester_ < VLat. *_admonestare,_ var. of Lat. _admonēre_ : _ad,_ to + _monēre,_ to warn.] —**ad·mon' ish·er** _n._ —**ad·mon'ish·ing·ly** _adv._ —**ad·mon'ish·ment** _n._

Synonyms: admonish, reprove, rebuke, reprimand, reproach. These verbs refer to adverse criticism intended as a corrective. _Admonish_ stresses the act of advising or warning so that a fault may be rectified or a danger avoided. _Reprove_ usually implies gentle criticism and constructive intent. _Rebuke_ refers to sharp, usually angry, criticism, as does _reprimand,_ which often also implies an official or otherwise formal act. _Reproach_ usually refers to sharp criticism made regretfully or unhappily out of a sense of disappointment.

anon. anonymous.

a·non·y·mous (ə-nŏn'ə-məs) _adj._ **1.** Having an unknown or unacknowledged name. **2.** Having an unknown or withheld authorship or agency. [LLat. _anonymus_ < Gk. _anōnumos,_ nameless : _an-,_ without + _onoma,_ name.]

baker's dozen _n._ A group of 13. [From the former custom of bakers to add an extra roll as a safeguard against the possibility of 12 weighing light.]

caus·tic (kô'stĭk) _adj._ **1.** Capable of burning, corroding, dissolving, or otherwise eating away by chemical action. **2.** Marked by sharp and bitter wit; cutting:

"Her new clothes were the subject of caustic comment" (Willa Cather). **3.** Of or pertaining to light emitted from a point source and reflected or refracted from a curved surface. _n._ A caustic material or substance. [Lat. _causticus_ < Gk. _kaustikos_ < _kaiein,_ to burn.] —**caus·ti·cal·ly** _adv._ —**caus·tic'i·ty** (kô-stĭs'-ĭ-tē) _n._

con·ceive (kən-sēv') _v._ **-ceived, -ceiv·ing, ceives.** —_tr._ **1.** To become pregnant with. **2.** To form or develop in the mind; devise: _conceive a plan to increase profits._ **3.** To apprehend mentally; understand: _can't conceive your meaning._ **4.** To think or believe; hold an opinion: _didn't conceive that such a tragedy could occur._ —_intr._ **1.** To form or hold an idea: _Ancient peoples conceived of the earth as flat._ **2.** To become pregnant. [ME _conceiven_ < OFr. _concevoir_ < Lat. _concipere_ : _com-_ (intensive) + _capere,_ to take.] —**con·ceiv'-a·bil'i·ty, con·ceiv'a·ble·ness** _n._ —**con·ceiv'a·ble** _adj._ —**con·ceiv'a·bly** _adv._ —**con·ceiv'er** _n._

rec·ti·fy (rĕk'tə-fī') _tr.v._ **-fied, -fy·ing, -fies. 1.** To set right; correct. **2.** To correct by calculation or adjustment. **3.** _Chem._ To refine or purify, esp. by distillation. **4.** _Elect._ To convert (alternating current) into direct current. **5.** To adjust (the proof of alcoholic beverages) by adding water or other liquids. [ME _rectifien_ < OFr. _rectifier_ < Med. Lat. _rectificare_ : _rectus,_ right + _facere,_ to make.] —**rec'ti·fi'a·ble** _adj._ —**rec'ti·fi·ca'tion** (-fə-kā'shən) _n._

spoon·er·ism (spōō'nə-rĭz'əm) _n._ An unintentional transposition of sounds of two or more words, as _Let me sew you to your sheet_ for _Let me show you to your seat._ [After William A. _Spooner_ (1844–1930).]

EXERCISE 3

USING A DESK DICTIONARY

Answer the questions by referring to the dictionary entries that follow the questions.

1. What is a "**valid** argument"?

   _____

   Complete sentences 2–5 using the words **asserted, affirmed, avowed,** and **alleged.**

2. The salesperson _____ that our furniture would be delivered on Saturday before noon.

3. The instructor _____ that some students had cheated while taking an examination.

4. The mayor _____ that she would bring a halt to rising city taxes.

5. Tom _____ his objections to registering for the draft in an outspoken letter that was published in a local newspaper.

6. How do **confidant** and **confidante** differ in meaning?

   _____

   _____

7. What does it mean to say "Bob will **contend** for the Ping-Pong championship"?

   _____

8. What does it mean to say "they **contend** abortion should be illegal"?

   _____

9. What is meant by "pasta, **e.g.**, spaghetti"?

   _____

10. What is meant by **narcissism** in everyday usage?

_____

_____

11. What is the etymological source of **narcissism?**

_____

_____

12. What is a "**valid** driver's license"?

_____

as·sert (ə-sûrt´) *tr.v.* **-sert·ed, -sert·ing, -serts. 1.** To state or express positively; affirm. **2.** To defend or maintain (one's rights, for example). **3. assert oneself.** To express oneself forcefully or boldly. [Lat. *asserere, assert-,: ad-*, to + *serere*, to join.] —**as·sert´a·ble, as·sert´i·ble** *adj.* —**as·sert´er, as·ser´tor n.**

Synonyms: assert, asseverate, declare, affirm, aver, avow, allege. These verbs all mean to state; they differ principally in emphasis. To *assert* is to state one's position boldly, and to *asseverate* is to add even greater emphasis to the position taken. *Declare* has the approximate force of *assert,* but may suggest formality of statement and authority in the speaker. *Affirm* and *aver* imply less forcefulness, but stress the speaker's confidence in the validity of his statement. *Avow* emphasizes moral commitment to the statement. *Allege* refers to making a controversial charge or statement without presentation of proof.

con·fi·dant (kŏn´fĭ-dănt´, -dănt´, kŏn´fĭ-dänt´, -dänt´) *n.* One to whom secrets or private matters are confided. [Fr. *confident* < Ital. *confidente* < Lat. *confidens,* p.part. of *confidere,* to rely on. —see CON-FIDE.]

con·fi·dante (kŏn´fĭ-dănt´, -dänt´, kŏn´fĭ-dänt´, -dänt´) *n.* A woman to whom secrets or private matters are confided. [Fr. *confidente,* fem. of *confident,* confidant.]

con·tend (kən-tĕnd´) *v.* **-tend·ed, -tend·ing, -tends.** —*intr.* **1.** To strive, as in battle, fight. **2.** To compete, as in a race; vie. **3.** To strive in controversy or debate; dis-

pute. —*tr.* To maintain or assert. [ME *contenden* < Lat. *contendere : com-,* with + *tendere,* to strive.] —**con·tend´er** *n.*

e.g. *Lat.* exempli gratia (for example).

nar·cis·sism (när´sĭ-sĭz´əm) also **nar·cism** (när´sĭz´əm) *n.* **1.** Excessive love or admiration of oneself. **2.** *Psychoanal.* An arresting of development at or a regression to the infantile stage of development in which one's own body is the object of erotic interest. [After NARCISSUS.] —**nar´cis·sist** *n.* —**nar´cis·sis´tic** *adj.*

Nar·cis·sus (när-sĭs´əs) *n.* **1.** *Gk. Myth.* A youth who pined away in love for his own image in a pool of water and was transformed into the flower that bears his name. **2. narcissus,** *pl.* **-cis·sus·es** or **-cis·si** (-sĭs´ī´, -sĭs´ē). Any of several widely cultivated plants of the genus *Narcissus,* having narrow, grasslike leaves and usually white or yellow flowers characterized by a cup-shaped or trumpet-shaped central crown. [Lat. < Gr. *Narkissos.*]

val·id (văl´ĭd) *adj.* **1.** Well-grounded; sound: *a valid objection.* **2.** Producing the desired results; efficacious: *valid methods.* **3.** Legally sound and effective; incontestable: *valid title.* **4.** *Logic.* **a.** Containing premises from which the conclusion may logically be derived: *a valid argument.* **b.** Correctly inferred or deduced from a premise: *a valid conclusion.* **5.** *Archaic.* Of sound health; robust. [Fr. *valide* < OFr. < Lat. *validus,* strong < *valēre,* to be strong.] —**va´lid·ly** *adv.* —**va´lid·ness** *n.*

EXERCISE 4

USING A DESK DICTIONARY

Answer the questions by referring to the dictionary entries that follow the questions.

Complete sentences 1–4 using the words **dexterous, deft, adroit,** and **nimble.**

1. It is well for a dentist to be _____ .

2. It is a pleasure to observe a _____ quarterback in action.

3. A secretary of state must be _____ .

4. A ballet dancer must be _____ .

5. What does it mean to "**emerge** the winner"?

_____

6. What does it mean to "**emerge** from behind a hill"?

_____

7. What is an "**eminent** ecologist"?

_____

8. What is meant by "*Keys,* Harriet Krantz, **et al.**" in a footnote?

_____

9. What is the meaning of **regression** in the study of psychoanalysis?

_____

10. In modern usage, what is a **scapegoat**?

_____

11. What Old Testament event is the source of the word **scapegoat**?

_____

12. What custom is the etymological source of **whipping boy**?

_____

dex·ter·ous (děk′stər-əs, -strəs) also **dex·trous** (-strəs) *adj.* **1.** Adroit or skillful in the use of the hands, body, or mind. **2.** Done with dexterity. [<Lat. *dexter*, skillful, on the right side.] —**dex′ter·ous·ly** *adv.* —**dex′ter·ous·ness** *n.*

   Synonyms: *dexterous, deft, adroit, handy, nimble.* These adjectives refer to skill and ease in performance. *Dexterous* most often applies to manual ability. *Deft* suggests quickness, sureness, and lightness of touch in physical or mental activity. *Adroit* implies ease and natural skill, especially in meeting difficult situations. *Handy* implies a more modest aptitude, principally in manual work. *Nimble* stresses quickness and liveliness in physical or mental performance.

e·merge (ĭ-mûrj′) *intr.v.* **e·merged, e·merg·ing, e·merg·es. 1.** To rise up or come forth from or as if from immersion. **2.** To become evident or obvious. **3.** To issue, as from obscurity. **4.** To come into existence. [Lat. *emergere* : *ex-*, out + *merg-ere*, to immerse.]

em·i·nent (ĕm′ə-nənt) *adj.* **1.** Towering or standing out above others; prominent. **2.** Outstanding in performance, rank, or attainments; distinguished: *an eminent historian.* **3.** Possessing or displaying em-inence; noteworthy. [ME < OFr. or < Lat. *eminens,* pr.part. of *eminēre,* to project.] —**em′i·nent·ly** *adv.*

et al. *Lat.* et alii (and others).

re·gres·sion (rĭ-grĕsh′ən) *n.* **1.** Reversion; retrogression. **2.** Relapse to a less perfect or developed state. **3.** *Psychoanal.* Reversion to a more primitive or less mature behavior pattern. **4.** *Statistics.* The tendency for the expected value of one of two jointly correlated random variables to approach more closely the mean value of its set than the other. **5.** *Astron.* Retrogradation.

scape·goat (skāp′gōt′) *n.* **1.** In the Old Testament, a live goat over whose head Aaron confessed all the sins of the children of Israel and which was sent into the wilderness symbolically bearing their sins on the Day of Atonement. **2.** A person or group bearing blame for others. —*tr.v.* **-goat·ed, -goat·ing, -goats.** To make a scapegoat of. [(E)SCAPE + GOAT, as transl. of Heb. *azāzēl,* goat of Azazel, construed as *ēz-ōzēl,* goat that escapes.]

whipping boy *n.* **1.** A scapegoat. **2.** A boy formerly raised with a prince or other young nobleman and whipped for the latter's misdeeds.

EXERCISE 5

USING A DESK DICTIONARY

Answer the questions by referring to the dictionary entries that follow the questions.

1. What is **camaraderie?**

   _____

2. What is the etymological source of **camaraderie?**

   _____

3. What is the meaning of "page 120, **ff.**" in the index of a book?

   _____

4. What does it mean to be "**immersed** in work"?

   _____

5. What does it mean to "**immerse** metal in acid"?

   _____

Complete sentences 6–9 using the words **jovial, blithe, jocular,** and **convivial.**

6. They are _____ who often tell amusing stories.

7. Happy children, free of care, are _____ .

8. Santa Claus is a _____ character.

9. One who enjoys camaraderie is _____ .

10. What is the meaning of **niche** in the study of ecology?

    _____

11. What does it mean to say "Jim is a **Wasp**"?

    _____

12. What is the etymological source of **Wasp?**

    _____

ca·ma·ra·der·ie (kä′mə-rä′də-rē, kăm′ə-răd′ə-) *n.* Good will and lighthearted rapport between or among friends; comradeship [Fr. < *camarade*, comrade < OFr., roommate. —see COMRADE.]

ff. 1. folios. **2.** following.

im·merse (ĭ-mûrs′) *tr.v.* **-mersed, -mers·ing, -mers·es. 1.** To cover completely in a liquid; submerge. **2.** To baptize by submerging in water. **3.** To involve profoundly; absorb. [< Lat. *immersus*, p.part. of *immergere*, to immerse : *in-*, in + *mergere*, to dip.]

jol·ly (jŏl′ē) *adj.* **-li·er, -li·est. 1.** Full of merriment and good spirits; fun-loving. **2.** Exhibiting or occasioning happiness or mirth; cheerful. **3.** Greatly pleasing; enjoyable. —*adv. Chiefly Brit. Informal.* Very; extremely: *a jolly good cook.* —*v.* **-lied, -ly·ing, -lies.** —*tr.* To keep amused or diverted for one's own purposes; humor. —*intr.* To amuse oneself with humorous or teasing banter. —*n., pl.* **-lies. 1.** *Chiefly Brit.* A good or festive time. **2. jollies.** *Slang.* Amusement; kicks: *However you get your jollies is fine with me.* [ME *joli* < OFr.] —**jol′li·ly** *adv.* —**jol′li·ness** *n.*

Synonyms: jolly, jovial, merry, blithe, jocular, convivial. These adjectives describe persons who show good humor or high spirits or who are companionable in general. *Jolly* and *jovial* are especially associated with outward display of good cheer that invites friendship and promotes camaraderie. *Merry* suggests love of fun and laughter, and *blithe* implies buoyancy and freedom from care. *Jocular* refers to one who is sportive or given to joking and *convivial* to one who derives great pleasure from the cheerful companionship of others.

niche (nĭch, nēsh) *n.* **1.** A recess in a wall, as for holding a statue. **2.** A cranny, hollow, or crevice, as in rock. **3.** A situation or activity specially suited to a person's abilities or character. **4.** *Ecol.* **a.** The set of functional relationships of an organism or population to the environment it occupies. **b.** The area within a habitat occupied by an organism. —*tr.v.* **niched, nich·ing, nich·es.** To place in a niche. [Fr. < OFr. < *nichier*, to nest < VLat. *nidicare* < Lat. *nidus*, nest.]

Wasp or **WASP** *n.* A white Protestant of Anglo-Saxon ancestry. [W(HITE) + A(NGLO)-S(AXON) + P(ROTESTANT).] —**Wasp′ish** *adj.* —**Wasp′y** *adj.*

EXERCISE 6

USING A DESK DICTIONARY

Answer the questions by referring to the dictionary entries that follow the questions.

1. What is a "**flagrant** lie"?

   _____

2. What is meant by "orthography, **i.e.** spelling"?

   _____

3. What is meant by "**induced** to work for less money"?

   _____

4. What does it mean to "**induce** the solution to a problem"?

   _____

5. What does the following statement, printed on the container of a cleaning product, mean? "**Induce** vomiting if swallowed."

   _____

6. What is meant by **modification** in the study of linguistics?

   _____

Complete sentences 7–10 using the words **offended, insulted, affronted,** and **outraged.**

7. He was _____ when he learned that his car had been stolen and destroyed in an accident.

8. She was _____ by somebody in a crowd who had a foul body odor.

9. He was _____ when his best friend did not invite him to a party at her house.

10. She was _____ when she was unjustly accused of being unkind to her grandmother.

11. What does it mean to "**tantalize** an admirer"?

_____

12. What is the etymological source of **tantalize**?

_____

_____

_____

fla·grant (flā′grənt) _adj._ **1.** Extremely or deliberately conspicuous; shocking: _a flagrant miscarriage of justice._ **2.** _Obs._ Flaming; blazing. —See Usage note at **blatant.** [Lat. _flagrans, flagrant-,_ pr.part. of _flagare,_ to burn.] —**fla′gran·cy, fla′grance** _n._ —**fla′grant·ly** _adv._

i.e. _Lat._ id est (that is).

in·duce (ĭn-doos′, -dyoos′) _tr.v._ **-duced, -duc·ing, -duc·es. 1.** To lead or move by influence or persuasion: _finally induced him to give up smoking._ **2. a.** To bring about the occurrence of; cause. **b.** To arouse by stimulating. **3.** To infer by inductive reasoning. **4.** _Physics._ To produce (an electric current or magnetic effect) by induction. [ME _inducen_ < Lat. _inducere,_ to bring in : _in-,_ in + _ducere,_ to lead.] —**in·duc′er** _n._ —**in·duc′i·ble** _adj._

mod·i·fi·ca·tion (mŏd′ə-fĭ-kā′shən) _n._ **1.** The act of modifying or the condition of being modified. **2.** The result of modifying. **3.** A small alteration, adjustment, or limitation. **4.** _Biol._ A physical change in an organism due to environment or activity. **5.** _Ling._ **a.** A change undergone by a word as it passes from language to language. **b.** The linguistic change of a morpheme from one construction to another. —**mod′i·fi·ca′tor** _n._ —**mod′i·fi·ca′to·ry** (-kā′tə-rē), **mod′i·fi·ca′tive** (-kā′tĭv) _adj._

of·fend (ə-fĕnd′) _v._ **-fend·ed, -fend·ing, -fends.** —_tr._ **1.** To create or excite anger, resentment, or annoyance in. **2.** To be displeasing or disagreeable to: _Onions offend his sense of smell._ **3. a.** To transgress; violate. **b.** To cause to sin. —_intr._ **1.** To cause displeasure: _Bad manners may offend._ **2. a.** To violate a moral or divine law, sin. **b.** To violate a rule or law; _offend against the law_ [MF _offenden_ < OFr. _ofendre_ < Lat. _offendere._] —**of·fend′er** _n._

Synonyms: offend, insult, affront, outrage. _Offend_ is the least specific of these verbs denoting the act of giving displeasure; it often makes no implication regarding intent. _Insult_ applies to a deliberate act calculated to cause humiliation; _affront_ adds to this a stress on openness of attack, a sense of an insult to one's face. _Outrage,_ stronger still, emphasizes that which causes extreme resentment by flagrantly violating one's standards of right and decency.

tan·ta·lize (tăn′tə-līz′) _tr.v._ **-lized, -liz·ing, -liz·es.** To excite (another) by exposing something desirable while keeping it out of reach. [After _Tantalus._] —**tan′ta·li·za′tion** _n._ —**tan′ta·liz′er** _n._ —**tan′ta·liz′ing·ly** _adv._

Tan·ta·lus (tăn′tə-ləs) _n._ **1.** _Gk. Myth._ A king who for his crimes was condemned in Hades to stand in water that receded when he tried to drink, and with fruit hanging above him that receded when he reached for it. **2. tantalus.** A locked-up stand in which decanters are displayed. [Lat. < Gk. _Tantalos._]

USING A DESK DICTIONARY

Answer the questions by referring to the dictionary entries that follow the questions.

1. What is meant by "wine is an **aphrodisiac**"?

   _____

2. What is the etymological source of **aphrodisiac**?

   _____

3. What does it mean to "**integrate** the music, story, dancing, scenery, and costumes of a musical comedy"?

   _____

4. What does it mean to have "the **latitude** to buy what one wants to buy"?

   _____

5. What is the meaning of **latitude** in the study of geography?

   _____

6. What is meant by the **malapropism** "He's retarded on a pension"?

   _____

7. What is the etymological source of **malapropism**?

   _____

8. What does it mean to have been "**manipulated** into giving somebody five dollars"?

   _____

9. What does "Sigmund Freud **op. cit.**" mean in a footnote?

   _____

Complete the following sentences using the words **obtuse, dense,** and **crass.**

10. They are _____ who arrive to work late after having been told daily to arrive on time.

11. It is _____ of a teacher to tell students uncomplimentary things about their work or behavior in the presence of other students.

12. It is _____ to pick one's nose, spit, or belch in the presence of others.

aph·ro·dis·i·ac (ăf′rə-dĭz′ē-ăk′) *adj.* Stimulating or intensifying sexual desire. —*n.* An aphrodisiac drug or food. [Gk. *aphrodisiakos* < *aphrodisia,* sexual pleasures < *Aphroditē,* Aphrodite.] —**aph′ro·di·si′a·cal** (ăf′rə-dĭ-zī′ə-kəl) *adj.*

Aph·ro·di·te (ăf′rə-dī′tē) *n.* **1.** *Gk. Myth.* The goddess of love and beauty. **2. aphrodite.** A brightly colored butterfly, *Argynnis aphrodite,* of North America. [Gk. *Aphroditē.*]

in·te·grate (ĭn′tĭ-grāt′) *v.* **-grat·ed, -grat·ing, -grates.** —*tr.* **1.** To make into a whole by bringing all parts together; unify. **2.** To join with something else; unite. **3.** To open to people of all races or ethnic groups without restriction; desegregate. **4.** *Math.* **a.** To calculate the integral of. **b.** To perform integration upon. **5.** To bring about the integration of (personality traits). —*intr.* To become integrated or undergo integration. [Lat. *integrare, integrat-,* to make whole < *integer,* complete.] —**in′te·gra′tive** *adj.*

lat·i·tude (lăt′ĭ-tōōd′, -tyōōd′) *n.* **1.** Extent; breadth. **2.** Freedom from normal restraints, limitations, or regulations. **3. a.** The angular distance north or south of the equator, measured in degrees along a meridian, as on a map or globe. **b.** A region of the earth considered in relation to its distance from the equator: *temperate latitudes.* **4.** *Astron.* The angular distance of a celestial body north or south of the ecliptic. [ME < OFr. < Lat. *latitudo* < *latus,* wide.] —**lat′i·tu′din·al** (-tōōd′n-əl, -tyōōd′-) *adj.* —**lat′i·tu′di·nal·ly** *adv.*

mal·a·prop·ism (măl′ə-prŏp-ĭz′əm) *n.* A ludicrous misuse of a word. [After Mrs. *Malaprop,* a character in *The Rivals,* a play by Richard B. Sheridan (1751–1816).] —**mal′a·prop′i·an** (măl′ə-prŏp′ē-ən) *adj.*

ma·nip·u·late (mə-nĭp′yə-lāt′) *tr.v.* **-lat·ed, -lat·ing, -lates. 1.** To operate or control by skilled use of the hands; handle: *manipulated the lights to get just the effect she wanted.* **2.** To influence or manage shrewdly or deviously: *He manipulated public opinion in his favor.* **3.** To tamper with or falsify (financial records) for personal gain. [Back-formation < MANIPULATION.] —**ma·nip′u·la·bil′i·ty** *n.* —**ma·nip′u·la·ble** (-lə-bəl) *adj.* —**ma·nip′u·la′tive, ma·nip′u·la·to′ry** (-lə-tôr′ē, -tōr′ē) *adj.* —**ma·nip′u·la′tor** *n.*

op. cit. *Lat.* opere citato (in the work cited).

stu·pid (stōō′pĭd, styōō′-) *adj.* **-er, -est. 1.** Slow to apprehend; dumb. **2.** Showing a lack of intelligence. **3.** Dazed or stunned. **4.** *Informal.* Pointless; worthless: *a stupid job.* —*n. Informal.* A stupid person. [Fr. *stupide* < Lat. *stupidus* < *stupēre,* to be stunned.] —**stu′pid·ly** *adv.* —**stu′pid·ness** *n.*

   Synonyms: stupid, dumb, slow, dull, obtuse, dense, crass. These adjectives mean lacking mental acuity. *Slow* and the informal *dumb* imply chronic sluggishness of perception or understanding; *stupid* and *dull* occasionally suggest a merely temporary state. *Stupid* and *dumb* also can refer to individual actions that are extremely foolish. *Obtuse* implies insensitivity or unreceptiveness to instruction. *Dense* suggests a mind that is virtually impenetrable or incapable of grasping even elementary ideas. *Crass* refers especially to stupidity marked by coarseness or tastelessness.

8. LEARN NEW WORDS

On the average, students learn the meanings of about 1,500 words each year they are in college. They need to know new words to understand the subjects they study, and college stimulates their desire to enlarge their vocabularies. This chapter explains how to undertake a systematic program for learning new words.

LOCATE WORDS TO LEARN

Learn the meanings of words instructors explain in classes. Write down in class notes everything they say about word meanings. Words that teachers discuss in class are usually important words to know. Methods for taking good class notes are explained in Chapter 16.

Also, of course, learn the meanings of words that are explained in textbooks. The most important words to learn may be listed at the beginning or end of chapters, in a **glossary,** or they may be printed in italics, boldface, or a special color (such as red). The important terminology in *RSVP* is printed in boldface, and it is defined in a glossary at the back of the book.

As you study required reading materials, you will come across such words as *tenacious, presupposition,* and *convivial,* which are used in exercises for Chapters 5–7 of *RSVP.* Words such as these are known by most third- and fourth-year college students. If you don't know them, why not learn them?

MAKE NOTES FOR WORDS

One way to learn new words is to make notes of the type illustrated in Figure 8.1 and to study the notes using methods explained in Chapter 20.

The notes for *ostracize* in Figure 8.1 are written on a 3-by-5-inch card, though they could have been written on a 3-by-5-inch piece of paper.

© 1984 by Houghton Mifflin Company

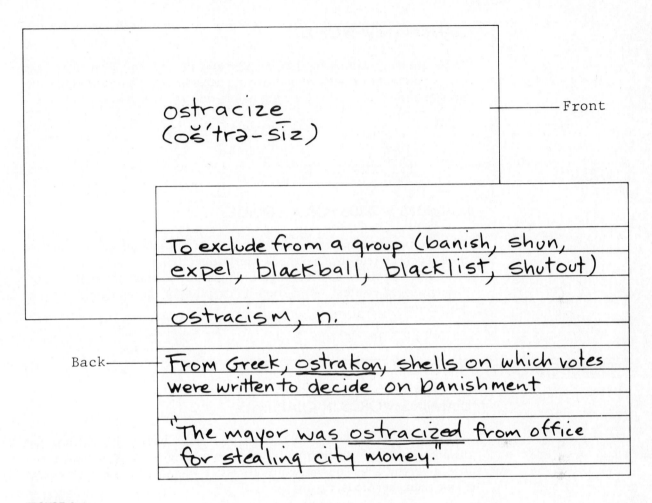

ostracize
(ŏsˊtrə-sīz)

— Front

To exclude from a group (banish, shun, expel, blackball, blacklist, shutout)

ostracism, n.

From Greek, ostrakon, shells on which votes were written to decide on banishment

"The mayor was ostracized from office for stealing city money."

Back —

FIGURE 8.1

Notes for learning a word

They include (1) the correct spelling of *ostracize*, (2) its pronunciation, (3) its definition, (4) some of its synonyms, (5) its noun form, (6) its etymology, and (7) a sentence that illustrates how it is used.

It is not necessary that notes always be as complete as those in Figure 8.1. In some instances notes may include only the correct spelling of a word and its meaning. Include in notes only the information that you want to learn about a word.

The information on the back of the card in Figure 8.1 is written upside-down in relation to *ostracize*, written on the front. Using this procedure, information on the back is in the proper position for reading when the card is turned over.

Notes may, of course, be written on notebook paper rather than on cards. A good form for notes on notebook paper is to write words on the left side of the red margin and information about them on the right side of the margin. In this way, definitions can be covered to learn word meanings, using methods explained in Chapter 20.

LEARNING NEW WORDS

Use the suggestions in this chapter and in Chapter 20 to learn the words you want or need to add to your vocabulary. The following exercises provide practice for learning words that are worthwhile to know.

EXERCISE 1

LEARNING WORDS FOR A COURSE

Locate twenty important terms printed in italics, boldface, or a special color (such as red) in a textbook you are studying for another course. Make notes of the type illustrated in Figure 8.1 to learn their meanings. You will need *twenty* 3-by-5-inch index cards or pieces of paper to do this exercise.

EXERCISE 2

LEARNING WORDS IN CHAPTER 5

Use methods explained in this chapter and Chapter 20 to learn the meanings of 80 words printed in boldface in Chapter 5. Your instructor may give you a list of the words to assist you in preparing for a quiz about their meanings.

EXERCISE 3

LEARNING WORDS IN CHAPTER 6

Use methods explained in this chapter and Chapter 20 to learn the meanings of 75 words printed in boldface in Chapter 6. Your instructor may give you a list of the words to assist you in preparing for a quiz about their meanings.

EXERCISE 4

LEARNING WORDS IN CHAPTER 7

Use methods explained in this chapter and Chapter 20 to learn the meanings of 55 words printed in boldface in Chapter 7. Your instructor may give you a list of the words to assist you in preparing for a quiz about their meanings.

EXERCISE 5

LEARNING WORDS IN CHAPTERS 13 AND 14

Use methods explained in this chapter and Chapter 20 to learn the meanings of 57 words printed in italics in questions 3–5 for Exercises 1–10 in Chapter 13 and Exercises 6–14 of Chapter 14. Your instructor may give you a list of the words to assist you in preparing for a quiz about their meanings.

III. READ WITH UNDERSTANDING

In a typical term of study, full-time college students read five, six, or more textbooks. The chapters in this part of *RSVP* explain how to read textbooks efficiently and with good comprehension. You will learn

1. how to gather quickly a great deal of information about what you will read before you actually read it.
2. how to locate the major and minor details about topics discussed in books.
3. how to identify the six types of information that frequently appear in textbooks.
4. how to find information that is hinted at or suggested in books as well as the information that is directly stated in them.
5. how to evaluate the merits of the things you read.
6. how to interpret tables and graphs.

These reading skills are illustrated using excerpts from books of the type you are studying, or will soon be studying, in college. And, you will practice the skills by applying them to passages from college textbooks to help you meet the challenge of reading books that are more difficult than the ones you read in high school.

9. PREVIEW BEFORE READING

Previewing is the first of seven steps in reading textbooks with good comprehension.

1. **Preview before reading.**
2. Locate major details.
3. Find minor details.
4. Identify expository patterns.
5. Infer implied meanings.
6. Make evaluations.
7. Interpret tables and graphs.

Most students prepare to read a chapter in a textbook by counting the pages in it. There is a much better method—it's called previewing.

Preview a book before you read it. A **preview of a book** includes reading the preface or introduction and the table of contents to learn how it is organized and what its major features are. Then, before you read a chapter in a book, preview it as well. A **preview of a chapter** includes reading the title, introduction, headings, and summary. It takes only a few minutes to preview, but the time is well spent because it is proper preparation for reading with good comprehension.

PREVIEW BOOKS

Use the following procedures to preview textbooks soon after you purchase them at the beginning of each term.

1. Read the **title page,** which is the page at the beginning of a book that gives information about the title, author, and publisher. Information about authors of textbooks usually includes the colleges or universities where they teach. Information about publishers includes the cities in which books are published. When more than one city is listed, the book was published in the first city in the list.

2. Read the **copyright page,** which is the page following the title page—it states the year a book was published. If more than one year is listed, the copyright year is the most recent year.
3. Study the **table of contents,** which lists the chapters of a book, the major headings in chapters, and indicates whether chapters are grouped into parts. A table of contents is usually located immediately after a title page, but sometimes it follows an introduction or preface.
4. Examine the **introduction** or **preface;** they give the author's explanations of why a book was written, and they often give a summary of the purpose, philosophy, or contents of a book. They are located immediately after or before a table of contents.
5. Determine if the book has an **appendix,** which is supplementary materials or information. When a book has an appendix, it is located in the back of the book, usually immediately following the last chapter.
6. Observe if the book has a **glossary**—a list of important terms used in the book and their definitions. When a book has a glossary, it is usually located following the last chapter or the appendix; however, some textbooks have short glossaries in each chapter.
7. Determine if a book has an **index,** which is an alphabetical listing of the topics in a book and the page numbers on which they are discussed. It is always located at the very end of a book. Some textbooks have a subject index and a *name index,* or *author index.* When this is the case, the name index comes before the subject index. When you do not find a person's name in an index, look to see if the book has a name index. For instance, if you do not find "Sigmund Freud" listed in the index of a psychology textbook, look for it in the name index.

Exercises 1 and 3 at the end of this chapter provide practice for previewing books.

PREVIEW CHAPTERS

Before you read a chapter of a textbook, preview it by reading the chapter title, introduction, headings, and summary. Also study the figures or tables in the chapter and lists of important terminology, learning goals, or review questions. The following discussions explain how to preview the chapters of textbooks.

Title and Introduction

Begin a preview by reading the chapter title and introduction. A chapter title states what the chapter is about, and the introduction usually explains the main purpose of the chapter. Following are the title and introduction for a chapter in a psychology textbook.

CHAPTER 11: LEARNING AND INSTRUCTION

Henry Adams once said of children: "They know enough who know how to learn." There is much to be said for this view, for complex learning does not take place automatically. Carefully planned instruction is often helpful.

In this chapter we move beyond theory and research to consider the application of learning principles in practical situations. The central question is this: Given a certain task to be learned, such as a geography unit, how does one go about planning the learning environment?

Notice that the first sentence in the second paragraph of this introduction explains how the chapter is related to other chapters in the book. The last sentence of the second paragraph states the question that is answered by the chapter. Those who find the answer to the question as they read the chapter will have a good understanding of the information in it.

Whether an introduction to a chapter is short or long, read it carefully as part of your preview.

Headings

Continue a chapter preview by reading headings. When you preview headings, you learn the topics discussed in a chapter and the emphasis given to each topic. The number of pages devoted to a topic often provides a clue about its importance or complexity; the longer the discussion, the more important or complex it is likely to be.

Figure 9.1 is a page from a history textbook that illustrates one of the many ways major headings and subheadings are shown. Notice in Figure 9.1 on page 108 that the major heading, "The Watergate Scandal," is in large type and printed above a column of print but the subheadings are in small type and printed in boxes.

Following are some ways to determine the relationships among headings in a textbook:

1. If headings are printed in different sizes of type, the larger the type, the more important the heading.
2. If headings are printed in the same size type but some are printed IN ALL CAPITAL LETTERS and others are not, the headings printed in all capital letters are more important.
3. If headings are printed in the same size type but some are printed in **boldface** and others are not, the headings printed in boldface are more important.
4. If headings are printed in the same size type but some are printed in black ink and others are printed in another color (such as red), the headings printed in the other color are more important.

Textbooks often have headings in addition to major headings and subheadings. Use hints in this list to help in understanding the relative importance of headings in a book that has three or four types of headings.

FIGURE 9.1

Major heading and sub-
headings in a textbook

**Major
heading**

**Sub-
headings**

return to old-fashioned morality and a balanced budget. He blamed government for fettering American economic creativity. America could again be what it once was, he declared, and Americans wanted to believe him.

The Watergate scandal

Watergate actually began in 1971, with the establishment by the White House not only of CREEP but of the overlapping Special Investigations Unit, known familiarly as the Plumbers. Created to stop the leaking of confidential information to the press following publication of the Pentagon Papers, the Plumbers burglarized the office of Daniel Ellsberg's psychiatrist in an attempt to find information that would discredit him. It was the Plumbers who broke into the Democratic National Committee's headquarters to photograph documents and install wiretaps. And it was CREEP that raised the money to pay the Plumbers' expenses both before and after the break-in. CREEP's official duty was to solicit campaign contributions. The committee had managed to collect $60 million, much of it donated illegally by corporations.

The arrest of the Watergate burglars generated furious activity in the White House. Incriminating documents were shredded, E. Howard Hunt's name was expunged from the White House telephone directory, and tens of thousands of dollars in $100 bills were removed from safes and paid as hush money to the burglars. In addition, Nixon ordered his chief of staff, H. R. Haldeman, to discourage the FBI's investigation into the burglary on the pretext that it might compromise national security.

Soon after the break-in the Democrats filed a damage suit against CREEP and the five burglars for invasion of privacy. John Mitchell, the chairman of Nixon's re-election campaign, called the suit "another example of sheer demagoguery." CREEP "did not authorize and does not condone the alleged actions of the five men apprehended there," Mitchell said. Later, Nixon announced to the press that his White House

*White House
cover-up*

counsel, John W. Dean III, had conducted a "complete investigation," and that no one in the administration "was involved in this very bizarre incident." At the same time, Nixon authorized CREEP payments in excess of $460,000 to keep Hunt and others from implicating the White House in the crime.

Thanks to White House efforts to cover up the scandal, the break-in went practically unnoticed by the electorate. Meanwhile, Nixon's "dirty tricksters" were active in the primaries, sabotaging Democratic candidates' campaigns. Funded by CREEP, they forged press releases and campaign handouts, set off stink bombs, heckled speakers, and cut telephone lines. They falsely accused Senators Hubert Humphrey and Henry Jackson of sexual improprieties, and they made special efforts to offend racial, religious, and ethnic minorities. As one of the tricksters explained, "The idea was to get the [Democratic] candidates backbiting each other."

Had it not been for the diligent efforts of reporters, government special prosecutors, federal judges, senators and congressional representatives, and an aroused public, Nixon might have succeeded in disguising his involvement in Watergate. Slowly, however, the ball of fabrications and distortions began to unravel. In spring 1973, U.S. District Court Judge John Sirica tried the burglars, one of whom, James McCord, implicated his superiors in CREEP and at the White House. In April the acting director of the FBI, L. Patrick Gray, resigned after confessing that he had confiscated incriminating documents, taken them home, and burned them. Meanwhile, the Senate Select Committee on Campaign Practices, chaired by Senator Sam Ervin, heard testimony from White House aides. John Dean acknowledged not only that there had been a cover-up, but that the president had directed it. Another aide, Alexander Butterfield, shocked the committee and the nation by disclosing that Nixon had had a taping system installed in the White House, and that conversations about Watergate had been recorded.

Nixon feigned innocence, but on April 30 he announced the resignations of his two chief White House aides, John Ehrlichman and H. R. Haldeman. Speaking to a nationwide television audience, the president pledged that he would determine the facts

*Watergate
hearings and
investigations*

Figures and Tables

Photographs, drawings, diagrams, graphs, charts, and other graphic materials are included, often at great expense, to summarize or illustrate information in textbooks. As you preview a chapter, examine figures and tables and read the titles and captions for them; you will find that they frequently summarize the information in a section of a chapter.

For example, Figure 9.2 is a pictorial summary of the main topic and subtopics discussed on ten pages of a meteorology textbook; students who study the figure are provided with a summary of the ten-page discussion.

Methods for interpreting tables and graphs are explained in Chapter 15.

Important Terminology

A chapter may begin or end with a list of the important **terminology,** or words, that is introduced in it. Terminology may be listed under a heading such as "Key Terms," "Important Words," "Key Concepts," or

FIGURE 9.2

The hydrologic cycle

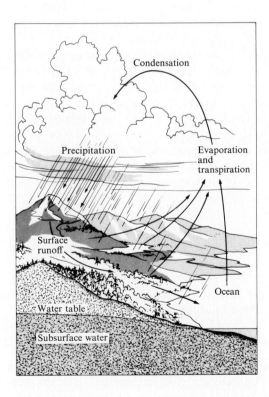

"Terms Used in This Chapter." Following is an example of the lists of terms that appear at the end of chapters in an astronomy textbook.

Key Concepts

Asterism	Circumpolar constellations	Precession
Autumnal equinox	Constellation	Summer solstice
Celestial equator	Declination	Vernal equinox
Celestial pole	Ecliptic	Winter solstice
Celestial sphere		Zodiac

When there is a list of terminology at the beginning or end of a chapter, study it as part of your preview. If there is no list of terms, **scan** the pages of the chapter as you preview to locate the important words introduced in it; they are likely to be printed in italics, boldface, or a special color (such as red). In *RSVP,* terminology is printed in boldface, and it is defined in a glossary at the back of the book.

Learning Goals and Review Questions

A chapter may begin or end with a list that summarizes what should be learned when the chapter is read and studied. A list at the beginning of a chapter may have a heading such as "Learning Goals," "Learning Objectives," "Performance Goals," "Study Guides," or "Chapter Preview." A list at the end of a chapter may have a heading such as "Questions," "Exercises," "Review Questions," or "Discussion Questions."

Figure 9.3 shows learning goals on the first page of a chapter in a chemistry book. The first goal is: "Describe Dalton's atomic theory, Thomson's model of the atom, and Rutherford's model of the atom." Students who study the chapter to achieve this goal and the other seven goals in the list are likely to learn almost everything they are expected to learn in the chapter.

Whether a list is at the beginning or at the end of a chapter, read it as part of a chapter preview. After reading the chapter, study the items in the list again to make certain that you have learned everything you were supposed to learn.

Summaries

A textbook chapter may end with a summary. It is helpful to read the summary *before* reading the chapter. Read the following summary from the end of a chapter in a business textbook.

SUMMARY: DEVELOPING POSITIVE FIRST IMPRESSIONS

In a business setting positive first impressions are important because they contribute to repeat business and greater customer loyalty. People tend to form impressions quickly at the time of the initial meeting,

FIGURE 9.3

Learning goals in a
chemistry textbook

111

CHAPTER 4

Atomic theory, or what's in an atom?

For besides that which happens in the generation, corruption, nutrition, and wasting of bodies, that which we discover partly by our microscopes of the exstream littlenesse of even the scarce sensible parts of concretes; and partly by the chymical resolutions of mixt bodies, and by divers other operations of spagyrical (alchemical) fires upon them, seems sufficiently to manifest their consisting of parts very minute and of differing figures. And that there does also intervene a various local motion of such small bodies, will scarce be denied.

Robert Boyle
THE SCEPTICAL CHYMIST, 1661

LEARNING GOALS

After you've worked your way through this chapter, you should be able to:

1. Describe Dalton's atomic theory, Thomson's model of the atom, and Rutherford's model of the atom.

2. Give the charge and mass of the electron, proton, and neutron.

3. Find the number of protons, electrons, and neutrons in an atom of an element or an isotope.

4. Define an isotope and give examples.

5. Use the standard notation for isotopes.

6. Calculate the average atomic weight of an element when you're given the relative abundances of the isotopes.

7. Calculate the percent abundance of two isotopes when given the atomic weight of each isotope and the average atomic weight.

8. Using the table of relative abundances of isotopes, calculate the number of atoms or grams of a particular isotope present in a given sample.

and these first impressions tend to be preserved. Leonard and Natalie Zunin describe the four-minute barrier as the average time people spend together before a relationship is either established or denied. In a business setting this time interval is often reduced to seconds.

The impression you form of another person during the initial contact is made up of assumptions and facts. When meeting someone for the first time, people tend to rely more heavily on assumptions. Many of your assumptions can be traced to early cultural conditioning. Assumptions are also based on "surface language." The Zunins describe surface language as a pattern of immediate impressions conveyed by appearance. The clothing and jewelry you wear, your hair style, the fragrances you use all combine to make a statement about you to others.

Egon Von Furstenberg, author of *The Power Look*, contends that discrimination on the basis of appearance is still a fact of life in the business world. The clothing you wear is an important part of the image you communicate to others. Three things tend to influence your choice of clothing for work: (1) the products or services sold by the employer, (2) the type of customer served, and (3) the desired image projected by the firm.

In addition to clothing, research indicates that facial expressions strongly influence whether you like or dislike someone. The expression on your face can quickly trigger a positive or negative reaction. Likewise, your voice, handshake, and manners also contribute to the image you project when meeting others.

When a summary is easy to understand, read it when you preview the chapter. However, a summary may be difficult to understand because it includes many technical words that are learned as a result of reading a chapter. When this is the case, read the summary *after* you read the chapter.

PREVIEWING BEFORE READING

Use the following procedures to preview books soon after purchasing them:

1. Read the title page.
2. Read the copyright page.
3. Study the table of contents.
4. Examine the introduction or preface.
5. Determine if there is an appendix.
6. Observe if it has a glossary.
7. Locate the index or indexes.

Also, preview a chapter before reading it:

1. Read the title and introduction.
2. Read the headings and subheadings.
3. Examine the figures and tables.

4. Read the list of important terminology, or find terms that are printed in italics, boldface, or a special color (such as red).
5. Study learning goals or review questions.
6. Read the summary if it is easy to understand.

The following exercises provide practice for previewing textbooks and chapters in textbooks.

EXERCISE 1

QUICK PREVIEW OF TWO BOOKS

Write the titles of two of your textbooks over the columns on the right. Then, answer the following questions about the books. If an answer is no or none, write "no" or "none."

1. _____   2. _____

1. Does the title page give information about the title, author, and publisher?

   _____   _____

2. In what year was the book published?

   _____   _____

3. How many chapters are listed in the table of contents?

   _____   _____

4. Are the chapters grouped in parts? If so, how many parts are there in the book?

   _____   _____

5. How many pages long is the introduction or preface?

   _____   _____

6. Is there a special preface for students?

   _____   _____

7. Does the book have an appendix? If so, what is in it?

   _____   _____

8. Does the book have a glossary at the back? If not, is there a glossary in each chapter?

   _____   _____

9. Does the book have an index?

   _____   _____

10. Is there a name index or author index?

    _____   _____

EXERCISE 2

QUICK PREVIEW OF TWO CHAPTERS

Preview one chapter in each of the two books that you previewed when you did Exercise 1. Write the titles of the chapters over the columns on the right. Then, answer the following questions about the chapters. If the answer to a question is no or none, write "no" or "none."

1. _____   2. _____

1. Does the title state clearly what the chapter is about?

2. Does the introduction state the purpose of the chapter?

3. How many major headings are there in the chapter?

4. Do subheadings follow some major headings?

5. How many figures, tables, or pictures are in the chapter?

6. Is there a list of important terms? If so, how many terms are in the list?

7. Are learning goals listed at the beginning of the chapter?

8. Are discussion questions listed at the end of the chapter?

9. Is there an easy-to-understand summary at the end of the chapter?

EXERCISE 3

IN-DEPTH PREVIEW OF A BOOK

Do this exercise using the textbook that you found to have the most features when you completed Exercise 1.

Find the information for questions 1–6 on the title page and the copyright page of the book.

1. Title _____

2. Author(s) _____

3. School affiliation of author(s) _____

   _____

4. Publisher _____

5. City of publication _____

6. Date of publication _____

Find the answers for questions 7–9 by referring to the table of contents of the book.

7. If the chapters of the book are organized into parts, what is the title of the first part of the book? If the chapters are not organized into parts, write "no parts."

   _____

8. List the titles of the chapters in the first part of the book. Or, if the book is not organized into parts, list the titles for the first four chapters.

   _____

   _____

   _____

9. List the first six major headings in the first chapter of the book.

   _____

   _____

_____

_____

_____

_____

The introduction or preface is located before or after the table of contents.

10. What two types of information in the introduction or preface are most interesting to you?

  a. _____

  b. _____

An appendix is usually located immediately after the last chapter of a book.

11. If the book has an appendix, what type of supplementary material is included in it? If it has no appendix, write "no appendix."

  _____

A glossary is usually located immediately after the last chapter or the appendix of a book. Sometimes there is a short glossary in each chapter of a book.

12. If the book has a glossary, approximately how many terms are defined in it? If it has no glossary, write "no glossary."

  _____

An index is always located at the very end of a book.

13. If the book has an index, how many pages long is it? If it has no index, write "no index."

  _____

14. If the book has a name index, how many pages long is it? If it has no name index, write "no name index."

  _____

EXERCISE 4

IN-DEPTH PREVIEW OF A CHAPTER

Do this exercise using the textbook that you found to have the most features when you did Exercise 2. Preview a chapter that you have not yet read.

1. What is the title of the textbook?

   _____

2. What is the title of the chapter you are previewing?

   _____

3. How many pages long is the chapter?

   _____

4. A major purpose of the chapter should be stated in the introduction. What is the major purpose of the chapter?

   _____

   _____

5. How many major headings are there in the chapter?

   _____

6. List the first four major headings in the chapter.

   _____

   _____

   _____

   _____

7. List the subheadings under one of the major headings on the following lines. Write the major heading and indent the subheadings under it.

   _____

   _____

_____

_____

_____

_____

8. Describe the information in the most interesting figure or table in the chapter.

_____

_____

9. If there is a list of terminology in the chapter, how many terms are in the list. If there is no list of terminology, write "no list."

_____

10. If terminology is printed in italics, boldface, or a special color (such as red) in the chapter, write four of the terms on the following lines.

a. _____   b. _____

c. _____   d. _____

11. If there is a list of learning goals at the beginning of the chapter, how many goals are listed? If there is no list, write "no learning goals."

_____

12. If there is a list of discussion questions at the end of the chapter, how many questions are listed? If there is no list, write "no discussion questions."

_____

13. If there is a summary at the end of the chapter, how many paragraphs long is it? If there is no summary, write "no summary."

_____

14. If there is a summary, is it easy to read and understand?

_____

© 1984 by Houghton Mifflin Company

10. LOCATE MAJOR DETAILS

After previewing a chapter, read it a section at a time to learn about topics by locating major details.

1. Preview before reading.
2. **Locate major details.**
3. Find minor details.
4. Identify expository patterns.
5. Infer implied meanings.
6. Make evaluations.
7. Interpret tables and graphs.

Major details are information that is subordinate to, or beneath, topics stated in headings. The topic of the following passage is "Steps in the Selling Process." The major details in the passage are underlined.

STEPS IN THE SELLING PROCESS

Many businesses have as their primary function the selling of a product or service; selling may be viewed as a four-step process.

First, the selling business wants to find buyers. Buyers are attracted to a product or service through advertising, the availability of the product or service, or the efforts of salespeople. Department stores find buyers by advertising and by being located where customers shop. Encyclopedias are often sold through advertising and the efforts of salespeople.

After potential buyers have been found, a product or service must be presented in the most attractive and convincing way possible. Expensive perfume is offered for sale in attractive and expensive-looking bottles. Low-cost vacation trips are sold in offices that convince customers they will receive a bargain; it would not be convincing to sell low-cost travel in an office that is decorated with rare objects of art and expensive furniture.

Once buyers have been found and the product or service has been presented in an attractive and convincing way, the salesperson must

121

create the customer's desire to buy. This is usually achieved by persuading customers that their lives will be better when they make a purchase. Another technique salespeople use is to establish rapport with customers so they buy because they like the salesperson rather than because they need or want what they purchase.

   The final step in the selling process is to close the sale. Once the customer has the desire to buy, the salesperson will do something to motivate the customer to put out money for a purchase. A clothing salesperson might ask, "Will you take the brown sweater or the blue one?" A travel salesperson might close a sale by asking, "Shall I book you hotel rooms in London, Paris, and Rome, or have you decided not to stop in Paris?"

The major details are four steps in the selling process.

This chapter illustrates methods for locating the major details that explain or elaborate upon topics stated in textbook headings.

INTRODUCTIONS

A heading in a textbook may be followed by an introduction that names the major details presented in following paragraphs. An arrow indicates the location of a list of major details in the following introduction:

AGENCIES OF SOCIALIZATION

   The socialization process involves many different influences that affect the individual throughout life. The most important of these influences are *agencies of socialization*, institutions or other structured situations in which socialization takes place. Four agencies of socialization—the family, the school, the peer group, and the mass ◄ media—are especially important in modern societies, for they affect almost everyone in a powerful and lasting way.

The four major details discussed in following paragraphs are named in the last sentence of this introduction: (1) the family, (2) the school, (3) the peer group, and (4) the mass media. The details enumerate agencies of socialization.

   Sometimes introductions state the number of details discussed in following paragraphs without naming them. An arrow indicates the location of a statement about the number of major details in the following introduction.

PRODUCT DEVELOPMENT

   Between the time a product idea is born and the time the finished products actually arrive in the marketplace, the concept may undergo many changes. The end result reflects decisions made during product development, which may include up to eight stages. ◄

The last sentence of this introduction states that eight major details are discussed in following paragraphs—they are stages in the development of a new product.

When an introduction gives information about major details, use it to guide reading. For instance, if an introduction states that a passage explains eight stages of product development, use the information to read the selection for the purpose of learning about each of the eight stages.

SUBHEADINGS

Often major details are indicated by subheadings that follow a major heading. Read the introduction to the following passage and place an arrow next to the place where the number of major details is stated in it. Then, underline the subheadings that are used to further emphasize the major details.

STAGES OF PREGNANCY

A normal pregnancy can last between 240 and 300 days, with about 266 days the average length. Most literature divides pregnancy into three, three-month periods called *trimesters.*

First Trimester

During the first trimester many women experience tiredness, upset stomach, and the need to urinate frequently. Psychologically this is a time of acknowledging and "owning" the pregnancy. During this time most women experience both negative and positive feelings about being pregnant.

Second Trimester

During the second trimester the pregnancy begins to show. The weight of the uterus increases about twenty times during pregnancy, with most of this increase occurring before the twentieth week as the fetus rapidly increases in size . . . . During the fourth or fifth month fetal heartbeats become audible through a stethoscope. Fetal heartbeats are much more rapid than those of the mother, about 120 to 140 beats per minute compared to her 70 to 80. The movements of the fetus become perceptible during the second trimester and by late in the trimester become visible as momentary protrusions and movements of the mother's abdomen. Any nausea or strong needs to nap that were present during the first trimester usually diminish and disappear during the second. By mid-pregnancy a woman's breasts, stimulated by hormones, have become functionally complete for nursing.

Third Trimester

The uterus becomes increasingly large during the third trimester, and a woman may become increasingly uncomfortable. The stomach and other internal organs become crowded. Pressure on the bladder may again cause frequent urination. Feelings of wanting to nap may return. The baby will frequently be felt moving, kicking, sometimes even hiccupping.

You should have placed an arrow next to the second sentence of the introduction and you should have underlined the subheadings "First Trimester," "Second Trimester," and "Third Trimester."

WORDS IN ITALICS OR BOLDFACE

Words printed in italics, boldface, or a special color (such as red), are also often used as clues to major details. Read the following passage, and underline the words printed in italics that name the major details discussed in it.

TYPES OF SOCIAL MOBILITY

Social mobility can take several forms. *Horizontal mobility* involves a change from one status to another that is roughly equivalent—say, from that of a plumber to that of a carpenter. *Vertical mobility* involves a change from one status to another that is higher or lower—for example, from plumber to corporation president, or vice versa. *Intragenerational mobility* involves a change in status (horizontal or vertical) during an individual's career, while *intergenerational mobility* involves a change (horizontal or vertical) in the status of family members from one generation to the next. Sociologists are especially interested in vertical intergenerational mobility, which occurs, for example, when a plumber's child becomes a corporation president or vice versa. The amount of this intergenerational mobility in a society is of great significance, for it tells us to what extent inequalities are built into the society. If there is very little intergenerational mobility, people's life chances are for the most part being determined at the moment of birth. If there is a good deal of mobility from one generation to the next, people are clearly able to achieve new statuses through their own efforts, regardless of the circumstances of their birth.

You should have underlined the words "horizontal mobility," "vertical mobility," "intragenerational mobility," and "intergenerational mobility," where they are printed in italics.

NUMBERS

Major details in a passage may also be indicated by words such as "first," "second" or "third" or by Arabic numerals, such as "1," "2," and "3."

Numbers are used to indicate how many major details there are in the following passage. Read the passage and then underline the sentences that state tactics food quacks use.

TACTICS OF FOOD QUACKS

Many erroneous food claims are based on the idea that the virtues of a particular food are necessary for medicinal reasons, vitality and youthfulness, or sexual rejuvenation. The food quack promotes the single food as a cure-all that has magical properties, to the exclusion of other highly nutritious foods. A dietary plan that does not involve a food selection plan based on the basic four food groups (milk, meat, vegetables and fruit, and cereal) should be considered highly dubious.

A second tactic of the food quack is to recommend the omission of certain foods because they may be injurious to the health. He or she may cite fortified foods, foods grown with chemical fertilizers, or foods that have been commercially prepared as being unfit for human consumption. The truth is that these are the same foods that most Americans eat and have eaten for years and with which they seem to have prospered fairly well. Over the years, the average height and weight of Americans have increased; although this is not exclusively due to good nutrition, the use of fortified foods and improved methods of food storage and processing have had a great deal to do with it.

A third argument used by the food quack is the appeal to "natural" foods. The prices of these naturally grown foods are outlandish, and the nutritional benefits are no greater than those of regular foods.

You should have underlined the second sentence of the first paragraph and the first sentences of the second and third paragraphs.

FIRST SENTENCES OF PARAGRAPHS

Sometimes the number of major details in a passage is not indicated by an introduction, subheadings, words printed in italics or boldface, or numbers. In such instances, they may be stated in the first sentences of paragraphs.

Read the following passage and underline in it the first sentences of paragraphs that state a norm for eye behavior.

NORMS FOR EYE BEHAVIOR

One of the first things many of us learn as children is that people who lie do not look straight into our eyes. There are many folk tales like this one about eye behavior. As you might guess, some are based on myth, including this one. While our eye behavior communicates many things, the degree to which we are telling the truth is not one of them. And if you don't believe us, ask a good poker player like former world champion Amarillo Slim.

One of the most pervasive norms concerns attention. When we communicate with a person we assume that if he or she looks us in the eyes the person is paying attention. We should realize, though, that maintaining strict eye contact is uncomfortable for some people and, as a result, is not necessarily indicative of attentiveness.

Another norm in our culture is that sustained eye contact is an invitation to communicate. Have you ever been called on in class when you did not want to be called on? Chances are you made and briefly sustained eye contact with your teacher. Most students intuitively realize this and avoid eye contact with a teacher when they are unsure about responding to the question.

Finally, eye contact in our culture commonly is associated with physical attraction. Depending on the environment, males frequently assume that if a female is looking at him, she finds him physically attractive. Lest females take this as another indication of the macho needs of males, females frequently draw an identical conclusion when being "checked" out by a male. The truth of the matter is, though, people stare. If we notice we are the primary object in another's field of vision, it does not necessarily mean the person is enamoured with our physical appearances.

You should have underlined the first sentences of the second, third, and fourth paragraphs. The first paragraph is an introduction; it does not state a norm for eye behavior or how many norms for eye behavior (details) are discussed in the passage.

LOCATING MAJOR DETAILS

Read textbooks to find the major details that are presented for topics stated in headings. One or more of the following may give help:

1. An introduction
2. Subheadings
3. Words printed in italics, boldface, or a special color (such as red)
4. A number or numbers
5. First sentences of paragraphs

The following exercises provide practice for locating details in textbook passages.

EXERCISE 1

DEFENSE MECHANISMS

Preview "Defense Mechanisms" and circle the numbers in front of items in the following list that help in locating the exact number of major details in it.

1. An introduction
2. Subheadings
3. Words printed in italics
4. A number or numbers
5. First sentences of paragraphs

Then, underline the locations of the major details in the passage.

DEFENSE MECHANISMS

So many adults confront the problems of life in similar ways that these ways of coping with frustration have been identified and collectively named defense mechanisms. **Defense mechanisms** are emotional reactions that serve the important purpose of helping people to feel good about themselves in situations which have the potential for making them feel that they are not very worthwhile. Rationalization, projection, sublimation, and compensation are four common types of defense mechanisms.

Rationalization is the giving of logical reasons or excuses for an action or behavior to make ourselves appear to have acted rationally when we have acted irrationally. For example, a student who received a low grade in a course because he did not study, claimed to himself that he received the low grade because his "teacher didn't like him." A young woman was seldom asked for a date more than once because she spent her time with men talking about nothing except herself, but she convinced herself that men rejected her because she was too intelligent for them.

Projection is a kind of lie we tell ourselves when we see our unacceptable characteristics in others, but do not see them in ourselves. For example, an office worker who wasted several hours of each work day, constantly complained about her fellow workers "goofing off." A store clerk who was disagreeable with customers spent much of his time complaining to co-workers and family about the rudeness of customers. The office worker found it unacceptable that she wasted so much time and the store clerk disapproved of the poor treatment he gave customers, but it would have made them feel badly about themselves if they had recognized that they were unacceptable people. They used the defense mechanism of projection; they found their unacceptable characteristics in others.

Sublimation and compensation are more constructive types of defense mechanisms. In *sublimation* a socially accepted activity is used to do something that would otherwise not be socially acceptable. For example, since it is socially unacceptable for a man to physically injure another man, some men may play tackle football as a socially acceptable way to injure others. Also, it is socially unacceptable to ask people questions about their private lives, but it is one job of social workers to learn about other people's lives. It is possible that some social workers have found a socially acceptable way to satisy the socially unacceptable desire to pry into the private affairs of others. *Compensation* is another constructive defense mechanism in which one makes up for an inadequacy in one activity by being outstanding in another activity. For example, a boy who is not good at sports may become an excellent student, or a girl who does not consider herself to be pretty may cultivate a charming personality.

The defense mechanisms of rationalization, projection, sublimation, and compensation are used by most people at some time in their adult lives.

EXERCISE 2

MEASURES OF CENTRAL TENDENCY

Preview "Measures of Central Tendency" and circle the numbers in front of items in the following list that help in locating the exact number of major details in it.

1. An introduction
2. Subheadings
3. Words printed in italics
4. A number or numbers
5. First sentences of paragraphs

Then, underline the locations of the major details in the passage.

MEASURES OF CENTRAL TENDENCY

When psychologists give tests to measure intelligence, aptitude, or personality characteristics, they want to know how people scored on the tests. They use measures of **central tendency** to help find this information.

The Mean

The most widely used measure of central tendency is the familiar average score, also referred to as the *arithmetic mean*. This score is obtained by adding together all the scores and dividing by the total number of scores. For the scores 2, 3, 4, 5, 6, 7, 8, and 9, the arithmetic mean is the sum of the scores (44) divided by the number of scores (8), which equals 5.5. One problem in using the arithmetic mean is that it may be influenced by extremely high or low scores that are not typical of the group. Say, for example, that out of 100 people who take a test, 90 score between 80 and 85, and 5 score between 0 and 10. These very low scores, which are obviously exceptions rather than the rule, pull down the arithmetic mean, so that it does not reflect the true central tendency of the scores.

The Median

Another measure of central tendency, which is not as greatly influenced by extreme scores, is the *median*—the middle score above and below which the same number of scores fall. For the scores 2, 3, 40, 45, 50, 55, and 60, the median score is 45, since three scores fall above it and three scores fall below it. But the arithmetic mean of this group is 36.4, since it has been influenced by the extreme scores (2 and 3). Note that 45 is a more accurate indicator of central tendency in this case than is 36.4. However, if only the median is used to describe the central tendency, it gives no information about what is happening at the upper and lower ends of the set of scores. Thus, it is advisable to use both the mean and the median.

The Mode

A third measure of central tendency is the *mode*, which is the score that occurs most frequently; on a graph, it is the score at the highest point of the curve. Generally, the mode is not as good an indicator of central tendency as the mean or median. The mode is the measure most preferred, for example, by dress manufacturers, who want to know which size occurs most frequently among the customers to whom they wish to sell their garments.

EXERCISE 3

PACKAGING FUNCTIONS

Preview "Packaging Functions" and circle the numbers in front of items in the following list that help in locating the exact number of major details in it.

1. An introduction
2. Subheadings
3. Words printed in italics or boldface
4. A number or numbers
5. First sentences of paragraphs

Then, underline the locations of the major details in the passage.

PACKAGING FUNCTIONS

Effective packaging involves more than simply putting products in containers and covering them with wrappers. A package performs several tasks—including protection, economy, convenience, and promotion.*

Packaging materials serve four primary functions. First, they protect the product or maintain it in a functional form. The Pringles package, for example, protects potato chips so that they can't be broken or crushed. Fluids such as milk, orange juice, and hair spray need packages that preserve and protect them. Second, the protection of the product should be effective in reducing damage that could affect its usefulness and increase costs (economy). Third, consumers often look for convenience. The size or shape of a package may relate to the product's storage, convenience, or replacement rate. Small, single-serving cans of vegetables may prevent waste and facilitate storage. The fourth function of packaging is to promote a product by communicating its features, uses, benefits, and image.

* Philip Kotler, *Marketing Management: Analysis, Planning, and Control*, 3rd ed. (Englewood Cliffs, N.J.: Prentice-Hall, 1976), p. 216.

EXERCISE 4

MONEY MANAGEMENT

Preview "Money Management" and circle the numbers in front of items in the following list that help in locating the exact number of major details in it.

1. An introduction
2. Subheadings
3. Words printed in italics or boldface
4. A number or numbers
5. First sentences of paragraphs

Then, underline the locations of the major details in the passage.

MONEY MANAGEMENT

Because many college students don't have a lot of extra money, they need to be especially effective in this area of management. Poor money management may cause you constantly to be in debt and unable to take advantage of some significant opportunities, such as attending a concert or going out on the town with a date. We've known several students whose money management was so poor that their creditors were constantly prodding them to pay up. These students were barely able to stay one step ahead of collection agents. This kind of situation can cause a great deal of tension and frustration, which of course will reduce your efficiency in other areas of responsibility.

Record keeping is unusually important in managing your money . . . . Record all of your spending—the amount you spend and what you spend it for. If your expenditures follow a monthly pattern because you are paid monthly, you should establish a baseline for a whole month. If you record your spending patterns for only a week, you could get a very unrealistic picture of that spending. Imagine, for example, the potential difference between your spending the week after payday and the week before payday. Your baseline, of course, will indicate that certain spending is fixed (rent, utilities, laundry) but that considerable spending may fall in the incidental and impulsive category. It is from this latter category that you will gain considerable latitude in adjusting your expenditures.

Your game plan in money management will almost always involve the preparation of a budget. Use your baseline record and, if available, your financial records for the past several months to determine how much you have been spending in various areas—food, cleaning supplies, paper products, and personal-health and grooming items (all things you buy in a grocery store); housing; transportation; utilities; insurance; medical costs; clothing; laundry and dry cleaning; entertainment; fixed monthly payments on loans or large purchases.

Scrutinize each area to determine where and how you can cut down—ride a bus or get into a car pool; take your lunch; go to matinees instead of more expensive evening performances. Try to find ways to reduce impulse spending, such as planning your menus in advance and buying only items needed for the menus. Avoid certain stores in which the temptation is greatest to buy unneeded items—or just stay out of stores except when your schedule calls for shopping. Draw up a list of nonperishable items that you regularly use and stock up on these items when they're on sale. If credit cards are your downfall, put them in a safe place for a while instead of having them constantly with you. Cut your expenses in as many categories as possible when you're making out your new budget.

11. FIND MINOR DETAILS

After you have located the major details about a topic, find the minor details.

1. Preview before reading.
2. Locate major details.
3. **Find minor details.**
4. Identify expository patterns.
5. Infer implied meanings.
6. Make evaluations.
7. Interpret tables and graphs.

Minor details are information that is subordinate to, or beneath, major details.

CHARACTERISTICS OF MINOR DETAILS

The word *minor* is often used to mean "not very important," as in "I have a minor head cold." However, *minor* in the term *minor detail* is used to explain a relationship among details, not to identify whether details are important or unimportant. A minor detail in one context may be a major detail or even a topic in other contexts. For instance, *history* and *chemistry* are minor details in the following context.

Some College Subjects

Major details
I. Humanities
  A. History
  B. Philosophy
II. Natural sciences
  A. Chemistry
  B. Physics
  C. Biology
Minor details

While *history* and *chemistry* are minor details in this context, they are major details in the following context.

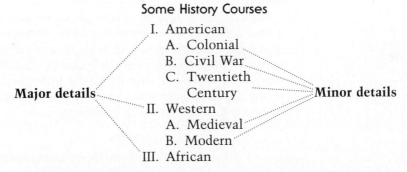

In yet other contexts, *history* or *chemistry* are topics with major and minor details subordinate to them. For instance,

Some History Courses

I. American
   A. Colonial
   B. Civil War
   C. Twentieth
      Century
II. Western
   A. Medieval
   B. Modern
III. African

Major details ←→ **Minor details**

To summarize, the terms *major details* and *minor details* are used to explain a relationship among details in a specific context, not to identify whether they are important or unimportant. That which is a minor detail in one context may be a major detail or a topic in other contexts.

MINOR DETAILS IN TEXTBOOKS

Figure 11.1 on page 134 shows a textbook passage and an outline for it. In that outline, major details are labeled with Roman numerals and minor details are labeled with capital letters. Compare the outline with the passage in Figure 11.1 to observe that the outline clearly illustrates the relationships among the major and minor details that are presented for the topic, "Types of Families," in the passage.

FINDING MINOR DETAILS

The following exercises provide practice for locating minor details in some of the textbook passages in Chapter 10. Exercises in Chapter 19 provide additional practice for locating and writing major and minor details in well-organized notes.

FIGURE 11.1

A passage and an out-
line showing the rela-
tionships among major
and minor details in the
passage

TYPES OF FAMILIES

A **nuclear family** consists of a married couple and their children. Most people are born into a nuclear family—their family of orientation—and then go on to establish a nuclear family of their own—their family of procreation. The only possible members of a *family of orientation* are a mother, father, brothers, and sisters. Your *family of procreation* may include your husband or wife, sons, and daughters.

The **extended family** is another term sociologists use to describe family relationships. Exactly who is considered a member of an extended family differs from country to country, but in the United States the extended family is usually considered to include children, parents, and other relatives who live with them in the same house or very near by.

Families may also be viewed in terms of the number of partners in a marriage. In our country we have **monogamous families**—there is only one husband and one wife in a marriage partnership. In some societies, though, there are **polygamous families** with more than two marriage partners. Polygyny is the form of polygamy in which there is one husband and two or more wives; polyandry is the form in which one wife has two or more husbands.

Types of Families

I. Nuclear family—married couple and their children
   A. Family of orientation—mother, father, brothers, and sisters
   B. Family of procreation—husband, wife, sons, and daughters
II. Extended family
   A. Children
   B. Parents
   C. Relatives who live with them or near by
III. Monogamous family—one husband and one wife
IV. Polygamous family—more than two marriage partners
   A. Polygyny—one husband and two or more wives
   B. Polyandry—one wife and two or more husbands

Major details

Minor details

EXERCISE 1

STEPS IN THE SELLING PROCESS (pages 121–122)

Refer to the passage named above and write the minor details on the lines that are not already filled out in the following outline.

Steps in the Selling Process

I. Find buyers

    A. _____

    B. *Make the product easily available. Ex) department stores*

    C. _____

II. Present the product attractively and convincingly

    A. _____

    _____

    B. _____

    _____

III. Create the customer's desire to buy

    A. _____

    _____

    B. _____

    _____

IV. Close the sale

    A. _____

    B. _____

    _____

EXERCISE 2

STAGES OF PREGNANCY (pages 123—124)

Refer to the passage named above and write the minor details on the lines that are not already filled out in the following outline.

Stages of Pregnancy

   I. First trimester (1–3 months)

      A. _____

          _____

      B. *Women admit to "owning" the pregnancy*

      C. _____

  II. Second trimester (4–6 months)

      A. _____

      B. _____

      C. _____

      D. _____

      E. *Nausea and need to nap diminish or disappear*

      F. _____

 III. Third trimester (7–9 months)

      A. _____

      B. _____

      C. _____

      D. _____

      E. _____

EXERCISE 3

SOCIAL MOBILITY (page 124)

Refer to the passage named above and write the minor details on the lines that are not already filled out in the following outline.

Social Mobility

I. Horizontal mobility

A. _____

_____

B. (Ex) Plumber becomes a carpenter

II. Vertical mobility

A. _____

_____

B. _____

C. (Ex) Corporation president becomes a plumber

III. Intragenerational mobility

A. A change in status during an individual's career

B. _____

IV. Intergenerational mobility

A. _____

_____

B. _____

C. _____

D. If there is little intergenerational mobility in a society, life changes are determined at birth

E. _____

_____

EXERCISE 4

DEFENSE MECHANISMS (pages 127–128)

Refer to the passage named above and write the minor details on the lines that are not already filled out in the following outline.

Defense Mechanisms

I. Rationalization

    A. _____

    _____

    B. _____

    _____

    C. (Ex) *Woman rejected by men for talking only of herself believed it was because she was too intelligent for them.*

II. Projection

    A. _____

    _____

    B. _____

    C. _____

III. Sublimation

    A. _____

    _____

    B. _____

    C. _____

IV. Compensation

    A. _____

    _____

    B. _____

    C. _____

EXERCISE 5

MEASURES OF CENTRAL TENDENCY (pages 128–129)

Refer to the passage named above and write the minor details on the lines that are not already filled out in the following outline.

Measures of Central Tendency

I. The mean

     A. _____

     _____

     B. _____

     _____

     C. Problem: the mean may be influenced by high or low scores that are not typical of the group

II. The median

     A. _____

     _____

     B. (EX) In 2, 3, 40, 45, 50, 55, and 60, the median is 45

     C. _____

     _____

III. The mode

     A. _____

     B. _____

     _____

12. IDENTIFY

EXPOSITORY

PATTERNS

Chapters 10 and 11 illustrate how to locate the *number* of major and minor details in textbook passages. This chapter explains how to identify the *kinds* of details in textbooks.

1. Preview before reading.
2. Locate major details.
3. Locate minor details.
4. **Identify expository patterns.**
5. Infer implied meanings.
6. Make evaluations.
7. Interpret tables and graphs.

The writing in textbooks is **exposition**—writing that gives explanations and information. The explanations are usually presented in one of six **expository patterns.** Information in textbooks may be about

1. *categories,* or types of things.
2. *sequences* in which events occur or happen.
3. *methods* for doing certain things.
4. *causes,* or the reasons things are as they are.
5. *effects,* or the results of actions or events.
6. *comparisons,* or similarities and differences.

This chapter explains how to identify these six expository patterns.

CATEGORIES

Categories are divisions created to organize or classify facts and concepts so that they can be understood more easily. For instance, to help in understanding textbooks, this chapter identifies six expository patterns: categories, sequences, methods, causes, effects, and comparisons.

Most textbooks explain categories. Art history textbooks describe various types of art, business textbooks identify assorted kinds of corporate financing, biology textbooks classify plants and animals, and so on.

When scholars classify, they usually do not consider it essential for items to be placed in one category, and one category only. For example, a psychology textbook may identify three types of psychotics: manic-depressives, schizophrenics, and paranoids. However, a psychotic person may exhibit characteristics of two—or even all three—of the basic types of psychoses: he or she may be manic-depressive, schizophrenic, and paranoid. This overlapping is typical of many classifications in college textbooks.

The passage in Exercise 1 classifies the types of conflicts people experience.

EXERCISE 1

CONFLICT

Preview "Conflict" and circle the numbers in front of items in the following list that help in locating the exact number of major details in it.

1. An introduction
2. Subheadings
3. Words printed in italics
4. A number or numbers
5. First sentences of paragraphs

Then, underline the locations of the major details in the passage.

CONFLICT

Conflict occurs whenever we are faced with a choice that involves the pairing of two or more competing motives or goals. Kurt Lewin (1935) described conflict situations that were later conceptualized in terms of learning principles by Dollard and Miller (Miller, 1944). These are called approach-approach, avoidance-avoidance, approach-avoidance, and double approach-avoidance conflicts.

Approach-Approach Conflict

An *approach-approach conflict* occurs when an individual is faced with a choice between two positive goals, both equally attractive. For example, Joan is accepted at two Ivy League colleges, Barnard and Radcliffe, and cannot decide which to attend. Fred is buying his first new car and cannot decide between a Datsun or a Toyota. These are relatively easy kinds of conflict to deal with; since both the alternatives are positive ones, no matter what the decision, you end up with something you want. Usually, this type of conflict is resolved when one alternative becomes more positive and the other more negative. In Joan's case, she talks to students at both colleges and finds that the courses in the major field of her choice are better at one school than the other. In Fred's case, a salesman convinces him that one of the cars would require fewer repairs than the other.

Avoidance-Avoidance Conflict

An *avoidance-avoidance conflict* involves making a choice between two unpleasant alternatives. For instance, in making up her program, Sally finds that the only courses still open are two that she dislikes—math and science—and she must choose between them. Carl, whose school is on the honor system, is being compelled either to name the student who stole a copy of the final exam and face the loss of his best friend (who is the culprit) or to lose his scholarship.

Behavior in this type of conflict situation is characterized by *vacillation*; that is, the individual approaches first one goal, then the other. The nearer one gets to each alternative, the stronger is the avoidance response. If the strength of one of the avoidance responses is increased, the person withdraws from the most disliked or feared situation and overcomes the conflict. If both alternatives remain equally unpleasant, however, the individual often attempts to "leave the field," as Lewin (1935) puts it—either literally, by running away, or figuratively, by daydreaming—instead of facing up to the situation. This type of situation is resolved when one alternative becomes more positive than the other. Sally chooses to take math when she learns that her best friend, who is good in math, will be in that class. Carl, on the other hand, chooses to leave the field by quitting school and not facing up to the situation.

Approach-Avoidance Conflict

An *approach-avoidance conflict* involves a single goal that has both positive and negative characteristics. This is the most difficult of the three types of conflicts to resolve and tends to evoke a great deal of anxiety. For example, Ellen does not like the shape of her nose and believes that if she had plastic surgery, she would look beautiful. At the same time, she has a very low tolerance for pain, and she has been told that this kind of surgery involves a lot of postoperative pain.

Double Approach-Avoidance Conflict

Often, two goals have both good points and bad points. A young woman must choose between taking a good job or going to graduate school. If she takes the job, she will make a good deal of money but will never get a master's degree, which she values. If she goes to school instead, she will obtain a degree but will forfeit an excellent salary for four years. This is known as a *double approach-avoidance conflict*. In life, most conflicts fall into this category, since most of our choices have both positive and negative features. Unfortunately, there is never a completely satisfactory solution to this conflict, because each alternative has disadvantages that we would like to avoid. When we finally make a decision, we are likely to feel some regret afterwards.

References

Lewin, K. *A Dynamic Theory of Personality.* Trans. D. K. Adams and K. E. Zener. New York: McGraw-Hill, 1935.

Miller, N. E. "Experimental Studies in Conflict." In *Personality and Behavior Disorders.* Ed. J. McV. Hunt. New York: Ronald Press, 1944.

SEQUENCES

A **sequence** is the order in which things follow each other in time, space, rank, or some other dimension.

Time sequences are explained in many textbooks, including those for the study of history. To think intelligently about the history of the United States, for instance, it is necessary to understand the order in which presidents were in office and the sequence in which major wars were fought. This type of sequence is called *time sequence, chronological sequence,* or *temporal sequence*—all three terms have the same meaning.

Spatial sequences are important in the study of such subjects as astronomy and geography. For instance, those who know the order of planets in space know that a rocket flying away from earth must pass the orbits of Mars and Jupiter before reaching Saturn.

In *hierarchical sequences,* items are arranged by complexity, importance, or rank. In biology, for instance, forms of life are organized in a hierarchical sequence, beginning with the least complex and advancing to the most complex. In this arrangement of animal life, the one-celled protozoa are at the bottom, and apes are very near the top of the hierarchy.

Textbooks also often use *logical sequences,* which progress according to a rational ordering of events or tasks. Vocabulary chapters in *RSVP* are arranged in a logical sequence: "Study Context," "Analyze Word Structure," and "Use a Dictionary." It is logical to study context first, because the meanings of words in textbooks are more likely to be determined in this way than by analyzing word structure. It is logical to analyze word structure before using a dictionary because when the meaning of a word can be determined by analyzing word structure, it is not necessary to refer to a dictionary.

The passage in Exercise 2 explains the sequence of emotional stages that terminally ill people often experience.

EXERCISE 2

DEATH AND DYING

Preview "Death and Dying" and circle the numbers in front of items in the following list that help in locating the exact number of major details in it.

1. An introduction
2. Subheadings
3. Words printed in italics
4. A number or numbers
5. First sentences of paragraphs

Then, underline the locations of the major details in the passage.

DEATH AND DYING

In her book *On Death and Dying,* Elisabeth Kübler-Ross presents a great deal of clinical information on the process of dying. She obtained this information directly from patients who knew they were dying and who revealed their emotions and thoughts. Dr. Ross identifies five stages through which dying people generally progress.

1. *Denial.* The patient's first reaction may be a temporary state of shock in which his or her only response is "no, it can't be happening to me." Death is almost inconceivable for most of us because in our unconscious minds we are all immortal. After a while, the patient stops denying the reality of death and turns to less extreme defense mechanisms. Much depends on how the person is told about the approach of death, how much time there is to come to a gradual acknowledgment of the inevitable, and how the person has been prepared throughout life to cope with stressful situations.
2. *Anger.* Denial is often replaced by feelings of anger, rage, envy, and resentment. The question is now "why me?" or "who is responsible for this death?" This is a very difficult stage for the family and hospital staff to cope with, because the person's anger is displaced and projected onto various people. The patient may complain that "the doctors are just no good," and the visiting family members may be received with little cheerfulness.
3. *Bargaining.* In this stage there is an attempt to postpone the inevitable by requesting a reward "for good behavior" or by setting a self-imposed deadline (for example, "Just one more month so I can attend my son's wedding"). This request usually contains an implicit promise that no more requests will be made if this one postponement is granted. Most such bargains are not mentioned explicitly, but only hinted at.
4. *Depression.* Depression is often used by the dying person as a way of preparing for the impending loss of all love objects. During this stage, encouragement to look at the sunny side of things should *not* be given, because this would mean that he or she should not

contemplate approaching death. It would be incongruent to tell the person not to be sad when all of his or her loved ones are sad. The dying person is losing everything and everybody he or she loves. If allowed to express this sorrow, final acceptance of death may be easier.

5. *Acceptance.* If there has been enough time (that is, if it is not a sudden, unexpected death) and the dying person has been helped through the preceding stages, a stage can be reached where he or she is neither depressed nor angry about his fate. The person will be able to contemplate death with a degree of acceptance because previous feelings, envy for the living and the healthy, and anger will have been dealt with in a meaningful way.

Dr. Kübler-Ross's research in recent years has focused on the question of life after death. Speaking at Earlham College in Indiana in 1975, she expressed a conviction that there is a life after death. This conviction is based on talks with hundreds of people who had experienced bodily death (for example, during surgery) but had been brought back to life (*New York Times*, April 20, 1976).

METHODS

Methods are the procedures or processes used to do something. Some textbooks are devoted almost entirely to explaining the ways things are done—textbooks for mathematics and foreign language courses, for instance. *RSVP* explains methods for improving vocabulary, reading, study, and test-taking skills.

Some textbooks explain methods for students to use; others inform about methods that are used by professionals. For instance, an introductory psychology textbook explains methods psychologists use to determine whether people are "normal" or "abnormal." The purpose of the explanations is to inform students of methods psychologists use, not to train them in how to do the things that practicing psychologists do.

The passage in Exercise 3 explains methods you may use to improve listening skills.

EXERCISE 3

IMPROVING YOUR LISTENING SKILLS

Preview "Improving Your Listening Skills" and circle the numbers in front of items in the following list that help in locating the exact number of major details in it.

1. An introduction
2. Subheadings
3. Words printed in italics
4. A number or numbers
5. First sentences of paragraphs

Then, underline the locations of the major details in the passage.

IMPROVING YOUR LISTENING SKILLS

While there are no hard and fast rules for good listening, there are some general guidelines that can help you improve your listening skills.

1. *Develop listening responses.* Nodding your head occasionally, re-marking, "I see . . . I understand," and so on indicate that you are paying attention and are actively involved in the conversation.
2. *Learn how to phrase your questions.* Questions can be *open* or *closed.* Closed questions tend to elicit a "yes" or "no" response and yield a minimum of information. When listening to an employee complain about the department's work schedule, a manager may ask, "Do you think the schedule is made for your personal benefit?" Open questions encourage more productive responses and will not, as a rule, put the other person on the defensive. The same manager could ask, "How would you arrange the schedule if it were up to you?"
3. *Avoid making value judgments.* A critical listener can bring a conversation to a quick end. Good listening means creating an atmosphere of trust, mutual respect, and warmth.
4. *Don't anticipate.* Resist the temptation to finish a speaker's sentences or jump to conclusions when you've heard part of an argument or discussion. Most of the time your guess will be wrong. Give the speaker time to find the right words.
5. *Ask for clarification; restate important points.* Make sure you understand the terms the other person is using. Restate what they've said in your own words so you understand the points as the speaker intended. Don't assume you know what they mean.
6. *Be ready to give feedback.* When asked, give feedback as soon as you can. Be as specific as possible and speak from an "I" framework. Instead of saying, "Your thinking seems fuzzy here," pinpoint what you think can be changed or needs to be done. "I feel an important step has been overlooked. I would suggest checking with inventory before planning that large an order."

CAUSES

Causes are reasons given to explain why things are as they are. Some history textbooks explain what caused the United States to fight in World War II, and some sociology textbooks explain what causes people to become criminals.

Causes, or reasons, may be facts or theories. **Facts** are things that are known to be true. The question "Why did we fight in World War II?" can be answered by listing events that are known to have caused us to fight in this war. Many times, though, reasons are **theories,** which are possible, but not certain, explanations. We do not know for certain how the planet earth came to be; however, scientists offer theories to explain its origin. Also, we do not know for certain what causes people to become criminals, but sociologists have formulated theories in an attempt to understand and explain antisocial behavior.

The passage in Exercise 4 explains possible causes of lightning.

EXERCISE 4

THEORIES ABOUT LIGHTNING

Preview "Theories About Lightning" and circle the numbers in front of items in the following list that help in locating the exact number of major details in it.

1. An introduction
2. Subheadings
3. Words printed in boldface
4. A number or numbers
5. First sentences of paragraphs

Then, underline the locations of the major details in the passage.

THEORIES ABOUT LIGHTNING

Ever since Benjamin Franklin, scientists have been investigating the exact nature of **lightning.** It is the most spectacular show that the atmosphere puts on. Lightning results from a build-up of electrical charges in neighboring parts of a cloud, or in portions of the Earth that are adjacent to a charged region of the atmosphere. The charges seem to build up most frequently when violent updrafts of air sweep through a cloud. When the water droplets and ice crystals in the clouds fall and collide with other droplets in supercooled water vapor, they accumulate regions of like electrical charges. When there is a discharge of electricity between adjacent positive and negative fields, lightning occurs.

One common theory about the origin of lightning is that, as the larger droplets of water in a cloud break apart, they accumulate electrical charges. Small droplets, which are near the center of the cloud, accumulate negative charges (electrons). Larger droplets, which are near the outermost regions of the cloud, are left with positive charges.

Another theory about lightning is that positive charges build up on ice crystals near the top of cumulonimbus clouds, while in the lower portions of the clouds water droplets maintain a positive charge, surrounded by other droplets that have negative charges. The Earth is usually negatively charged with respect to the air. However, a low-lying, negatively charged cloud, as it moves over the surface, induces a positive charge on the Earth because it repulses the negative charges. Now air is a poor conductor of electricity, so the electric current does not flow through it easily. Therefore a tremendous electrical potential builds up between the Earth and the cloud. Lightning occurs only when the potential is large enough to overcome the air resistance.

EFFECTS

Effects are the results or consequences of actions or events. For instance, some of the effects, or results, of the increased cost of oil and gasoline have been higher prices for airline tickets, shorter automobile trips during vacation periods, and lower temperatures in homes and public buildings during winter months. One effect of using efficient study procedures is that more is learned in less time.

The passage in Exercise 5 explains some of the effects of the economic depression in the United States during the 1930s.

EXERCISE 5

THE GREAT DEPRESSION

Preview "The Great Depression" and circle the numbers in front of items in the following list that help in locating the exact number of major details in it.

1. An introduction
2. Subheadings
3. Words printed in italics
4. A number or numbers
5. First sentences of paragraphs

Then, underline the locations of the major details in the passage.

THE GREAT DEPRESSION

The stock market crash in the autumn of 1929 led off the greatest economic disaster in the nation's history, and radically altered the lives of millions of Americans. For the great depression which followed was a tragedy of lost jobs, lost income, lost homes, lost careers, lost hopes, abrupt changes in standards of living. It is the story of people in hunger and want, often worrying where their next meal was coming from, worrying whether their children had adequate clothing, worrying about the electricity being cut off, worrying about the mortgage payment when there was no money to meet it. The anxiety, misery, and despair cannot be adequately told, but we can gain some idea of what the depression meant by a few glimpses into the early thirties when the catastrophe was at its peak.

The job market was calamitous. By 1932 Chicago had 660,000 unemployed, New York City over 1 million. The desperate search for jobs found men trying to get jury duty for the pittance it paid per diem and turning up on the streets as shoeshine boys, necktie and toy salesmen, or hawkers of vegetables trundling handcarts. In 1931, when the Soviet Union advertised in the United States for 6,000 skilled workers, their New York office received over 100,000 applications from 38 states. When Birmingham, Alabama, advertised for 750 men at 20 cents an hour to do pick-and-shovel labor on a local relief project, over 12,000 applied. The desperate and near-hopeless search for jobs was the same everywhere.

It is impossible to estimate how many, in losing their jobs, also lost their savings, their homes, and other property, but the number was substantial. Throughout the nation, on the fringe of cities and towns, dispossessed families built shacks out of packing crates, boxes, sheets of old metal, chicken wire, and anything to keep the weather out, calling these communities "Hooverville" in honor of that President's refusal to grant public relief. People slept in empty freight cars, shut-down factories, abandoned buildings, subways, caves, and parks. The Commissioner of Public Welfare in Chicago found several hundred unemployed women sleeping in the city's parks at night. *The New York Times* reported that police had found a woman and her sixteen-year-old daughter in the woods near Danbury, Connecticut, "huddled beneath a strip of canvas stretched from a boulder to the ground. Rain was dripping from the improvised shelter, which had no sides." They had been living there for days, subsisting on wild berries and apples. Iowa farmer Johannes Schmidt lost his farm, home, livestock, and equipment, and after filing for bankruptcy he and his family had only a wagon, an old team of horses, two cows, five hogs, a few pieces of furniture, and no place to go.

Thousands of single men and women, and even families, wandered aimlessly about the country, often traveling illegally in railroad box-cars. By 1932 an estimated one to two million were on the road, living on handouts from relief missions or by begging. Many a small-town household knew that when they heard a freight train stop in town within a few minutes someone would be knocking at the door and asking for food. One Midwesterner, recalling those days, wrote to a friend, "I can't remember how many fried-egg sandwiches I made as an eleven-year-old and handed out to those be-deviled people who showed up on our back porch, to say nothing of what my mother cooked for them if they came when she was home."

Ironically in a nation of vast agricultural abundance, food itself became a problem. Millions went hungry while tons of food were wasted or destroyed. A witness testifying before a Congressional committee reported that while he had seen women picking scraps from the refuse piles of Seattle's main market, in lower Oregon thousands of bushels of apples rotted in the orchards because the price was so low they were not worth harvesting. He had seen men, he reported, fighting over meat scraps in the garbage cans of Chicago, while a sheep-raiser he knew in the West had killed his entire flock and dumped the bodies down a canyon because he could not afford to feed them or ship them to market. People prowled in garbage dumps, picked up leavings and spoiled vegetables in market places, stood in line in charity soup kitchens. A newspaper reporter told the mayor of Youngstown, Ohio, that he could not believe what his neighbors were subsisting on. "The mother mixes a little flour and water and cooks it in a frying pan. That is their regular meal."

COMPARISONS

Comparisons are explanations of similarities and differences. For instance, political science textbooks make comparisons when they explain the similarities or differences among democracy, socialism, and communism.

Comparisons tend to emphasize differences, or **contrasts,** rather than similarities. Comparisons of skin diseases in microbiology textbooks, for instance, emphasize differences rather than similarities among them. Similarly, in comparing battles of the Civil War, history textbooks explain more how they were different than how they were alike.

The passage in Exercise 6 is a comparison of romantic love and mature love that emphasizes the differences between them.

EXERCISE 6

ROMANTIC AND MATURE LOVE

Preview "Romantic and Mature Love" and circle the numbers in front of items in the following list that help in locating the exact number of major details in it.

1. An introduction
2. Subheadings
3. Words printed in italics
4. A number or numbers
5. First sentences of paragraphs

Then, underline the locations of the major details in the passage.

ROMANTIC AND MATURE LOVE

Romantic love is based on a sense of need or lack of completeness so that an individual desperately seeks the one perfect person who will give the love that will fill that need. In contrast, mature love proceeds, not from need, but from a sense of wholeness and a self-acceptance. Mature love honestly respects the total individuality of each person, including fears and faults as well as joys and strengths. Because mature love is based on acceptance of a total person rather than unrealistic idealization, it can increase with continuing intimacy.

A romantic lover wants to possess the loved one completely. In mature love there is no idea of possession. Each person allows the other complete freedom to grow and develop her or his potential to the fullest, even when this means they have less time to spend together. Mature lovers know that time together can be more enjoyable when each person has more interests and joy of life to bring to the relationship.

When romantic lovers are apart they may suffer real pain or "withdrawal" symptoms, because, without the other person each is incomplete. In contrast, mature lovers feel complete whether alone, together, or in the company of others.

Romantic lovers expect to feel love and passion only for each other. But mature love is a part of the love one feels for all persons. It is not expected to be exclusive. There may be a commitment that the sexual relationship will be reserved for the two partners, but loving feelings will be shared with all others.

Within a relationship based on mature love, sexual expression can reach its greatest potential. In these relationships, sex is a means of physically expressing the high degree of caring, acceptance, and intimacy of both the physical aspects and the feeling aspects of the relationship. In this setting it can reach its most complete and joyous expression.

COMBINED PATTERNS

Earlier in this chapter it is stated that many of the classifications in textbooks do not allow for clear-cut categorization. This statement also applies to the expository patterns they use.

A passage may be written using a combination of patterns. The *category* and *comparison* patterns are often combined, as in the passage entitled "Romantic and Mature Love" in Exercise 6, which identifies two types of love and explains differences between them. The *method* and *sequence* patterns are also often used in combination. For instance, when English textbooks explain the methods for writing term papers, they arrange the methods in a sequence: select a topic, narrow the topic, prepare an outline, write a draft, and so on.

Sometimes it is essential to attend to both patterns. To understand how to write term papers, it is necessary to understand how to accomplish each step *and* the sequence in which to do the steps. On the other hand, it is often clear that one pattern is more important than another. "The Great Depression," in Exercise 5, includes dates that suggest the sequence pattern, but it is clear that the more important information in the passage concerns the effects of the depression, not a sequence of events.

IDENTIFYING EXPOSITORY PATTERNS

After previewing a chapter in a textbook, read it a section at a time to locate details and to identify expository patterns. Passages in textbooks may be about

1. *categories*, or types of things.
2. *sequences* in which events occur or happen.
3. *methods* for doing certain things.
4. *causes*, or the reasons things are as they are.
5. *effects*, or the results of actions or events.
6. *comparisons*, or similarities and differences.

The following exercises provide practice for identifying expository patterns and additional practice for locating major details.

EXERCISE 7

SQ3R

Preview "SQ3R" and then circle the numbers in front of items in the following list that help in locating the exact number of major details in it.

1. An introduction
2. Subheadings
3. Words printed in italics
4. A number or numbers
5. First sentences of paragraphs

Next, read the passage and circle the number in front of the title in the following list that best states the expository pattern of the passage.

1. Five Types of Study Methods
2. Steps of the SQ3R Study Method
3. Reasons for Using the SQ3R Study Method
4. Effects of Using the SQ3R Study Method

Then, underline the locations of the major details in the passage.

SQ3R

The following explanation of SQ3R has been developed for students who are having academic trouble. SQ3R is a mnemonic for certain action words or steps used in one study method. These steps are survey, question, read, recite, review.

Survey

Look over the material to get a feel for it. Look at the titles and the headings of major chapter divisions. If there is a summary at the end of the chapter, read it through quickly. The point is to get a quick, one-minute idea of what the major themes of a unit are. This will help you to cluster your ideas around the organization of the topic. It will also help you to start questioning.

Question

Having read the summary or gotten a quick idea of the topic and its coverage, go back to the beginning of the unit. Your job now is to turn all the major headings into questions. Go through the entire unit again, writing each question down. This questioning does two things: It makes you respond actively to each heading. It also arouses your curiosity by raising questions in your mind.

Read

Start at the beginning again and read with a purpose. You are now looking for answers to the questions you have written in your study notes. Pay attention only to the material that will help you to organize your answers. Don't mess around with tables, charts, or diagrams unless they refer directly to your question. Use a pencil or a marking pen to outline main ideas. Underlining the main thought in each paragraph and bracketing the supporting material might help you. Many students use a light-colored marking pencil to highlight an idea on the page without blotting it out. Put a star in the margin to mark an important point.

Recite

As soon as you have finished reading the material concerning your first question, turn away from the book and try to answer it. As you recite, write down what you say. Leave space in your notes so you can add any material you may have missed. You'll find that you'll need space when you go back and compare what the book says with your own answer. Fill in the space. In this way, you will express the whole idea in your own words. Don't go overboard on this outline; keep it short and stick to the main point.

Review

After you have finished reading the lesson, look over your notes. Check your recollection of each point by going over it until you are satisfied that you know it.

The beauty of this method is that you will wind up with a set of notes and a list of questions similar to those the instructor will use in tests, with answers in your own words. The amount of memory loss you will have will depend on how often and how thoroughly you review.

EXERCISE 8

LOW-LEVEL CLOUDS

Preview "Low-Level Clouds" and then circle the numbers in front of the items in the following list that help in locating the exact number of major details in it.

1. An introduction
2. Subheadings
3. Words printed in boldface
4. A number or numbers
5. First sentences of paragraphs

Next, read the passage and circle the number in front of the title in the following list that best states the expository pattern of the passage.

1. How to "Read" the Clouds
2. Causes of Cloud Formations
3. Stages of Cloud Formation
4. Four Types of Clouds

Then, underline the locations of the major details in the passage.

LOW-LEVEL CLOUDS

If you want to find out what's going on in the weather, look at the clouds. Clouds are one of the best indicators of the activity of the air just above the Earth's surface. There is, of course, no foolproof system of judging what weather changes are going to take place. However, studying clouds is the best way of making some judgments on possible weather conditions in the immediate future. Clouds are classified according to such factors as height and formation. Low-level clouds range upward from the Earth's surface to a height of about 2100 m (6900 ft), or more than a mile. Figure 12.1 on page 156 shows some examples of low-level clouds.

1. **Stratus clouds** are gray, uniformly layered clouds that often cover the sky completely. They may be composed of ice crystals and may yield drizzle or snow grains, although they usually are not associated with precipitation. Stratus clouds are more often composed of minute water droplets. They tend to produce threatening skies. Their form parallels the contours of the land below them, as they often result from radiational cooling of the air above a given land area. When strong winds break up stratus clouds and give them a ragged appearance, they are called *scud clouds.*

2. **Cumulus clouds** are dense, woolly, detached (that is, they appear singly), vertical mounds. Often they tower far above other low-level clouds, although a small, flattened type called *cumulus humilis* exists. Cumulus clouds are more often dome-shaped and whitish near the top, with a darker, flattened base. Owing to local updrafts, they usually do not merge with other clouds, but appear as separate "piles." The flattened bottoms indicate convective uplift to the condensation level; cumulus clouds are often domed above that level. Cumulus clouds are generally made up of water droplets. When they are in the form of vertical towering clouds, they may release showers. Cumulus clouds—though they are often viewed as summer clouds—may appear at any time of year.

3. **Nimbostratus clouds** are thick, grayish or white clouds that appear in the form of a patchy series of sheetlike masses in the sky. They are usually composed of water droplets, occasionally of ice crystals. When you see nimbostratus clouds, rain—or some other form of

FIGURE 12.1

(a) Stratus clouds, (b) cumulus clouds, (c) stratocumulus clouds, (d) nimbostratus clouds (All photographs courtesy NOAA)

precipitation—is likely. (The kind of precipitation depends on temperature.)

4. **Stratocumulus clouds,** which result from convection currents and air turbulence, are globular and exhibit lumpy crests. The outlines of these crests are elongated and point in the direction of the prevailing winds. Precipitation may occur from the lower portions, at which point the cloud is transformed and becomes nimbostratus.

EXERCISE 9

HELPFULNESS

Preview "Helpfulness" and then circle the numbers in front of items in the following list that assist in locating the exact number of major details in it.

1. An introduction
2. Subheadings
3. Words printed in italics
4. A number or numbers
5. First sentences of paragraphs

Next, read the passage and circle the number in front of the title in the following list that best states the expository pattern of the passage.

1. Comparison of Helpful Actions
2. Effects of Helping Behavior
3. Reasons People Help Others
4. How to Be Helpful to Others

Then, underline the locations of the major details in the passage.

HELPFULNESS

Although we read frequently about people's indifference to others in trouble, and experiments have shown that individuals in groups are often reluctant to take action in an emergency, we must remember that almost every day, individuals do perform acts of genuine heroism. In Europe, during the Second World War, many people put their lives in jeopardy to help Jews escape from the Nazis. In the 1960s hundreds of young American men and women participated in voter registration drives in the Deep South, at great personal risk. Frequently we read of people who rush into burning buildings or jump into deep water to rescue someone in danger. Why are some people more likely to help than others? The reasons vary, depending on the particular situation. Three approaches to explaining altruism are reviewed by Middlebrook (1974): a normative explanation, a cost analysis, and the influence of moods and feelings.

The Normative Explanation

During socialization, children learn the rules of appropriate conduct, which include two norms of helping behavior. The first is the *norm of social responsibility*, which states that people should help others who need help because it is the right thing to do. Studies have shown that people will be helpful if they see another person helping someone else (Bryan & Test, 1967), because observing this behavior makes the social responsibility norm salient. However, research has shown that this norm is not a strong determinant of helping behavior (Berkowitz, 1972). The second norm, called the *norm of reciprocity*, holds that people should treat others as the others have treated them. This means that we help the person who previously did a favor for us, and if a person has denied us help in the past, we deny it to that person when he or she needs it. Gouldner (1960) suggested that this is a universal norm, and many subsequent studies have demonstrated the norm of reciprocity (Kahn & Tice, 1973).

The Cost Analysis Approach

The *cost analysis* approach holds that helping behavior is most likely to occur when the rewards for helping outweigh the costs. Costs would be the negative consequences and rewards the positive consequences to the individual. Darley and Latané (1970) have shown that the relative cost of the help requested influences the incidence of helping. Ninety-three of their social psychology students went out on the streets of New York and made a number of different requests of passersby. They found that what was asked made a significant difference as to whether or not people complied with the request. For example, people were much more likely to give change for a quarter (73 percent) than to tell their name (39 percent), which involves a certain personal risk in a large metropolis. Thus, the number of people complying decreases as the costs of helping increase.

Helping is much less likely to occur if it involves the threat of danger. In large cities, such as New York, people may be inhibited from helping because of urban crime statistics, which lead to lack of trust in others. This theory was illustrated in a study that compared helping behavior in New York City with that of individuals in several small towns in New York State. The investigators, working singly, rang doorbells, asking the occupants if they could use the telephone. In the city, 75 percent of the residents did not open their doors, whereas in the small towns, about 75 percent admitted the strangers (Altman, Levine, Nadien & Villena, unpublished, in Milgram, 1970).

The Mood Approach

The third, or *mood,* approach suggests that moods and feelings influence the extent to which people are willing to help others. A person in a good mood is more likely to offer assistance or act in a generous manner to others than is a person in a bad mood (Berkowitz, 1972; Rosenhan, Underwood & Moore, 1974). Helping others also minimizes one's feelings of guilt. If you have wronged someone, you may want to make it up by doing something nice for the person. Feelings of equity might also cause you to correct a wrong, even if you are not responsible for it; for seeing somone unjustly hurt disturbs your belief that the world is a fair place. Sympathy—compassion for an injured person—may also stimulate helping behavior.

References

Berkowitz, L. "Social Norms, Feelings, and Other Factors Affecting Helping and Altruism." In *Advances in Experimental Social Psychology.* Vol. 6. Ed. L. Berkowitz. New York: Academic Press, 1972, pp. 63–108.

Bryan, J., and M. Test. "Models and Helping: Naturalistic Studies in Aiding Behavior." *Journal of Personality and Social Psychology,* 6 (1967), 400–407.

Darley, J., and B. Latané. "Norms and Normative Behavior: Field Studies of Social Interdependence." In *Altruism and Helping Behavior: Social Psychological Studies of Some Antecedents and Consequences.* Eds. J. Macaulay and L. Berkowitz. New York: Academic Press, 1970, 83–101.

Gouldner, A. W. "The Norm of Reciprocity: A Preliminary Statement." *American Sociological Review,* 25 (1960), 161–178.

Kahn, A., and T. Tice. "Returning a Favor and Retaliating Harm. The
Effects of Stated Intentions and Actual Behavior." *Journal of Experimental Social Psychology,* 9 (1973), 43–56.

Middlebrook, P. N. *Social Psychology and Modern Life.* New York:
Knopf, 1974.

Milgram, S. "The Experience of Living in Cities." *Science,* 167 (1970),
1461–1468.

Rosenhan, D. L., B. Underwood, and B. Moore. "Affect Moderates Self-
gratification and Altruism." *Journal of Personality and Social Psychology,* 30, No. 4 (1974), 546–552.

EXERCISE 10

PRISONS

Preview "Prisons" and then circle the numbers in front of items in
the following list that help in locating the exact number of major details
in it.

1. An introduction
2. Subheadings
3. Words printed in italics
4. A number or numbers
5. First sentences of paragraphs

Next, read the passage and circle the number in front of the title in the
following list that best states the expository pattern of the passage.

1. The Reasons for Prisons
2. Comparison of Prisons' Effects
3. How to Reform Our Prisons
4. Types of Prisons in America

Then, underline the locations of the major details in the passage.

PRISONS

A major question for those who would reform criminal sentencing
is trying to figure out what sending people to prison is supposed to
accomplish.

Protecting Society

One argument is that we send people to prison because they are
dangerous to society if they are not in prison. They have a record of

attacking property or people. And they will steal or do violence again if they are not imprisoned. Public safety, then, is what criminal sentencing and prisons are all about.

But policy based solely on public safety will not get us very far in deciding what kinds of sentences to impose. If we used prisons simply to remove from society those who, if left free, would commit other crimes, "then white middle-aged, middle-class wife murderers should be released instantly and black, young, drug-addicted auto thieves should be kept locked up indefinitely. It is virtually a statistical certainty that the former will not kill again but that the latter will steal again." The author of this quotation, a perceptive student of criminal processes, concludes that such a policy is obviously silly. In effect we would be saying "that a human life is worth nothing, and a stolen car is worth everything."[1]

Deterrence

A second reason for putting criminals in prisons is deterrence: The threat of prison is supposed to keep people from commiting crimes. It is as if society is saying, "We know you are tempted to cheat on your income tax or steal a car, but resist that temptation because if you are caught you are going to pay for it." Some critics of the criminal-justice system think that sentences are too light and that this is why crime is increasing. If sentences were more severe, and more certain, then those who are tempted to commit crimes would take notice and would be deterred.

However, there is little evidence that imprisoning criminals contributes much to deterrence. This is true whether one speaks of general deterrence or of individual deterrence. General deterrence assumes that the example of punishment will be a lesson to others. Putting one criminal in prison will keep someone else from becoming a criminal. But except for white-collar crimes, the idea of general deterrence does not seem to have much effect on criminal behavior. Perhaps criminals do not learn by example; perhaps they believe that they will not get caught.

Individual deterrence assumes that if you catch someone at a crime and punish that person, he or she won't repeat the act. Here common sense is misleading. The number of criminal repeaters (the *recidivism rate*) is so high as to suggest that imprisonment does not have this individual deterrent effect.

This is not to reject the deterrence argument, but it is to warn against basing sentencing only on this criterion. For if deterrence were the goal it would be tempting for a society to impose harsher and harsher penalties as a way to reduce crime. Logic would even suggest making the penalties very visible. We would not only hang and torture but hang and torture in the city square.

---

[1]James Q. Wilson, "Changing Criminal Sentencing," *Harper's,* November 1977, p. 20.

Punishment and Justice

There is another reason for prisons, one that goes beyond protecting society or deterring would-be criminals. Prisons punish people. They punish people who have done some wrong against society. Criminal laws constitute a moral code. They identify certain behaviors that society has decided are simply wrong. The criminal justice system, then, is supposed to find the people who have done these wrong things and make them pay for it. This is why the wife murderer, who is not likely to repeat his crime, is locked up along with the car thief.

In this argument punishment is justice and prisons do justice. Society punishes not out of a sense of revenge but in order to establish a moral order.

13. INFER IMPLIED MEANINGS

Chapters 9–12 explain how to locate information that is stated in textbooks, but it is also important to infer meanings that are only suggested, or implied, by them.

1. Preview before reading.
2. Locate major details.
3. Find minor details.
4. Identify expository patterns.
5. **Infer implied meanings.**
6. Make evaluations.
7. Interpret tables and graphs.

Instructors ask test questions to determine if students understand information in required reading material. Some questions can be answered by recalling words printed in books, but others have answers that are only suggested, hinted, or **implied** by statements in them. When the answer to a question is implied, it must be **inferred**—information that is stated must be used to conclude the answer.

This chapter illustrates the differences between questions with answers that are stated in books and those with answers that are implied by statements in them.

STATED INFORMATION

When the answer to a question is stated, it can be given by copying, restating, or reading aloud words in printed material. Read the following passage to answer four questions by copying information in it.

PHONEMES

The various sounds found in all languages are surprisingly similar, considering the wide variety of noises that human beings are capable of making. In English there are 46 basic sounds, called *phonemes*;

some languages use considerably fewer, while others have almost twice as many. Phonemes are the meaningful sound units that can be distinguished in a language. For example, the word "cat" has three phonemes—k, a, and t, using phonetic notation. "Sat" also has three—s, a, and t. "Scat" has four—s, k, a, and t, but "seat" only has three—s, e, and t.

Write answers to the following questions.

1. What is a phoneme?

   _____

2. How many phonemes are there in the English language?

   _____

3. Do all languages have the same number of phonemes?

   _____

4. How many phonemes are there in the word "sat"?

   _____

Write answers to the questions before reading the following explanations.

1. The answer is "basic sounds," or "meaningful sound units [that can be distinguished in a language]." These answers are stated in the second and third sentences.
2. The answer is "46"; it is stated in the second sentence.
3. The answer is "no" or "no, some languages have fewer while others have more [or almost twice as many]." The answer is stated in the second sentence.
4. The answer is "three"; it is stated in the next-to-the-last sentence.

These answers may be copied from the passage about phonemes.

IMPLIED INFORMATION

When the answer to a question is implied, it cannot be answered by copying words. The answers to the following questions about "Phonemes" are implied. Use statements in the passage to infer their answers.

1. What is the approximate number of phonemes in the language that has the most phonemes?

   _____

2. Which letter in the word "cast" does not represent an English phoneme?

_____

3. Of the words "eye," "say," and "be," which contains only one phoneme?

_____

4. How many phonemes are there in the word "blow"?

_____

Write answers to the questions before reading the following explanations.

1. The answer is a number that is slightly less than 92 (91, 90, or 89, for example). It is concluded by using two facts that are stated in the passage: (1) English has 46 phonemes, and (2) some languages have almost twice as many [phonemes as English]. The word "almost" is a clue that the answer is a number slightly less than 92 (2 × 46 = 92).

2. The answer, "c," is found by (1) observing that the passage states that the three phonemes in "cat" are _k_, _a_, and _t_ and (2) concluding that, if "c" is not a phoneme in "cat," then it must not be a phoneme in "cast." The letters _a_, _s_, and _t_ in "cast" are identified as phonemes in the last two sentences. (All letters except _c_, _q_, and _x_ represent phonemes.)

3. The answer, "eye," is found by (1) understanding that a phoneme is a language sound unit and (2) analyzing the words to decide which has only one language sound unit. "Say" has two (sā), "be" has two (bē), but "eye" has only one (ī).

4. The answer, "three," is found by (1) understanding that a phoneme is a language sound unit and (2) analyzing "blow" to conclude that it has three of them (blō).

These answers cannot be copied from the passage about phonemes; statements in the passage must be used to infer the answers.

STATED AND IMPLIED INFORMATION

Exercises at the end of this chapter and Chapter 14 include multiple-choice questions with answers that are stated in or implied by information in textbook passages. Read the following passage and then answer the multiple-choice questions, which are the type you will answer when you do the exercises in this chapter.

TYPES OF ADVERTISING

There are three basic types of advertising. *Selective advertising* promotes the sale of specific brand name products, such as Bayer aspirin, Ford automobiles, and Maxwell House coffee. *Primary demand advertising* encourages the total demand for a product without promoting any specific brand. The advertisements for Florida oranges are examples of this; those ads seek to increase the sale of Florida oranges without concern if consumers purchase fresh oranges or any specific brand of frozen or bottled orange juice. The third type, *institutional advertising*, has as its purpose to create good will toward the advertiser. For example, when an oil company runs an ad that explains what the company is doing to keep fuel costs low, this is an example of institutional advertising. Any ad designed to make you think well of a company or organization, and that does not request you to make a specific purchase, is an example of institutional advertising.

Answer the following questions and *also* circle the numbers in front of questions whose answers are implied by the passage but are not directly stated in it.

_____ 1. Selective advertising is used to promote the
    a. sale of a specific brand name product.
    b. demand for a general type of product.
    c. good will of consumers toward an advertiser.
    d. purchase of any product or service.

_____ 2. Selective advertising is used to sell
    a. American cars.
    b. Wisconsin cheeses.
    c. Japanese computers.
    d. Timex watches.

_____ 3. Selective advertising is *not* used to sell
    a. Bayer aspirin.
    b. Ford automobiles.
    c. Florida oranges.
    d. Maxwell House coffee.

_____ 4. A telephone company does *not* use institutional advertising when it publishes an advertisement about
    a. women who do "men's" work.
    b. the times long-distance calls are cheapest.
    c. an employee who saved a person's life.
    d. a movie it will sponsor on public television.

Answer the questions before reading the following explanations.

1. The answer, *a,* is stated in the second sentence.
2. The answer, *d,* is not stated; you should have circled "2." It is decided by knowing that selective advertising is used to promote the sale of

specific brand name products and by concluding that "Timex" is the only brand name product among the choices.

3. The answer, *c*, is found using information that is stated in the passage. The passage states that the products following *a*, *b*, and *d* are promoted using selective advertising but that Florida oranges are promoted using product-demand advertising.

4. The answer, *b*, is not stated; you should have circled "4." It is decided by understanding that institutional advertising serves the purpose of creating good will toward advertisers and by concluding that the examples following *a*, *c*, and *d* serve the purpose of creating good will. The purpose of the example following *b* is to encourage people to make more long-distance telephone calls.

INFERRING IMPLIED MEANINGS

In the following exercises, textbook passages are followed by ten multiple-choice questions. In each exercise, the first question is about locating major details in the passage (Chapter 10); the second question is about the expository pattern of the passage (Chapter 12); the third, fourth, and fifth questions are about the meanings of words in the passage (Chapters 5–8); and the remaining five questions are about information that is implied by or stated in the passage.

EXERCISE 1

ODD-EVEN PRICING

Odd-even pricing assumes that more of a product will be sold at $99.99 than at $100.00. Customers are supposed to think that the store could have charged $100 but instead cut the price to the last cent, to $99.99 or $99.98 (which is also an odd price, though an even number). Odd prices seem to have little genuine effects on sales, except that they do force the cashier to use the cash register.

A second approach to odd-even pricing is based on the attractiveness of the numbers themselves. It is believed that certain numbers are physically more attractive to people. Thus, the symmetrical 8 could 3 be used in the price 88 cents. This is believed by some to be a better price than, say, 77 cents or 44 cents, numbers that have harsh edges and points.

Another pricing theory based on this concept has its roots in the 4 well-known book *The Naked Ape.* Author Desmond Morris declares that human beings are attracted to round figures and letters and that a sign which uses the word *good,* for example, will get more attention than one which uses pinched letters such as *l, f,* or *w.* This is so, Morris writes, since human beings are driven to glance at open figures (*o*) because the primal self is ever on the alert for eyes, which might 5 belong to a predator. Thus, a sign that advertises GOOD FOOD should get more attention than one that reads EATS, and a price of $10.01 should be more attractive than one of $9.77.

_____ 1. Major details are
     a. indicated in an introduction.
     b. indicated by words in italic type.
     c. indicated by a number.
     d. not indicated by items in *a, b,* or *c.*

_____ 2. Which title best states the expository pattern?
     a. Reasons for Using Odd-Even Pricing
     b. Effects of Using Odd-Even Pricing
     c. How to Price Using Odd-Even Numbers
     d. Three Odd-Even Pricing Theories

Circle the numbers in front of the questions whose answers are implied by the passage but are not directly stated in it.

_____ 3. *Symmetrical* means
     a. balanced in arrangement.
     b. synthetic or manufactured.
     c. unornamented or plain.
     d. pleasing or attractive.

_____ 4. A *concept* is a
              a. plan or proposal.
              b. division or category.
              c. notion or idea.
              d. book or paper.

_____ 5. *Primal* means
              a. primitive or original.
              b. cautious or careful.
              c. complex or multifaceted.
              d. essential or mandatory.

_____ 6. When odd-even pricing is used, a product is *not* sold for
              a. $16.95.
              b. $16.98.
              c. $16.99.
              d. $17.00.

_____ 7. An odd-even price for a product will
              a. encourage customers to carry change.
              b. encourage honesty among cashiers.
              c. increase its sales.
              d. lower its cost.

_____ 8. Which of the following prices should be most attractive to
             customers?
              a. 41¢
              b. 55¢
              c. 69¢
              d. 77¢

_____ 9. Desmond Morris believes we are attracted to the symbol *o*
             because we are
              a. pleased by its roundness and symmetry.
              b. attracted by its ancient simplicity.
              c. reminded by it of the moon and sun.
              d. searching for the eyes of enemies.

_____ 10. According to Morris's theory, which of the following should
            be the most eye-catching sign for a place where books are
            kept?
              a. LIBRARY
              b. BOOK ROOM
              c. BIBLIOTHECA
              d. STACKS

EXERCISE 2

WORDS AT PLAY

An **anagram** is a word or phrase spelled using the letters of another word or phrase. For example, *Satan* is an anagram spelled using the letters of *Santa*. *Abets*, which means "assists," is an anagram of four **3** words: *beast, beats, bates,* and *baste.* The phrase "they see" is an anagram of the phrase, "the eyes," and "no city dust here" is an anagram of "the countryside."

Palindromes are words, phrases, or sentences that spell the same backward and forward; for instance, *radar, deed, civic,* and *nun.* The first palindromic sentence is believed to have been created in the early 1600s. Here is a modern version of it.

Evil I did dwell; lewd did I live.   **4**

The most famous palindromic sentence is probably the one that Napoleon is supposed to have uttered when he went into exile: "Able was I ere I saw Elba." No palindrome tells a good story more succinctly **5** than the well-known "A man, a plan, a canal—Panama."

_____ 1. Major details are
   a. indicated in an introduction.
   b. indicated by words in italic type.
   c. indicated in first sentences of paragraphs.
   d. not indicated by items in *a, b,* or *c.*

_____ 2. Which title best states the expository pattern?
   a. Two Ways to Play with Words
   b. Methods for Writing Palindromes
   c. The History of Weird Word Games
   d. Some Reasons That Words Are Fun

Circle the numbers in front of the questions whose answers are implied by the passage but are not directly stated in it.

_____ 3. To *abet* is to
   a. gamble.
   b. waste.
   c. assist.
   d. hinder.

_____ 4. *Lewd* means
   a. indecent.
   b. thoughtful.
   c. beloved.
   d. unclothed.

_____ 5. *Succinct* means
     a. clear or obvious.
     b. vague or imprecise.
     c. brief or concise.
     d. long or verbose.

_____ 6. Which of the following is *not* an anagram of another word?
     a. ache
     b. kale
     c. vase
     d. glad

_____ 7. Which of the following is *not* an anagram of at least two other words?
     a. ought
     b. notes
     c. pares
     d. skate

_____ 8. Which of the following is an anagram of "The United States of America"?
     a. Unite to attain freedom's cause.
     b. Freedom of state attained here.
     c. Attaineth its cause: freedom!
     d. Armenians attained freedom there.

_____ 9. Which of the following is *not* a palindrome?
     a. A Toyota
     b. Don't give in.
     c. Dennis sinned.
     d. Madam, I'm Adam.

_____ 10. Which of the following is *not* a palindrome?
     a. Poor Dan is in a droop.
     b. Was it a car or a cat I saw?
     c. Pull up if I pull up.
     d. Did Mom read what Dad did?

EXERCISE 3

TELEVISION

Of the new luxuries, television was the most revolutionary in its effects. One man who grew up in the postwar era recalled the purchase of the first family TV set in 1950. "And so the monumental change **3** began in our lives and those of millions of other Americans. More than a year passed before we again visited a movie theater. Money which previously would have been spent for books was saved for the TV payments. Social evenings with friends became fewer and fewer still because we discovered we did not share the same TV program interests." By 1950 television had broken radio's grip on the American public. The number of households with TVs climbed from 8,000 in 1946 to 3.9 million in 1950 and 60.6 million in 1970.

Advertising was the foundation of the television industry, as it had also been for radio. The first TV commercial, made by the Bulova Watch Company in 1941, was a one-minute effort that cost nine dollars. By the end of the decade, American families were spending approximately five hours a day before the television set, and the bargain rates had vanished; annual expenditures for TV advertising totaled $50 million. By 1970 the figure had soared to $3.6 billion.   **4**

One obvious casualty of the stay-at-home suburban culture was the **5** motion picture. While Americans continued to buy paperbacks and comic books in large numbers, many of them stopped visiting movie theaters. After all, why fight traffic to go to a movie when you could watch TV in the comfort of your living room? Why pay a babysitter? From 1946 to 1948 Americans had attended movies at the rate of nearly 90 million a week. By 1950 the figure had dropped to 60 million a week; by 1960, 40 million. Thus the postwar years saw the steady closing of movie theaters—with the notable exception of the drive-in, which appealed to car-bound suburban families.

_____ 1. Major details are
   a. indicated in an introduction.
   b. indicated by a number or numbers.
   c. indicated in first sentences of paragraphs.
   d. not indicated by items in *a, b,* or *c.*

_____ 2. Which title best states the expository pattern?
   a. Reasons for the Popularity of TV
   b. Some of the Effects of Television
   c. Types of Television Viewing in America
   d. Similarities Between TV and Movies

Circle the numbers in front of the questions whose answers are implied by the passage but are not directly stated in it.

_____ 3. *Monumental*, in the passage, means
     a. unbelievable.
     b. praiseworthy.
     c. enduring.
     d. significant.

_____ 4. If you do not know the meaning of *billion*, consult a dictionary to determine its meaning.
     a. ten million
     b. one hundred million
     c. one thousand million
     d. ten thousand million

_____ 5. *Casualty*, in the passage, refers to something that
     a. suffered a loss.
     b. was destroyed completely.
     c. was killed.
     d. needed professional attention.

_____ 6. Between the years 1950 and 1970, the number of households with TV sets increased
     a. fivefold.
     b. tenfold.
     c. fifteenfold.
     d. twentyfold.

_____ 7. When people who are fifty years old today were ten years old, there were TV sets in
     a. almost all of their homes.
     b. more than half of their homes.
     c. about one-half of their homes.
     d. very few of their homes.

_____ 8. There have been paid commercials on television for
     a. more than fifty years.
     b. more than forty years.
     c. fewer than forty years.
     d. fewer than thirty years.

_____ 9. Between the late 1940s and 1970, expenditures for television advertising increased
     a. sixfold.
     b. thirtyfold.
     c. sixtyfold.
     d. ninetyfold.

_____ 10. Comparing movie theater attendance at the end of the 1940s
to 1950 and then to 1960, it was reduced first by
a. one-third, and then by more than half.
b. one-third, and then by about another third.
c. two-thirds, and then by more than half.
d. two-thirds, and then by another third.

EXERCISE 4

ENERGY FROM THE SUN

The ocean is the regulator of the impact of the sun's energy on the Earth. Gases in the atmosphere are exchanged with gases dissolved in the sea water. The exchanges of heat between the atmosphere and the sea water modify the temperatures of the atmosphere. Note: Water has a very high heat capacity. This makes it possible for sea water to absorb and store great quantities of heat, while at the same time experiencing little temperature change. The water in the sea can thus absorb solar energy and re-emit it in different locales, in which there is an energy deficit. Sea water is able to do this because it moves from 3 one location to another. It absorbs heat energy in areas of excess—such as the equatorial and tropical seas—and transports it to cooler regions at higher latitudes. The higher-latitude waters in turn move toward the warmer, lower-latitude areas.

The Northern hemisphere has warmer summers than the Southern hemisphere, due to its greater amount of land. For the same reason, it has colder winters. The lower specific heat of land causes land to heat faster than water and also to emit energy back to the atmosphere 4 faster than water does. It also causes land masses to cool faster than bodies of water.

The daily ranges of temperature over land are much more extreme than over water. In fact, temperature changes over the sea are almost nonexistent. Water's high specific heat causes it to absorb heat in large quantities without an appreciable change in temperature. Water's great 5 absorbing ability is due mainly to its high specific heat.

_____ 1. Major details are
   a. indicated in the introduction.
   b. indicated by a number or numbers.
   c. indicated in first sentences of paragraphs.
   d. not indicated by items in *a, b,* or *c.*

_____ 2. Which title best states the expository pattern?
   a. The Effects of the Sun on Land and Water
   b. A Comparison of Land and Ocean Surfaces
   c. How the Ocean Regulates Earth Temperatures
   d. Reasons for the Effectiveness of the Sun

Circle the numbers in front of the questions whose answers are implied by the passage but are not directly stated in it.

_____ 3. A *deficit* is a
   a. surplus.
   b. shortage.
   c. strength.
   d. weakness.

_____ 4. To *emit* is to
   a. give off.
   b. take in.
   c. close up.
   d. shut down.

_____ 5. *Appreciable* means
   a. measurable.
   b. appealing.
   c. well-liked.
   d. responsive.

_____ 6. The ocean regulates temperatures on earth by
   a. absorbing and distributing energy from the sun.
   b. absorbing and storing energy from the sun.
   c. moving warm water from the south to the north.
   d. moving cold water from the north to the south.

_____ 7. Northern countries are warmed by solar energy stored in
   a. southern land.
   b. northern land.
   c. tropical waters.
   d. arctic waters.

_____ 8. Compared to the Northern hemisphere, the Southern hemi-sphere has
   a. less land.
   b. more land.
   c. warmer summers.
   d. cooler winters.

_____ 9. Summers are warmer and winters are cooler on land than on water because land
   a. heats faster than water.
   b. emits energy faster than water.
   c. cools faster than water.
   d. has a lower specific heat than water.

_____ 10. Temperature changes over
   a. water are more extreme than over land.
   b. land are more extreme than over water.
   c. water are more frequent than over land.
   d. land are less frequent than over water.

EXERCISE 5

PROHIBITION

In 1920, the Eighteenth Amendment made it illegal to manufacture, transport, or sell alcoholic beverages. For fourteen years, Prohibition was the law of the land.

In the minds of many Americans, drinking was linked to corruption 3 in city politics, to immigration, to organized crime, to the decline in church attendance, and even to the increased divorce rate. In part, Prohibition was an attempt to find a single simple solution to these and other complex problems. Among the factors that combined to put 4 Prohibition into effect were the propaganda methods of the Anti-Saloon League and other reform organizations, the influence of rural-dominated state legislatures, and the need to use grain for food rather than for the manufacture of alcoholic beverages.

Prohibition did not prevent Americans from drinking, but it did change their drinking habits. Alcohol consumption was reduced, and 5 there was a shift from drinking hard liquor to drinking more beer and wine. Prohibition also gave organized crime an opportunity to become big business; money it earned selling illegal alcohol was invested in other businesses. Furthermore, the attempt to legislate drinking habits encouraged average citizens to break the law; Americans might vote for Prohibition, but this did not stop them from drinking. Unfortunately, the hypocrisy and corruption that resulted from Prohibition contributed strongly to the opinion that it is easier to break a disagreeable law than to change it.

_____ 1. Major details are
   a. indicated in the introduction.
   b. indicated by a number or numbers.
   c. indicated in first sentences of paragraphs.
   d. not indicated by items in *a, b,* or *c.*

_____ 2. Which title best states the expository pattern?
   a. Why Prohibition Became Law in America
   b. The Causes and Effects of Prohibition
   c. The Reasons Prohibition Did Not Last
   d. The History of Prohibition in America

Circle the numbers in front of the questions whose answers are implied by the passage but are not directly stated in it.

_____ 3. *Corruption,* in the passage, refers to
   a. deterioration.
   b. dishonesty.
   c. conclusiveness.
   d. wickedness.

_____ 4. A *factor* is
   a. a condition or circumstance.
   b. a policy for reform.
   c. an effect or result.
   d. a form of propaganda.

_____ 5. *Consumption*, in the passage, refers to
   a. illness.
   b. recovery.
   c. eating.
   d. drinking.

_____ 6. The Nineteenth Amendment made it illegal to
   a. make whiskey in distilleries.
   b. sell beer or wine in taverns.
   c. ship Scotch across country.
   d. deny women the right to vote.

_____ 7. Prohibition did *not* become law because of
   a. mass propaganda of reform organizations.
   b. widespread corruption in the liquor industry.
   c. state legislatures dominated by rural members.
   d. the need to use grain for food rather than drink.

_____ 8. The fundamental reason Prohibition became law was that many Americans wanted
   a. a simple solution to complex problems.
   b. a halt in the rising divorce rate.
   c. to reduce corruption in city politics.
   d. to increase attendance at churches.

_____ 9. Which of the following did *not* result from Prohibition?
   a. There was a shift to drinking more beer.
   b. Organized crime became big business.
   c. Disagreeable laws became easier to change.
   d. Average citizens became law breakers.

_____ 10. Prohibition probably came to an end because
   a. everybody's drinking could not be policed.
   b. drinking was made legal again in 1931.
   c. many Americans were dying from poisonous beer.
   d. The Nineteenth Amendment was enacted by Congress.

EXERCISE 6

RABIES

There is one factor that is extremely important in the transmission of rabies infection to humans: The vast majority of human cases involve dogs and cats. It is difficult to arrive at even a reasonably accurate estimate of the number of dogs and cats in the United States, but it is certainly a large number. People are exposed to the infectious agent largely through close association with these animals. If there were some means of controlling the disease in dogs and cats, its incidence in humans would decline.

What measures can be taken to control the incidence of rabies in 3 dogs and cats? First, the level of immunity of the dog and cat population can be increased. Many states require that dogs and cats be vaccinated against rabies annually. Second, leash laws can be enforced. Most municipalities in the United States have such laws, but they are 4 often poorly enforced. Such regulations and their enforcement are designed to reduce the possibility that a stray animal harboring the 5 disease will enter an area and infect other animals. Stated differently, the aim is to eliminate one of the potential reservoirs of the infectious agent.

Third, the public can be educated with respect to both the seriousness of the problem and what people can do to help solve it. Young children should be discouraged from petting unfamiliar dogs and cats, as well as wild animals, because they could easily be bitten by a rabid carrier. Adults should be made aware that they have a responsibility to advise the appropriate authorities (animal control officers or public health officials) whenever they observe any abnormal pattern of behavior in an animal.

_____ 1. Major details are
  a. indicated in an introduction.
  b. indicated in first sentences of paragraphs.
  c. indicated by a number or numbers.
  d. not indicated by items in *a*, *b*, or *c*.

_____ 2. Which title best states the expository pattern?
  a. Methods for Controlling Rabies
  b. Effects of Rabies on Humans
  c. Categories of Rabies Infection
  d. Comparison of Rabid Animals

Circle the numbers in front of the questions whose answers are implied by the passage but are not directly stated in it.

_____ 3. An *incidence* is
    a. an accident.
    b. an occurrence.
    c. an example.
    d. a consequence.

_____ 4. *Municipalities* are
    a. mayors.
    b. governors.
    c. countries.
    d. towns.

_____ 5. *Harboring,* in the passage, means
    a. holding or clinging to.
    b. being a dwelling place.
    c. quieting or calming.
    d. protecting or sheltering.

_____ 6. How many of the cases of rabies in humans are caused by animals other than dogs or cats?
    a. a vast majority
    b. a tiny minority
    c. about 75 percent
    d. about 25 percent

_____ 7. Rabies is controlled mostly by
    a. killing rabid animals.
    b. curing rabid animals.
    c. vaccinating humans.
    d. vaccinating animals.

_____ 8. Leash laws are
    a. enforced by states.
    b. enforced by counties.
    c. laws that forbid animals to roam free.
    d. laws that require the vaccination of pets.

_____ 9. For humans to be infected by rabies, it is necessary for them to be
    a. in contact with a rabid animal.
    b. bitten by a rabid animal.
    c. attacked by a rabid animal.
    d. especially susceptible to infection.

_____ 10. Leash laws are intended to reduce the spread of rabies
    a. among humans.
    b. among animals.
    c. within towns.
    d. within states.

EXERCISE 7

TESTS OF ABNORMALCY

Psychologists use three tests to determine what is "normal" and "abnormal": the tests of frequency, societal standards, and degree of disability.

The *test of frequency* may be used to determine abnormalcy of any characteristic on which people differ, such as weight, intelligence, and income. For example, when many people are weighed most of them fall in the middle range of weight, but a few are exceptionally heavy and a few are unusually light. By the frequency test, that which occurs infrequently is abnormal. For instance, those who are unusually intelligent or happy are abnormal when the test is used; therefore, the test of frequency must be used together with other tests.

The *test of societal standards* identifies what is abnormal in a society. In the United States, for example, it is abnormal and illegal to be married to more than one person at a time, but this practice is normal and legal in other societies. Also, there is censure against 3 murder, but we approve of soldiers killing the enemy in combat.

Perhaps the most important of the three tests is the *test of degree of disability.* When people are so incapacitated that they cannot meet 4 their everyday responsibilities, their disability is so great that their behavior is considered to be maladjusted, atypical, and abnormal. 5

_____ 1. Major details are *not* indicated
  a. in the introduction.
  b. by words in italic type.
  c. by a number.
  d. by words in boldface type.

_____ 2. Which title best states the expository pattern?
  a. Types of Abnormalcy in Society
  b. Causes of Abnormal Behavior Patterns
  c. Comparison of Abnormal Personalities
  d. Methods for Determining Abnormalcy

Circle the numbers in front of the questions whose answers are implied by the passage but are not directly stated in it.

_____ 3. *Censure* is
  a. disapproval.
  b. completeness.
  c. centrality.
  d. hostility.

_____ 4. *Incapacitated* means
     a. unavailable.
     b. disabled.
     c. heedless.
     d. minuscule.

_____ 5. *Atypical* means
     a. unusual.
     b. common.
     c. irrelevant.
     d. relevant.

_____ 6. Using the test of frequency, it is *not* abnormal for college students to
     a. be four feet tall.
     b. be extremely wealthy.
     c. get straight As.
     d. complain about tests.

_____ 7. Using the test of societal standards, it is *not* abnormal for college students to
     a. strike their teachers.
     b. work for good grades.
     c. eat human flesh.
     d. marry their parents.

_____ 8. College students who are frequently absent from classes, who do not do assignments, and who are absent from tests are abnormal using the
     a. test of frequency.
     b. test of societal standards.
     c. test of degree of disability.
     d. three tests stated in *a*, *b*, and *c*.

_____ 9. Using the test of frequency, it is *not* abnormal when parents
     a. always approve of their children's friends.
     b. dress their children in bizarre clothing.
     c. hope their children will fail in life.
     d. never forget their children's birthdays.

_____ 10. Using the test of societal standards, it is abnormal for
     a. teachers to correct students.
     b. students to correct teachers.
     c. employers to correct workers.
     d. parents to correct children.

EXERCISE 8

RELATIVES

Many people consider an uncle or grandparent to be as close a relative as a brother or sister. The fact is, however, that your **primary relatives** are only the members of your family of orientation (parents and siblings) and your family of procreation (husband or wife and sons **3,4** and daughters).

Your **secondary relatives** are the primary relatives of your primary relatives, who are not already primary relatives. For instance, your father is a primary relative of your mother; your mother is a primary relative of a primary relative. But your mother is not a secondary relative because she is already a primary relative. Your father's brother (uncle), your mother's father (grandfather), and your sister's daughter (niece) are some of your secondary relatives.

Now that you know what secondary relatives are, you should be able to guess the next type. **Tertiary relatives** are primary relatives of **5** secondary relatives who, of course, are not already primary or secondary relatives. Your father's brother's wife (aunt), your mother's father's father (great-grandfather), and your sister's daughter's son (great-nephew) are some of your tertiary relatives.

Those related to you by blood are *consanguineous* relatives, and those related to you by marriage are *affinal* relatives.

_____ 1. Major details are
    a. indicated in an introduction.
    b. indicated by words in boldface type.
    c. indicated in first sentences of paragraphs.
    d. not indicated by items in *a*, *b*, or *c*.

_____ 2. Which title best states the expository pattern?
    a. Three Types of Relatives
    b. How to Make a Family Tree
    c. Reasons for Closeness Among Relatives
    d. Comparison of Relatives by Blood and Marriage

Circle the numbers in front of the questions whose answers are implied by the passage but are not directly stated in it.

_____ 3. *Siblings* are
    a. mothers and fathers.
    b. wives and husbands.
    c. sons and daughters.
    d. brothers and sisters.

_____ 4. *Procreation* is
    a. amplification.
    b. reproduction.
    c. mystification.
    d. organization.

_____ 5. *Tertiary* means
    a. actual.
    b. supposed.
    c. distant.
    d. third.

_____ 6. Which of the following is *not* a primary relative?
    a. parent
    b. sibling
    c. uncle
    d. spouse

_____ 7. Which of the following is *not* a secondary relative?
    a. aunt
    b. cousin
    c. nephew
    d. grandfather

_____ 8. Which of the following is *only* a secondary relative?
    a. mother-in-law
    b. uncle
    c. nephew
    d. niece

_____ 9. Which of the following is *not* a tertiary relative?
    a. one's father's sister's husband
    b. one's father's mother's sister
    c. one's mother's father's daughter
    d. one's mother's brother's son

_____ 10. Husbands and wives are primary,
    a. affinal members of a family of procreation.
    b. affinal members of a family of orientation.
    c. consanguineous members of a family of procreation.
    d. consanguineous members of a family of orientation.

EXERCISE 9

HUMAN MOTIVATION

Abraham H. Maslow is one of the most respected students of human motivation.[1] He says that there are five basic needs, and that the lower- 3 level needs must be satisfied before satisfaction can be found for higher-level needs. The five needs, going from low to high, are: (1) *physiological*, such as the need for food, water, and shelter; (2) *safety*, including the need for security, stability, and structure; (3) *belongingness* and love, including the need for contact and association; (4) *esteem*, including the desires for a sense of adequacy or competence and for recognition, appreciation, and prestige; and (5) *self-actualiza-* 4 *tion*, including the urge for self-fulfillment as musician, painter, or as some other type of specialist. These five groups, Maslow explains, function as a hierarchy; that is, the lower needs must be satisfied, at 5 least to some extent, before satisfaction can be found for higher-level needs. For example, after human beings have satisfied the physiological needs, such as the needs for food, water, and shelter, then they can move on to satisfy safety needs. When safety needs are satisfied, satisfaction can then be found for belongingness needs, and so on up the ladder. Maslow adds that this step-by-step sequence is not rigid. A person may satisfy a higher-level need even though one of the lower-level needs is not completely satisfied.

[1] Abraham H. Maslow, *Motivation and Personality* (New York: Harper & Row, 1970), esp. pp. 35–47, 51–57.

_____ 1. Major details are *not* indicated
           a. by the number "five."
           b. by words in italic type.
           c. by the numbers 1, 2, 3, 4, and 5.
           d. in first sentences of paragraphs.

_____ 2. Which title best states the expository pattern?
           a. Reasons for Needs in Humans
           b. Comparison of Motivational Responses
           c. Maslow's Hierarchy of Human Needs
           d. Effects of Human Need Deprivation

Circle the numbers in front of the questions whose answers are implied by the passage but are not directly stated in it.

_____ 3. A *motivation* is a
           a. reason for action.
           b. behavior pattern.
           c. sly or secret activity.
           d. rationally inspired concept.

_____ 4. *Prestige* is
      a. a goal of human activity.
      b. status that brings respect.
      c. that which quiets or calms.
      d. a right bestowed at birth.

_____ 5. *Hierarchy*, in the passage, refers to a
      a. system of church government.
      b. bow-shaped arrangement.
      c. feature of architecture.
      d. ranked classification.

_____ 6. Abraham H. Maslow
      a. discovered the basic human needs.
      b. identified five needs as basic.
      c. explained how hierarchies function.
      d. devised one of the first hierarchies.

_____ 7. Which of the following does *not* directly satisfy a physiological need?
      a. proper clothing
      b. good employment
      c. sufficient sleep
      d. sexual activity

_____ 8. Which of the following does *not* directly satisfy a safety need?
      a. companionable acquaintances
      b. gainful employment
      c. unemployment insurance
      d. social security or pension

_____ 9. Friends and associates primarily satisfy
      a. physiological needs.
      b. safety needs.
      c. belongingness needs.
      d. esteem needs.

_____ 10. Fred, respected by most, has been long jobless and as a result his life lacks security and structure. What is the highest level of needs for which he is receiving satisfaction?
      a. physiological needs
      b. safety needs
      c. belongingness needs
      d. esteem needs

EXERCISE 10

THE AMERICAN LANGUAGE

Another factor that reinforced the American identity was language. Although the heavy tide of immigration brought a variety of languages to the United States, none rose in competition with English. The initial establishment of American society by English-speaking people made English the language of politics and government, trade and commerce, education and learning. Foreign-speaking immigrant groups often held tenaciously to their native tongue, seeking to retain it in their churches, their local schools, and their families. But the basic life of the nation was conducted in English, and however much first-generation immigrants might cling to the old and garble the new, their **3** children quickly discovered that English was the passport to getting ahead in America. The disunity that might well have come from a babel of languages was thus avoided. This is not to say that English **4** remained pure and unchanged in the new republic. Indeed, it was modified considerably in America, not only in the spelling and meaning of many words, but also in the many adaptations that came from the Indian and the variety of languages imported by the immigrants. As a matter of fact, some proponents of a distinct American nationality **5** hoped for a language quite separate from English, one clearly American in identity. Jefferson himself in 1813 declared that "The new circumstances under which we are placed call for new words, new phrases, and for the transfer of old words to new objects. An American dialect will therefore be formed." Many Englishmen would doubtless agree with George Bernard Shaw that the Americans have indeed achieved this goal of Jefferson's, that English hasn't been spoken here for years.

_____ 1. Major details are
   a. indicated in an introduction.
   b. indicated by a number or numbers.
   c. indicated by words in italic type.
   d. not indicated by items in *a, b,* or *c.*

_____ 2. Which title best states the expository pattern?
   a. How English Became the American Language
   b. Effects of Immigrants on the American Language
   c. The History of the English in America
   d. The Types of English Spoken in America

Circle the numbers in front of the questions whose answers are implied by the passage but are not directly stated in it.

_____ 3. To *garble* is to
   a. choke or gag.
   b. distort or scramble.
   c. chirp or sing.
   d. laugh or giggle.

_____ 4. *Babel*, in the passage, refers to
   a. noise and confusion.
   b. a confusion of voices.
   c. meaningless utterance.
   d. a confusion of languages.

_____ 5. A *proponent* is
   a. an idea, thought, or notion.
   b. an advocate or supporter.
   c. a backward-moving force.
   d. a reason to take action.

_____ 6. English became the American language because
   a. it is the most expressive of all languages.
   b. our society was founded by English speakers.
   c. it was the language of educated Europeans.
   d. there was no other language to compete with it.

_____ 7. First-generation immigrants did *not* use their native languages
   a. when speaking among family and friends.
   b. at their churches and local schools.
   c. as a second rather than a first language.
   d. to enter the mainstream of American society.

_____ 8. A multiplicity of languages in America was avoided because
   a. immigrants accepted the superiority of English.
   b. immigrants did not want to be viewed as ignorant.
   c. schools could not find books in other languages.
   d. children of immigrants decided to learn English.

_____ 9. Thomas Jefferson was among those who believed that
   a. America should create its own language.
   b. English should be the American language.
   c. immigrants should be made to learn English.
   d. Englishmen opposed our use of their language.

_____ 10. Some Englishmen seem to believe that Americans
   a. do not speak the English language.
   b. used to speak English, but stopped.
   c. speak a language devised by Jefferson.
   d. speak an inferior type of English.

14. MAKE EVALUATIONS

Comprehension of textbooks includes locating, inferring, and evaluating information in them.

1. Preview before reading.
2. Locate major details.
3. Find minor details.
4. Identify expository patterns.
5. Infer implied meanings.
6. **Make evaluations.**
7. Interpret tables and graphs.

To **evaluate** something is to analyze it to form an opinion about it. For instance, the answer to the following question requires an evaluation: "Why did you enjoy or not enjoy the last party you went to?" Your answer to this question is your evaluation of the last party you attended.

Two people may not evaluate the same event or information in the same way. A party you enjoyed may not have been a very enjoyable experience for others. Since people have different expectations, experiences, beliefs, preferences, and knowledge, they often do not agree in their evaluations.

The criteria, or standards, for evaluating written material vary depending on the type of writing that is evaluated. Different criteria are used to evaluate poetry and biography, for example. The most important criteria to consider when evaluating information in a textbook are answers to the following questions:

1. Is it understandable?
2. Is it complete?
3. Is it authoritative?
4. Is it factual?
5. Is it useful?

The following discussions explain how to decide the answers to these questions.

IS IT UNDERSTANDABLE?

You are the best judge of whether a textbook is understandable to you. Authors and editors usually take great care to make textbooks as understandable as possible.

1. They include descriptive headings and subheadings.
2. They identify major details in introductory paragraphs.
3. They place important statements in first sentences of paragraphs.
4. They print important words in italics, boldface, or a special color (such as red).
5. They define important terminology in context.
6. They use "first," "second," or "1," "2," and so on to indicate major details.
7. They avoid using words that are likely to be unfamiliar to most students.

They also include learning goals, discussion questions, lists of important terminology, and summaries in chapters to inform students of what they should learn. Chapters 9 and 10 of *RSVP* explain how to use these helps to read textbooks with better comprehension.

However, not all textbooks for a subject are equally understandable; some introductory chemistry textbooks, for instance, are much easier to understand than others. Also, some subjects are extremely complicated or technical and cannot be written about in an easy-to-understand manner. There are probably no books about advanced philosophical concepts or nuclear physics that most students would consider "easy" to read and understand.

EXERCISE 1

EVALUATING UNDERSTANDABILITY

Evaluate the understandability of two textbooks you are studying. Write the names of the books over the columns on the right. Then, answer the questions about the books by writing "yes" or "no" on the lines provided.

1. _____   2. _____

1. Are headings and subheadings usually descriptive of the information that follows them?   _____   _____

2. Are major details often
   identified in
   introductory paragraphs?   _____   _____

3. Are important
   statements often located
   in first sentences of
   paragraphs?   _____   _____

4. Are important terms
   printed in italics,
   boldface, or a special
   color (such as red)?   _____   _____

5. Are important terms
   defined in context?   _____   _____

6. Are "first," "second," or
   "1," "2," and so on
   sometimes used to
   indicate major details?   _____   _____

7. Does the book contain
   few words that are
   unfamiliar to you?   _____   _____

8. Which of the two books is easiest for you to understand?

   _____

IS IT COMPLETE?

A textbook seldom provides complete information about the topics discussed in it; the discussions in textbooks are usually brief summaries of large bodies of literature. For example, a thirty-page chapter about the origins of English words in an English textbook is not the complete information about this topic. Hundreds of books and articles have been written about the origins of English words.

Sometimes, of course, textbooks do provide complete information about topics. A two-page discussion in an English textbook about how to use commas correctly is likely to be complete information about this topic; so is a four-page discussion in a mathematics textbook about how to solve a specific type of problem.

However, for the most part, textbooks are not complete. An instructor selects a textbook because it is complete enough to teach a specific course, not because it includes everything that is known about the topics discussed in it. A textbook is complete enough for the specific purpose it was written to serve.

Most sources of information are complete enough for some purposes and not for others. Figure 14.1 shows two sources of information about Helen Keller: a dictionary entry and a biographical article. The dictionary entry is very brief, but it is complete enough for learning some basic facts about Helen Keller. The biographical article provides much more complete information about Helen Keller, but not everything that is known about her—several books and many articles have been written about this remarkable woman.

EXERCISE 2

EVALUATING COMPLETENESS

Study the dictionary entry and the article about Helen Keller in Figure 14.1. Then, on the lines provided below, write *D* if a question can be answered by referring to the *dictionary* entry. Write *A* if the biographical *article* must be consulted to answer the question; write *O* if some source *other* than the dictionary entry and biographical article must be consulted to answer it.

_____   1. The spelling of her complete name

_____   2. The place of her birth

_____   3. The years of her birth and death

_____   4. Places where she lectured

_____   5. Whether she was a writer

_____   6. Whether she was born blind and deaf

_____   7. Whether she attended college

_____   8. Whether she could speak

_____   9. Her feelings about blindness

_____ 10. Her exact age when she died

Dictionary Entry

Kel·ler (kĕl'ər), **Helen Adams.** 1880–1968. American author and lecturer, deaf and blind from infancy.

Biographical Article

Keller, Helen Adams (1880–1968), author and lecturer. Born on June 27, 1880, near Tuscumbia, Alabama, Helen Keller was afflicted at the age of 19 months with an illness that left her blind, deaf, and mute. She was examined by Alexander Graham Bell at about the age of six; as a result he sent to her a twenty-year-old teacher, Anne Mansfield Sullivan, from the Perkins Institution, which Bell's son-in-law directed. Miss Sullivan (later Mrs. John A. Macy), a remarkable teacher, remained with Helen from March 2, 1887, until her death in 1936. Within months Helen had learned to feel objects and associate them with words spelled out by finger signals on her palm, to read sentences by feeling raised words on cardboard, and to make her own sentences by arranging words in a frame. During 1888–1890 she spent winters in Boston at the Perkins Institution learning Braille. Then she began a slow process of learning to speak—feeling the position of the tongue and lips, making sounds, and imitating the lip and tongue motions—at Boston's Horace Mann School for the Deaf. She also learned to lip-read by placing her fingers on the lips and throat of the speaker while the words were simultaneously spelled out for her. At fourteen she enrolled in the Wright-Humason School for the Deaf in New York City, and at sixteen entered the Cambridge School for Young Ladies in Massachusetts. She won admission to Radcliffe College, entering in 1900, and graduated cum laude in 1904. Having developed skills never approached by any person so handicapped, she began to write of blindness, a subject then taboo in women's magazines because of the relationship of many cases to venereal disease. The pioneering editor Edward W. Bok accepted her articles for the *Ladies' Home Journal,* and other major magazines—*The Century, McClure's,* and the *Atlantic Monthly*—followed suit. She wrote of her life in several books, including *The Story of My Life,* 1902; *Optimism,* 1903; *The World I Live In,* 1908; *Song of the Stone Wall,* 1910; *Out of the Dark,* 1913; *My Religion,* 1927; *Midstream,* 1929; *Peace at Eventide,* 1932; *Helen Keller's Journal,* 1938; *Let Us Have Faith,* 1940; and *The Open Door,* 1957. In 1913 she began lecturing, primarily on behalf of the American Foundation for the Blind, for which she established a $2-million endowment fund, and her lecture tours took her around the world. Her efforts to improve treatment of the deaf and the blind were influential in removing the handicapped from asylums. She also prompted the organization of commissions for the blind in 30 states by 1937. Awarded the Presidential Medal of Freedom in 1963, she died in Westport, Connecticut, on June 1, 1968, universally acknowledged as one of the great women of the world.

FIGURE 14.1

A dictionary entry and a bibliographical article

IS IT AUTHORITATIVE?

A book is **authoritative** when it is written by an expert in the subject it discusses. When expert microbiologists write books about microbiology, the books they write are authoritative. Textbooks are written by authorities and read by other authorities before they are published—they are authoritative.

However, textbooks are seldom the most authoritative sources of information because they are usually secondary sources rather than primary sources. A **primary source** is a firsthand source; a **secondary source** is a source that gives information about a primary source. For example, the text of a speech given by Abraham Lincoln is a primary source of information about what he said, but a summary of the speech in a history textbook is a secondary source about things President Lincoln said. Textbooks are authoritative secondary sources for students who, in a term of study, have insufficient time to locate and read all the relevant primary sources.

EXERCISE 3

EVALUATING AUTHORITATIVENESS

Primary sources are generally considered more authoritative than secondary sources (see the preceding paragraph). Write the answers to the following questions on the lines provided.

_____ 1. Which of the following is a primary source of information about Martha Washington?
   a. a novel about her life with George
   b. an article in an encyclopedia
   c. a dress she wore

_____ 2. Which of the following is a primary source of information about an astronaut's experiences walking on the moon?
   a. a report in the *New York Times*
   b. notes in the astronaut's personal diary
   c. an article in *Newsweek* magazine

_____ 3. Which of the following is a primary source of information about the effects of smoking on health?
   a. statistical reports of the surgeon general
   b. articles in newspapers and magazines
   c. warnings printed on cigarette packages

_____ 4. Which of the following is a primary source of information about the spellings of English words?
   a. an English composition textbook
   b. a spelling or vocabulary book
   c. a standard desk dictionary

_____ 5. Which of the following is a primary source about public appearances made by President Jimmy Carter?
   a. a television recording of a speech he gave
   b. his family home in Georgia
   c. any report by somebody who saw him in person

IS IT FACTUAL?

The following statement appears in Chapter 12: "Facts are things that are known to be true." This statement is correct, but it is incomplete: **Facts** are things that are known to be true or regarded, as a result of observation, to be true. For example, it is known to be a fact that John F. Kennedy was president of the United States from 1961 until 1963. On the other hand, the First Law of Thermodynamics is regarded to be true.

The law states: Energy cannot be created or destroyed. There is not certain proof that the law is true, but, as a result of their observations, scientists regard it to be a fact.

Each discipline, or subject, has its own methods for establishing facts. To understand and accept the facts of a discipline, it is necessary to understand and accept the methodology the discipline uses to make observations and establish facts. For example, sociologists have established the fact that the death penalty is not a deterrent to crime. However, many people believe that the death penalty does deter crime; they do not understand or accept the methods sociologists use to make observations and establish facts.

Textbooks are written by authorities and approved by other authorities before they are published; as a result, they are factual in the opinion of those who write and approve them. If errors are found in a textbook, they are corrected when it is revised. College teachers do not require students to study books that they believe misrepresent the facts about their subjects. When information in a textbook seems inaccurate, instructors can usually explain why it is known or regarded to be correct.

EXERCISE 4

EVALUATING FACTUALITY

There are some facts about which informed people agree. For instance, those who know the facts agree that the jaguar, margay, and Utah prairie dog are among the endangered species in North America. On the other hand, there are some facts about which they do not agree. For instance, those who edit dictionaries do not agree which of the following is the preferred spelling: *good-by, good-bye,* or *goodbye!* Some of the following statements are facts about which informed people agree and others are statements about which they disagree. Place a check on the lines in front of statements about which you believe informed people are likely to *disagree.*

_____ 1. Energy cannot be created or destroyed.

_____ 2. The death penalty is an effective deterrent to crime.

_____ 3. Franklin Roosevelt was the first president to make effective use of the radio in communicating with the American public.

_____ 4. Vermont is the state with the smallest black population.

_____ 5. In comparison to other cities, New York provides the most favorable environment for the corporate offices of large businesses.

_____ 6. A one-ounce serving of cheddar cheese provides 115 calories.

_____ 7. Cheddar cheese and other foods high in saturated fat are the major cause of cardiovascular disease.

_____ 8. Pictures of men and women engaging in sexual intercourse are pornographic.

_____ 9. It is harmful to the mental health of children to observe their parents wearing no clothing.

_____ 10. Mt. Rainier, in Washington State, is 14,410 feet tall.

_____ 11. Women are working as firefighters in some major cities of the United States.

_____ 12. Women firefighters are as able in their work as male firefighters.

_____ 13. More Americans have been killed by privately owned firearms than by all the wars the United States has fought.

_____ 14. It is estimated that in 1978 there were 19,560 murders and 67,130 rapes in the United States.

_____ 15. Some of the things that Jesus taught were not original with him; they had been taught earlier by others.

_____ 16. It is essential to increase spending for research to learn how the sun may be used as an important source of energy.

IS IT USEFUL?

That which is useful is helpful, beneficial, serviceable, and often has practical utility. The information in *RSVP* should be useful to those who are interested in improving vocabulary, reading, study, or test-taking skills.

However, one common complaint of students is that they must study subjects that have little or no use to them. For example, students majoring in biology may fail to see the usefulness of studying a foreign language, and those majoring in a foreign language may complain that the study of biology is irrelevant to their needs.

College is a more rewarding and stimulating experience for those who study subjects that they view as useful and who understand why the subjects they study are useful and interesting to others. Why, for instance, is it useful to study biology or a foreign language such as Spanish? Those who study biology acquire a better understanding of plant and animal life—they increase their appreciation of the living things with which they will spend the rest of their lives. Those who study Spanish acquire an ability that enables them to communicate with 245 million people who speak the language; they also develop a skill they can offer to employers when they seek work.

Try to understand the usefulness of the things you study in college; you will enjoy studying more, and you will benefit more from your college experience.

EXERCISE 5

EVALUATING USEFULNESS

Are there subjects you are studying or are required to study in your curriculum that you believe are not useful or relevant to your needs? If so, list them on the following lines.

1. _____

2. _____

3. _____

Any subjects you may have listed are interesting and useful to some very intelligent people. Why can't they also be interesting and useful to you?

MAKING EVALUATIONS

This chapter explains five criteria for evaluating information in textbooks:

1. Is it understandable?
2. Is it complete?
3. Is it authoritative?
4. Is it factual?
5. Is it useful?

The second, third, and fourth questions are answered by experts who read textbooks before publication and by instructors when they select them for their classes. Instructors do not assign textbooks unless they are, in their opinions, authoritative, factual, and complete enough for the purposes of teaching specific courses.

Therefore, it is most important for you to evaluate whether information in textbooks is understandable and useful. If you are required to read a textbook that is very difficult to understand, find help by using one or more of the suggestions in Chapter 4 (pages 36–41). If you ever feel that the subject matter of a textbook has no use to you, try to understand why it is useful and interesting to others; you will benefit more from college if you do.

The following exercises are in the same format as exercises in Chapter 13 except that the reading selections are longer and the multiple-choice questions are followed by activities for evaluating information in textbooks.

6 MAKING ETHICAL DECISIONS

How are ethical decisions made? If ethical decisions are defined as 3 doing the right thing, how do we know what is right?

Fixed Rules

Throughout human history it has been possible to make ethical decisions on the basis of certain fixed rules. There have been, and still are, some principles that have stood the test of time, and these can offer guides for businesspeople as well as others. Perhaps the most influential set of fixed rules has been the Ten Commandments in the Book of Exodus (20:2–18). These rules have influenced many millions of Christians, Jews, and Moslems for thousands of years; and they have also influenced many people who are not formal adherents of 4 these faiths. The other religions of the world have offered similar ethical rules.

Stealing is forbidden by one of the Ten Commandments. Certainly this rule applies to a businessperson who sells shoddy goods as first-grade ones, or to one who accepts a job with another firm for a huge salary because of knowledge of his or her present employer's trade secrets. Advertisers might wonder if they are encouraging people to covet something that is their neighbor's.   5

Despite the general acceptance of the fixed rules, we do not go far before we run into exceptions. The advertisers just mentioned may decide that their work helps to stimulate the economy so that everyone has more; thus, a little coveting leads to better things. Before we call these people hypocritical, we should consider the fixed rules in their context. Exodus 20:13 (revised standard version), says plainly: "You shall not kill." In the very next chapter, however (21:12–17), various circumstances are cited in which killing is permissible—or even mandatory. The fixed rules exist, but since exceptions keep popping up, it is easy to deny the rules are binding.

Greatest Good for the Greatest Number

Another standard for making ethical decisions is to seek the greatest good for the greatest number. This principle was stated by the English philosopher Jeremy Bentham (1748–1832). Fixed rules are largely abandoned in favor of a calculation of maximizing good, or minimizing evil. Suppose you are driving a truck down a narrow mountain road with a cliff on one side. Your brakes have stopped working, and, ahead, a baby is sitting in the road. The only way you can avoid hitting the baby is to go off the cliff. If your truck were full of migrant workers, you could say that doing the greatest good for the greatest number would be to hit the baby and save the others. If you were alone in the truck, perhaps you would decide to drive off the cliff and jump out. This would give you a chance of survival, and it would save the baby (until the next vehicle came along).

In business, a manager might justify a somewhat deceptive advertisement on the grounds that the buyer will not be hurt badly and that the workers and managers of the firm need the sales to avoid a shutdown. The same manager might refuse to use a deceptive advertisement if the buyer could be badly hurt by using the product and business had been good.

Using Bentham's principle involves two primary problems. One is the obvious point that it is hard to measure the *greatest* good except in extreme cases, and it is not always easy to estimate the greatest number. Even more basic is the problem of personal bias. It is asking a lot to suggest that the lone driver should go off the cliff. Can we really expect such self-sacrifice? Can managers be expected to sacrifice their firms and the jobs of their employees and themselves just to avoid selling a poor product to a group of customers they do not know? It is easy to say that the firm should not be producing an inferior product, and this is true. It is also easy to say that one should never drive without thoroughly checking the car's brakes, but many people neglect to do so.

What Seems Right in the Situation

In recent years the idea of *situational ethics* has been advanced. Situational ethics do not claim that fixed rules will provide adequate guides and do not pretend to be able to measure the difference between the amount of good done to one group as opposed to the amount of possible harm to another group. The objective, instead, is to do what seems right in the situation as we live it. This may appear to be a position that lends itself to misuse through selfishness. To make the idea work at all, requires a very high and sensitive regard for other people. Situational ethics really says that we should ask ourselves: "What does love require me to do in this situation?" No one should attempt to answer this question without considerable thought and practice. It is unlikely that situational ethics could be properly used by someone under pressure who had never considered it before. For executives who do strive for awareness of their firms' effect on people everywhere, it may be usable.

EXERCISE 6

MAKING ETHICAL DECISIONS

Preview the passage and answer questions 1 and 2. Then, read the passage and answer the remaining questions.

_____ 1. Major details are indicated
          a. in the introduction.
          b. by three subheadings.
          c. by a number or numbers.
          d. in first sentences of paragraphs.

_____ 2. Which title best states the expository pattern?
          a. Steps in Making Ethical Decisions
          b. The Positive Effects of Ethical Decisions
          c. Three Ways to Make Ethical Decisions
          d. Reasons for Making Ethical Decisions

Circle the numbers in front of the questions whose answers are implied by the passage but are not directly stated in it.

_____ 3. _Ethical_ means
          a. unjustified.
          b. moral.
          c. artistic.
          d. logical.

_____ 4. _Adherent,_ in the passage, refers to
          a. a supporter or follower.
          b. an attentive listener.
          c. an indivisible object.
          d. a sticky substance.

_____ 5. To _covet_ is to
          a. hide from view.
          b. expose by uncovering.
          c. want or envy.
          d. reject or despise.

_____ 6. Fixed rules, such as the Ten Commandments, have influenced
          a. mostly Catholics and other Christians.
          b. Jews and Moslems, as well as Christians.
          c. followers of most of the world's religions.
          d. adherents to religions, and others as well.

_____ 7. The basic problem with using fixed rules to make ethical decisions is that
   a. too many people will not abide by rules.
   b. there are many exceptions to most of them.
   c. most are ancient and irrelevant for today.
   d. religions disagree about too many of them.

_____ 8. The most basic problem with making ethical decisions considering the greatest good for the greatest number is that
   a. it is often hard to measure the greatest good.
   b. the greatest number cannot always be measured.
   c. individuals disagree what is the greatest good.
   d. sometimes, as in war, it is necessary to do injury.

_____ 9. Those who advance the use of situational ethics claim that
   a. fixed rules provide sufficient guidance.
   b. good and harm to groups is measurable.
   c. most of us know what is good and bad.
   d. we should do what seems right at the time.

_____ 10. To use situational ethics, one need _not_ have
   a. sincere regard for other people.
   b. a great capacity for loving others.
   c. an extraordinarily high intelligence.
   d. insight into cause-effect relationships.

Making an Evaluation

The authors provide two equally important types of information in the passage. The first is descriptions of three methods for making ethical decisions, and the second is explanations of the problems associated with using each of the methods. However, it appears that the authors have not made the second type of information as obvious as they intend; when students make notes for the passage, most of them do not include all the explanations of problems with the methods unless they are specifically requested to. Write a third sentence for the introduction to the passage that alerts students to read the passage to locate and learn the _two_ types of information presented in it.

_____

_____

_____

_____

7 PROPAGANDA

An imbalance must be created among your attitudes in order that change may take place. Every day in your life, you are being bombarded by efforts to create such an imbalance. The persuasive techniques or propaganda devices used on radio and television and by salespeople, teachers, and others generally fall into seven categories:

1. *Transfer and testimony* involves having a famous person give a sales pitch for a product. The idea behind this technique is that if a person of a high status uses the product, you should also.
2. *Bandwagon* is an effort to get you to join the group: "Ninety-nine homemakers out of one hundred use Brand Y." Obviously, you are a creature to be pitied unless you too use Brand Y.
3. *Plain folks* is an attempt to establish a common bond between salesperson and customer. "Look, I am one of you, just an ordinary person. What's good for me should be good for you."
4. *Glittering generalities* is an effort to impress the client with high-sounding phrases: "Buy Brand Y because the makers of Brand Y stand four-square behind antipollution."
5. *Appeals to prejudice* try to get you to go for a product because people like you are using it. Not long ago Rheingold beer had a series of commercials that ran, "Ninety percent of the Italians in New York like Rheingold. We must be doing something right."
6. *Card stacking* involves rigging the facts so that the evidence points in favor of the product. "Nine out of ten doctors use Brand A." What this approach doesn't tell you is that the doctors who were selected were specifically chosen so that the results were sure to come out in the company's favor.
7. *Name calling* associates the product with something pleasant. "Drink Slurp! It's cool and refreshing." This sounds better when you are hot and thirsty than "Slurp—a soft drink."

If you want to have some fun, sit down with this list of techniques and watch TV commercials or listen to the radio. Check off the technique that is being used on you. But be careful, because some sales pitches are pretty sophisticated and hard to identify.

There are some variables in the use of propaganda and the tech- 3 niques of persuasion. One is the credibility of the source. Obviously 4 the more expert you consider the seller to be, the more willing you will be to listen. So if you want to convince somebody of something, you should first convince that person that you know what you are talking about. Then, as a speaker, you need to decide whether to use a one-sided message or a two-sided argument. In general, a two-sided argument is more effective in changing people's minds; a one-sided argument reinforces the opinions people already hold. Don't ask people to change their ideas just a little. If you shoot for a major change, you will be more effective. If you get people to participate actively in the argument as devil's advocates, you will tend to change their views 5 toward the side they are pretending to uphold. Most studies have shown that fear used as a persuasive device is not effective (this is the way your lungs will look if you smoke). If you want to scare people into changing, you must also give them some suggestions about ways to reduce their fear. Of course the higher the amount of fear you can arouse, the greater will be the change in their attitudes, unless you overplay your hand to the point where people ask, "What's the use?"

EXERCISE 7

PROPAGANDA

Preview the passage and answer questions 1 and 2. Then, read the passage and answer the remaining questions.

_____ 1. Major details are *not* indicated
   a. in the introduction.
   b. by the words in italic type.
   c. by subheadings.
   d. in first sentences of paragraphs.

_____ 2. Which title best states the expository pattern?
   a. Methods for Winning an Argument
   b. The Techniques of Persuasion
   c. Reasons People Fall for Propaganda
   d. Effects of Persuasion on Consumers

Circle the numbers in front of the questions whose answers are implied by the passage but are not directly stated in it.

_____ 3. *Variable,* in the passage, refers to
   a. a changeable circumstance or condition.
   b. something manipulated during experimentation.
   c. the believability of a source of information.
   d. that which is in a constant state of fluctuation.

_____ 4. *Credibility* is
   a. truthfulness.
   b. untruthfulness.
   c. believability.
   d. unbelievability.

_____ 5. *Devil's advocates* are people who
   a. pretend to agree when they disagree.
   b. pretend to disagree when they agree.
   c. express evil points of view in arguments.
   d. argue against evil to persuade others.

_____ 6. "Millions of women use Radiance soap for a lovelier complexion—you should too." What propaganda techniques are used in this statement?
   a. plain folks and name calling
   b. name calling and bandwagon
   c. bandwagon and transfer
   d. transfer and plain folks

_____ 7. In card stacking, information presented is
   a. for only one side of an argument.
   b. given at random, as in a card game.
   c. piled on top of other information.
   d. limited to what can be put on a card.

_____ 8. If an advertisement for a restaurant in your college newspaper states that it is the most popular one among students,
   the ad uses
   a. testimony.
   b. plain folks.
   c. appeal to prejudice.
   d. glittering generalities.

_____ 9. Television commercials for political candidates showing
   them at home with their families or playing with pets use
   a. bandwagon.
   b. transfer.
   c. card stacking.
   d. plain folks.

_____ 10. Which of the following is *not* a method to use when trying
   to convince others to change their minds?
   a. Convince others you know what you're talking about.
   b. Use a two-sided rather than a one-sided argument.
   c. Ask for a major rather than a minor change.
   d. Use fear as a motivation to make a change.

Making an Evaluation

Is the author correct that propaganda devices are used by advertisers,
teachers, and others? Examine newspapers and magazines to find advertisements that illustrate three of the propaganda methods explained in
the passage. Bring the advertisements to class and be prepared to explain
the types of propaganda used in them.

8 DRUG ABUSE

Drugs have been known to humanity since antiquity. Marihuana, for instance, has been traced back to 2700 B.C. Opium was known to the Egyptians as long ago as 1500 B.C. Opium has been used consistently as a painkiller since the eighteenth century. To the medical profession, opium was almost a universal panacea and was at different 3 times prescribed for pain of cancer, dysentery, gallstones, childbirth, and toothache.

The addictive properties of opium were not understood either by the ancients or by more recent doctors. Not until two refined products of opium—morphine and codeine—came into being in 1805 and 1832, respectively, were opium's addictive powers suspected. Strangely enough, it took a third advance, the invention of the hypodermic needle, to clarify the situation. During the Civil War, morphine and codeine were frequently injected. As a result, thousands of soldiers became addicted to these opiates, which were sold everywhere. The most devastating opium derivative, heroin, was synthesized in 1898. It too was available to everyone. Opium was not the only dependency-producing drug in common use. Until approximately 1902, Coca Cola contained a small dose of cocaine.

It might surprise you to learn that the levels of addiction today in no way equal those present in 1914, when the nation finally recognized the danger of opium and passed the Harrison Act to control it. At that time, it was estimated that one out of every four hundred people in our country was addicted. The estimate for 1965, in contrast, showed one in 3,300.

Several trends in drug use are quite disquieting. Before the 1940s, 4 most drug-dependent people were middle-aged or older and usually were not from the lowest socioeconomic class. Most of them came to be dependent through medical channels, although some artists also used drugs. The picture changed after World War II, when a shift in use from middle class to lower class occurred. This change also involved a shift to use by ethnic and minority groups, particularly in large cities. For example, in the northeastern United States, 90 percent of the narcotics arrests have involved blacks living in slums. On the West Coast, arrests have involved whites, blacks, and Mexican Americans. Another disturbing trend is the shift in drug use from the middle-aged and older to the young. From 1940 to 1962, there was a steady increase in the under-eighteen group and a decrease in the over-forty group. Today, drug abuse is spreading from the cities to the suburbs and is involving younger and younger people of all social classes. It is no longer an affliction of the poor in the slums.

Another trend has been the tendency among drug users to get away from the use of a single drug, such as an opiate derivative. Speed, goofballs, glue sniffing, banana peels, and LSD—almost any substances that might create a reaction—have been used singly and in tandem. 5

A major social problem that did not exist earlier is the combining of criminality and drug dependence. Although most addicts must steal and rob in order to support their habit, which often costs sixty or seventy dollars a day, some evidence shows that the excitement of performing a criminal act may be a part of the psychological life of a drug user. In some mysterious way, the outlaw feeling becomes important, so that lawlessness may not necessarily be a result of drug dependency; it may be part of a whole way of life.

EXERCISE 8

DRUG ABUSE

Preview the passage and answer questions 1 and 2. Then, read the passage and answer the remaining questions.

_____ 1. Major details are indicated
             a. in the introduction.
             b. by words in italic type.
             c. by a number or numbers.
             d. in first sentences of paragraphs.

_____ 2. Which title best states the expository pattern?
             a. Reasons for Increased Drug Use Among the Young
             b. Effects of Drug Abuse on the American Society
             c. The History of Drug Use Since 2700 B.C.
             d. Historical Facts About Drugs and Their Use

Circle the numbers in front of the questions whose answers are implied by the passage but are not directly stated in it.

_____ 3. A _panacea_ is
             a. a disadvantage.
             b. a cure-all.
             c. an opiate.
             d. an overview.

_____ 4. _Disquieting_ means
             a. noisy.
             b. troubling.
             c. muffling.
             d. relaxing.

_____ 5. Things done in _tandem_ are done
             a. together.
             b. secretly.
             c. accidentally.
             d. inconsiderately.

_____ 6. Marihuana has been used for approximately
             a. 2,500 years.
             b. 3,500 years.
             c. 4,500 years.
             d. 5,500 years.

_____ 7. Which of the following drugs came into use most recently?
   a. opium
   b. heroin
   c. morphine
   d. codeine

_____ 8. The percentage of Americans who were addicted to drugs in 1965 was
   a. much greater than fifty years earlier.
   b. much less than fifty years earlier.
   c. slightly greater than fifty years earlier.
   d. slightly less than fifty years earlier.

_____ 9. At one time cocaine was an ingredient in
   a. Coca Cola.
   b. Bayer aspirin.
   c. Hershey chocolate.
   d. Gordon's vodka.

_____ 10. It is *not* true that drug users now
   a. have increased in the lower classes.
   b. have increased among younger persons.
   c. are often associated with lawlessness.
   d. tend to use one rather than several drugs.

Making an Evaluation

Good test questions are often based on facts that are very different from what students are likely to guess the facts are. For instance, the following statement is a good true-false question because students are likely to guess it is false, even though it is true.

A powerful narcotic was, at one time, an ingredient in Coca Cola.

Referring to the passage, write two statements that students are likely to guess are false unless they know the facts.

1. _____

   _____

2. _____

   _____

9 HUMANS AND WEATHER

Air is the most important part of our daily intake. We can survive for long periods without food; people have even gone for days without water. But without air, no one can live for more than a few minutes.

As one rises higher into the atmosphere, there is less and less oxygen. At a height of 2 km (1.3 mi), lack of oxygen begins to affect the body. This lack causes headaches and nausea in people from lower elevations who try to carry out heavy physical tasks. At 6 km (3.8 mi), the lack of oxygen becomes more harmful. A pilot flying at this height without auxiliary oxygen would quickly become incoherent; some **3** people would also lose consciousness.

Yet some human beings have adapted to oxygen-deficient conditions. The natives of La Paz, Bolivia [height 3.5 km (2 mi)], survive quite well. And 175,000 people live in Lhasa, Tibet [height nearly 3.7 km (2.3 mi)], where there is only 62% as much oxygen in the air as there is at sea level.

So human beings vary markedly in their response to different environments, owing to different genetic inheritance and to their slow acclimatization to various conditions. All life forms that inhabit the Earth today have survived to the present because of their ability to adapt to changing conditions. But these adaptations and changes were slow, and required many thousands of years to be completed.

Human beings do not adapt quickly to changing climatic conditions. Furthermore it is not possible to experiment genetically with humans, as we do with plants, in order to breed people who can survive adverse **4** conditions of climate or atmosphere. We have survived to the present because we are adapted to present conditions, within certain limits, and because we have managed to make small adaptations to adverse conditions.

The U.S. armed forces have conducted much research into the ability of humans to survive in various kinds of climates. They have found that humans, like most animals, survive in cold climates only with great difficulty. Few birds or mammals, and no cold-blooded animals such as reptiles or amphibians, live in polar regions. The few animals that do are warm-blooded and have some body covering, such as fur or feathers.

The body builds of people throughout the world vary slightly from low to high latitudes. For example, people who live near the poles tend to be squatter and stockier than those living near the Equator. The stocky build tends to expose a smaller surface area to the air, and conserves body heat.

As humans migrated to various regions, they also managed to change the environment slightly to suit their needs. In the distant past, few areas of the world were suited to the survival of primitive people. The optimum conditions for humans are in central Africa, tropical South America, and Southeast Asia (Malaysia, Indonesia, and New Guinea). So, when humans migrated to colder areas, they built shelters to protect themselves from the cold. As the centuries went by, people's technological skills enabled them to improve their clothing and shelter and thus to increase their chances of survival.

Hot climates can threaten one's life also. The Noel Coward song "Mad Dogs and Englishmen Go out in the Noonday Sun" sums up the situation. The natives of tropical regions adapted to their climate by taking shelter from the extreme heat. But, when colonists entered these tropical climates, many of them tried to work all day, at the same pace as they had in temperate climates. It was not successful! To survive, one had to "go native"—that is, to adopt the long siesta of the natives. Natives of the tropics had learned to live with enervating heat by sleeping through the hottest midafternoon hours, often returning to work after dinner. They had learned to survive by avoiding those conditions they could do nothing about. 5

In hot, humid climates, it is very hard to do heavy work. Sweating, which is the body's normal adaptation to heat, is profuse. Yet the humidity prevents sweat from evaporating and the usual cooling effect does not work well. As the body's two million sweat glands exude sweat, the body quickly loses salt and water. In the early stages of **salt depletion,** this loss leads to fatigue; later, to cramps and circulation failure. Severe dehydration usually results in death. Yes, the siesta is a very wise adaptation to climatic conditions!

Studies show that, as temperatures rise above 32°C (90°F), physical tasks—and mental tasks such as learning in school—become more difficult. The time required for reflex action increases significantly as temperature and humidity rise. Investigations of industrial accidents reveal that the optimum temperature for people to work in is between 12°C (55°F) and 24°C (75°F).

In cold weather our circulatory systems cause blood vessels in the body's extremities to constrict in order to conserve body heat. Clothing traps air near the skin. Because air has a high specific heat, it is a good insulator. Thus a warm layer of clothing plus the trapped air protects us from cold. Long ago, people in cold climates learned that several layers of lighter clothing were more comfortable than one layer of heavy clothing, since layering traps more air.

In cold climates it is more important to cover the head than any other part of the body, because the head loses proportionately more heat than any other part of the body. Eskimos, for example, wear hoods for this reason.

Eskimos also build homes that retain heat efficiently. Conversely, natives in tropical regions build thatched huts that lose heat readily. The reason why people who live in these extreme climates are able to build shelters and wear clothes that are so efficient for their purposes is that experience is a wonderful teacher.

EXERCISE 9

HUMANS AND WEATHER

Preview the passage and answer questions 1 and 2. Then, read the passage and answer the remaining questions.

_____ 1. Major details are clearly
   a. indicated in the introduction.
   b. indicated by a number or numbers.
   c. indicated in first sentences of paragraphs.
   d. none of the above

_____ 2. Which title best states the expository pattern?
   a. The Effects of Weather on Humans
   b. How to Adapt to Changing Weather
   c. A Comparison of Hot and Cold Weather
   d. Why Humans Live in Ideal Climates

Circle the numbers in front of the questions whose answers are implied by the passage but are not directly stated in it.

_____ 3. _Incoherent_ means
   a. very ill and unable to move.
   b. unable to think or speak clearly.
   c. fearful, as of impending death.
   d. ascending, as in an airplane

_____ 4. _Adverse_ means
   a. publicized.
   b. contradictory.
   c. complicated.
   d. unfavorable.

_____ 5. _Temperate_, in the passage, means
   a. neither wet nor dry.
   b. neither hot nor cold.
   c. moderate and self-restrained.
   d. immoderate and unrestrained.

_____ 6. Which of the following statements is _false_?
   a. Some people become ill at 1.3 miles above sea level.
   b. Some people live at 2.3 miles above sea level.
   c. Humans adapt quickly to changing weather conditions.
   d. Responses are influenced by genetic inheritance.

_____ 7. Which of the following places provides the least ideal conditions for human life?
   a. central Africa
   b. tropical South America
   c. Southeast Asia
   d. Northeastern United States

_____ 8. One should not do heavy work in hot, humid climates because
   a. sweat does not evaporate.
   b. the body loses salt and water.
   c. circulation may slow or fail.
   d. all of the above

_____ 9. When the temperature is 32°C
   a. water freezes and turns to ice.
   b. the ocean emits a foggy vapor.
   c. learning in classrooms is difficult.
   d. exercise is needed for circulation.

_____ 10. For warmth in a cold climate, it is wise to wear
   a. several layers of clothing and a hat.
   b. a heavy wool or fur coat and a hat.
   c. clothing made of wool and animal skins.
   d. clothing designed by Alaskans.

Making An Evaluation

   Textbook authors can make what they write easier to understand by avoiding words that are likely to be unfamiliar to many students. The following four words are among words in the passage that are unfamiliar to many first-year college students, for whom the passage is intended.

1. enervating _____

2. profuse _____

3. exude _____

4. fatigue _____

Consult a dictionary to determine if the author could have used more familiar words than these. If so, write them on the lines provided.

10 SYPHILIS

The spiral-shaped bacterium (spirochete) that causes syphilis—*Treponema pallidum*—does not long survive the drying effects of air, but it will grow profusely in the warm, moist mucous membranes of the genital tract, the rectum, and the mouth. Sexual intercourse provides the best mode of transmission.

Primary Syphilis

The disease begins when a spirochete enters a tiny break in the skin. The infected person may show no sign of the disease for ten to twenty-eight days. The first sign is a lesion known as a *chancre* (pro- **3** nounced "shank-er"). The chancre is often an open lump or swelling about the size of a dime or smaller, teeming with microscopic spirochetes. The sore is moist, although there is no discharge, and it is generally painless. It usually appears in the site of infection in the genital region—on the shaft of the penis or on the vulva. Unfortunately, it can also develop in the recesses of the vagina, the rectum, or the male urethra. Thus many infected persons, women in particular, never know they have the disease during the initial phase. But visible or hidden, the chancre is dangerously infectious.

At this stage, a diagnosis can easily be made by a doctor and the disease can be treated. Even without treatment, the chancre disappears within several weeks. Many persons therefore gain a false sense of security, but, in fact, the infection has entered the blood and the spirochetes are being carried to all parts of the body.

Secondary Syphilis

Secondary-stage symptoms appear anywhere from a few weeks to six months—occasionally even a year—after the appearance of the chancre.

Symptoms of secondary syphilis may include a skin rash; small, flat lesions in regions where the skin is moist; whitish patches on the mucous membranes in the mouth and throat; spotty, temporary baldness; general discomfort and uneasiness; low-grade fevers; headaches; and swollen glands. These symptoms are easily mistaken for those of other diseases. It is therefore important to consult a physician if any of these signs appear, particularly if one has been exposed to syphilis during the preceding six months or so. Secondary syphilis, which lasts from three to six months, can always be diagnosed by blood tests.

The disease is most contagious during the secondary stage. All the lesions are filled with spirochetes; hence any contact with them— even without sexual intercourse—can transmit the disease.

Latent Syphilis

The third stage of syphilis is called the latent period. All signs and **4** symptoms of the disease disappear, but it is not gone; spirochetes are invading various organs, including the heart and the brain. This phase sometimes lasts only a few months, but it can also last for twenty years or until the end of life. In this stage, the infected individual appears disease-free and is usually not infectious, with an important exception—a pregnant woman can pass the infection to her unborn child. Although there are no symptoms, a blood test during this stage will reveal syphilis. And within the first two years the highly contagious secondary stage may recur.

Late Syphilis

The late stage of syphilis generally begins ten to twenty years after the beginning of the latent phase, but can occasionally occur earlier. In late syphilis, twenty-three percent of untreated patients become incapacitated. They may develop serious cardiovascular disease—many die of severe heart damage or rupture of the aorta—or they may suffer progressive brain or spinal cord damage, eventually leading to 5
blindness, insanity, or crippling.

Treatment

Syphilis is easily cured with antibiotics when the treatment is begun in the first two stages or even in the latent phase. Penicillin is used most often, but other antibiotics may be used when the patient is sensitive to penicillin. In the early 1970s the spirochete began showing some resistance to penicillin, although it still responds readily to other antibiotic treatment. Syphilis confers no immunity to succeeding infections, and there are no preventive vaccines. Thus, continual caution must be taken to ensure prompt and effective diagnosis and treatment after each possible exposure. To reduce the spread of the disease, prenatal and premarital tests are required by law in forty-five states.

EXERCISE 10

SYPHILIS

Preview the passage and answer questions 1 and 2. Then, read the passage and answer the remaining questions.

_____ 1. Major details are indicated
   a. in the introduction.
   b. by subheadings.
   c. by a number or numbers.
   d. by words in italic type.

_____ 2. Which title best states the expository pattern?
   a. How to Avoid Infection by Syphilis
   b. Four Types of Syphilis in Humans
   c. The Stages and Treatment of Syphilis
   d. The Causes of Syphilis in Humans

Circle the numbers in front of the questions whose answers are implied by the passage but are not directly stated in it.

_____ 3. A _lesion_ is
   a. damage to body tissue.
   b. any lump or swelling.
   c. a dime-sized body wound.
   d. always a chancre.

_____ 4. _Latent_ means
   a. third in rank or order.
   b. last in rank or order.
   c. not present or visible.
   d. present but not visible.

_____ 5. _Progressive,_ in the passage, means
   a. moving forward step by step.
   b. promoting the healing of injury.
   c. spreading and becoming worse.
   d. promoting or favoring social reform.

_____ 6. After infection, there is no sign of syphilis for
   a. two to four days.
   b. four to sixteen days.
   c. eight to twenty-one days.
   d. ten to twenty-eight days.

_____ 7. The chancre associated with syphilis is
a. painful.
b. microscopic.
c. not infectious.
d. often hidden.

_____ 8. Which of the following is *not* a symptom of secondary syphilis?
a. a rash on the skin
b. painful urination
c. fevers and headaches
d. white patches in the mouth

_____ 9. The latent stage of syphilis
a. usually lasts only a few weeks.
b. can be followed by the secondary stage.
c. is usually highly infectious.
d. cannot be detected by a blood test.

_____ 10. Those concerned whether they have syphilis should
a. abstain from sexual relationships.
b. visit a doctor for a blood test.
c. locate a source of penicillin.
d. check themselves for symptoms.

Making an Evaluation

Information about topics in textbooks is seldom complete. How much more information about syphilis is readily available in your college library?

1. Locate an article about syphilis in an encyclopedia. How many columns or pages long is the article?

_____

2. In the card catalogue, how many subject cards are there for syphilis?

_____

3. In the most recent annual volume of the *Readers' Guide to Periodical Literature,* how many magazine articles are listed for syphilis?

_____

11 THE PRINTED WORD

Within the past twenty-five years, two inventions have revolution-ized life for most Americans, television and the computer. By the late 1960s, the tired business executive or mechanic could return home in the evening, flip on "the tube," and while eating dinner watch battles in Vietnam or Israel that had occurred only a few hours before. The American tourist in Copenhagen or Florence or Tokyo who suddenly needs to draw on a bank account in New Orleans or Portland can have the account checked by computer in a matter of minutes. The impact of these relatively recent developments has been absolutely phenom-enal. The invention of movable type likewise transformed European society in the sixteenth century.

Sometime in the thirteenth century, paper money and playing cards from China reached the West. They were block printed, that is, Chinese characters or pictures were carved into a wooden block, inked, and the words or illustrations put on paper. Since each word, phrase, or picture was on a separate block, this method of reproducing an idea was extraordinarily expensive and time-consuming.

Around 1455, and probably through the combined efforts of three men—Johan Gutenberg (ca 1395–1468), Johan Fust (ca 1400–1465), and Peter Schoffer (ca 1425–1502), all experimenting at Mainz—mov-able type came into being. The mirror image of each letter (rather than entire words or phrases) was carved in relief on a small block. Individ- **3** ual letters, easily movable, were put together to form words; words separated by low-cast blank spaces formed lines of type; and lines of type were brought together to make up a page. The printer placed wooden pegs around the type for a border, locked the whole in a chase (or frame), and the page was then ready for printing. Since letters could be arranged into any format, an infinite variety of texts could be printed by reusing and rearranging the pieces of type.

Paper, by the middle of the fifteenth century, was no problem. The technologically advanced but extremely isolated Chinese knew how to manufacture paper in the first century A.D. This knowledge reached the West in the twelfth century, when the Arabs introduced the pro-cess into Spain. Europeans quickly learned that old rags could be shredded, mixed with water, placed in a mold, squeezed, and dried to make a durable paper, far less expensive than the vellum (calfskin) or parchment (sheepskin) on which medieval scribes had relied for cen-turies.

The effects of the invention of printing from movable type were not felt overnight. Nevertheless, within a half-century of the publication of Gutenberg's Bible in 1456, movable type brought about radical changes. The costs of reproducing books were drastically reduced. It took less time and money to print a book by machine than to make copies by hand. The press also cut the chances of error. If the type had been accurately set, then all copies would be correct no matter how many were reproduced. The greater the number of pages a scribe copied, the greater the chances for human error. Printing stimulated the literacy of the laity. Although most of the earliest books dealt **4** with religious subjects, students, businessmen, and upper- and middle-class people sought books on all kinds of subjects. Thus, intellectual interests were considerably broadened. International communication was enormously facilitated. The invention of printing permitted writers and scholars of different countries to learn about one another's ideas and discoveries quickly. Intellectuals working in related fields got in touch with each other and cooperated in the advancement of knowledge.

The very process of learning was made easier by printing from movable type. In the past, students had to memorize everything because only the cathedral, monastery, or professor possessed the book. The greater availability of books meant that students could begin to buy their own. If information was not at the tip of the tongue, knowledge was at the tip of the fingers, in the book. The number of students all across Europe multiplied. It is not entirely accidental that between 1450 and 1517 seven new universities were established in Spain, three in France, nine in Germany, and six new colleges were set up at Oxford in England.

Printing also meant that ideas critical of the established order in state or church could be more rapidly disseminated. In the early sixteenth century, for example, the publication of Erasmus's *The Praise of Folly* helped pave the way for the Reformation. After 1517, the printing press played no small role in the spread of Martin Luther's political and social views. Consequently, cartoons and satirical engravings of all kinds proliferated. They also provoked state censorship, 5 which had been very rare in the Middle Ages. The printed word eventually influenced every aspect of European culture: educational, economic, religious, political, and social.

EXERCISE 11

THE PRINTED WORD

Preview the passage and answer questions 1 and 2. Then, read the passage and answer the remaining question.

_____ 1. Major details are indicated
  a. in the introduction.
  b. by words in italic type.
  c. by a number or numbers.
  d. in first sentences of paragraphs.

_____ 2. Which title best states the expository pattern?
  a. Comparison of Printing in China and Europe
  b. The History of Printing in the Western World
  c. Effects of Printing's Arrival in Europe
  d. Reasons for China's Eminence in Printing

Circle the numbers in front of the questions whose answers are implied by the passage but are not directly stated in it.

_____ 3. _Relief,_ in the passage, refers to
  a. a lessening of pain or discomfort.
  b. figures raised from a flat surface.
  c. help in the form of money or food.
  d. one who takes over the duties of another.

_____ 4. _Laity_ refers to
  a. the poor illiterate masses of Europe.
  b. upper- and middle-class businessmen.
  c. people who do not belong to the clergy.
  d. priests and other members of the clergy.

_____ 5. _Provoke,_ in the passage, means to
  a. annoy or aggravate.
  b. cause or bring about.
  c. speak in favor of.
  d. publish and distribute.

_____ 6. How many years passed after the Chinese first manufactured paper before Europeans learned about the process?
  a. 200
  b. 500
  c. 800
  d. 1,100

_____ 7. The invention of printing using movable type brought major changes to all aspects of European life in the
   a. thirteenth century.
   b. fourteenth century.
   c. fifteenth century.
   d. sixteenth century.

_____ 8. Before students in Europe could purchase printed books, they learned information by
   a. borrowing books from churches.
   b. borrowing books from teachers.
   c. memorizing what they wanted to learn.
   d. taking careful lecture notes.

_____ 9. A major contribution to printing with movable type was *not* made by
   a. Johan Schmeller.
   b. Johan Gutenberg.
   c. Johan Fust.
   d. Peter Schoffer.

_____ 10. Which of the following did *not* occur in Europe by the time printing made books more widely available?
   a. Many new universities were established.
   b. Censorship of books by states decreased.
   c. Communication between countries increased.
   d. Businessmen read books on many subjects.

Making an Evaluation

Would the information in the passage be more readily accessible if it included subheadings? Following are five subheadings that could be used in the passage. Select the *two* that you believe are most helpful, and write them in the left margin of the passage next to the beginnings of paragraphs where you believe they should be placed.

1. Block Printing in China
2. Printing Develops in Europe
3. The Manufacture of Paper
4. The Effects of Printing
5. Printing and Censorship

Write your own subheadings in margins when they are not included in textbook passages.

12 THE SELECTION OF EMPLOYEES

The selection process involves matching the personnel needs of the firm with the available candidates and making the best possible hiring decision. Some form of job analysis precedes hiring, so that the features of a job and the skills of a person who can do it are known to the personnel department. If a job involves moving heavy castings by hand, a high degree of physical strength will be sought. For a typist some amount of speed and accuracy should be specified.

The **initial interview** is almost a universal feature of the hiring process. The recruiter can learn about candidates' interests and abilities by talking with them and can determine if the candidates are initially qualified. Few firms wish to hire people for any position, even at a low level of skill or responsibility, without an interview. Despite this fact, interviewers often find that people who look promising do not perform well; and sometimes those who are hired in a time of great need do well, though they made a bad impression on the interviewer. Future job performance is very difficult to predict.

Almost invariably candidates are asked to fill out a written employment **application,** which tells such things as the person's name, address, and personal history. Details of education and experience are sought, and typically the person will be asked to account for what he or she has done in the past. The person is asked to furnish the names of former employers, teachers, or others who can be contacted as references during the background investigation. If the candidate has left jobs, the reason for leaving is usually asked; in this way the personnel department hopes to spot people who have been fired. The amount of checking on details stated in the application will vary among firms and at different times. Usually extensive checking is done for the more responsible positions (plant guard). Less checking is done for routine positions (laborer), especially when there is a pressing, immediate need for workers. 3

Frequently, employers will want to use one or more **objective tests** to help determine which candidate is most qualified. Various forms of tests are available to assist managers in the selection process. Equal Employment Opportunity Commission guidelines require that all tests used must be directly related to the specific job in question. *Achievement or performance tests* are used often in such fields as typing, where it is possible to measure job-related skills. *Intelligence tests* are used to determine whether or not an employee is likely to be able to read and understand complicated written instructions; they are often used in hiring management trainees. *Aptitude tests* may be used to indicate a person's basic manual skill or interest in various types of work (inside versus outside, for example). Intelligence tests and aptitude tests are not perfect, and they must be interpreted with care. Some firms use them, not as an absolute measure, but as one indicator of how a candidate compares with successful present workers. A prospective salesperson, for example, might be rated, not on the basis of how high or low the scores were on the test itself, but on how 4 similar the scores were to those of the firm's best salespeople. However, testing should not be the deciding factor in selection. It is only one tool among the several we have considered.

A **physical examination** is often required for prospective employees 5 who appear suitable on the basis of their application and their personal interview. The examination, given by either a private physician or the company physician in larger plants, accomplishes at least three things. It can uncover ailments, such as lung disorders or hernias that could prevent a worker's functioning on the job. It can detect the presence of communicable diseases that endanger the health of coworkers and customers. It can also be a means of identifying preexisting ailments that might later be used as a financial claim by an employee who believed he or she was disabled on the job.

When a profile has been completed on each candidate, a manager must determine which candidate is more qualified to fill the available position. If a candidate did not qualify at any step in the selection process, he or she should have been rejected at that point. A candidate's profile will include the information gathered in the selection process. In addition to the employment application, there may be interviewer comments, test scores, reference information, and physical examination results.

Although the decision about whom to employ would appear to be fairly simple at this point, often it is as difficult and important a choice as the manager must make. Since the organization's destiny is determined by the people it employs, its future can be at stake if employment decisions are not taken seriously. The employment process must not be conducted too hastily.

EXERCISE 12

THE SELECTION OF EMPLOYEES

Preview the passage and answer questions 1 and 2. Then, read the passage and answer the remaining questions.

_____ 1. Major details are indicated
      a. in the introduction.
      b. by subheadings.
      c. by words in boldface type.
      d. by a number or numbers.

_____ 2. Which title best states the expository pattern?
      a. Steps in the Employee Selection Process
      b. How to Interview and Hire Employees
      c. Reasons for Difficulty in Finding Good Workers
      d. Effects of Good Employee Selection Procedures

Circle the numbers in front of the questions whose answers are implied by the passage but are not directly stated in it.

_____ 3. _Invariably_ means
      a. expensively.
      b. inexpensively.
      c. changeably.
      d. unchangeably.

_____ 4. _Objective_ means
      a. based on opinions.
      b. based on facts.
      c. projected.
      d. reflected.

_____ 5. _Prospective_ means
      a. favoring a more thorough search.
      b. opposing a more thorough search.
      c. expected or likely in the future.
      d. unexpected or unlikely in the future.

_____ 6. Professional interviewers of job applicants find that the way people will perform on jobs is
      a. difficult to predict from interviews.
      b. easy to predict from interviews.
      c. predictable for those who make bad impressions.
      d. unpredictable for those who make good impressions.

_____ 7. In general, much less time is spent checking job applications when
   a. positions are routine, such as that of laborer.
   b. positions are part-time or temporary.
   c. there are many jobs and few applicants.
   d. routine positions must be filled quickly.

_____ 8. One purpose of some testing programs is to identify job applicants who
   a. show willingness to work by taking tests.
   b. have test scores similar to those of successful employees.
   c. exhibit little anxiety while taking tests.
   d. know and utilize efficient test-taking skills.

_____ 9. A company does *not* give physical examinations to job applicants
   a. because it wants to care for their health problems.
   b. to spot disorders that make them unfit for work.
   c. to find potential health hazards for present workers.
   d. to detect ailments that might be blamed on the job later.

_____ 10. A profile for a job applicant does *not* usually include
   a. references.
   b. reviewer comments.
   c. physical examination results.
   d. the candidate's photograph.

Making an Evaluation

The passage explains four major steps in the selection of employees by large businesses. Write the steps on the following lines.

1. _____

2. _____

3. _____

4. _____

Based on your experience in applying for jobs, are these steps presented in the correct sequence?

13 PTOLEMY AND ASTROLOGY

A glance at the sky presents the very clear impression that the sky is a giant bowl, and that the sun, moon, stars, and planets are all circling around the earth, located at the center of this bowl. This very natural conception governed the first human attempt to decipher our place in the universe: the geocentric universe of classical civilization. This theory is usually associated with the name of Claudius *Ptolemy*, an ancient intellect who lived in Alexandria in the second century after Christ. Ptolemy, summarizing the ancient world view in his astronomy textbook *The Almagest*, actually added a number of refinements to an earlier theory. Most of the model had been worked out several centuries earlier by Greek thinkers, notably Aristotle and Hipparchus.

The Ptolemaic world view saw the universe as a gigantic planetarium.[1] The motions of celestial objects were produced by a system of wheels in the sky. These wheels were necessary to explain irregularities such as retrograde motion; by Ptolemy's time, after centuries of accumulated observations, the system's insistence on circular motion meant that well over 30 wheels were needed to explain the observations. Ptolemy himself did not believe that there were in fact 30-plus wheels up there in the sky. Rather, the whole system was regarded as a computing device that human beings could use to predict planetary positions. The reality of planetary motion was something known only to God, and not for mere mortals to try to understand.

One relic of Ptolemy's theory of the universe is astrology, which, unlike Ptolemy's description of planetary motion, is still with us. Astrology claims that the positions of the sun and planets in the heavens at the moment of a person's birth allow an astrologer to predict the person's fortune. Astrology has nothing whatever to do with astronomy, but as far as public exposure is concerned, astrology seems to receive as much attention as astronomy. (Sad but true: One of my astronomy students at Yale University insisted on turning in examination books marked "Astrology 10a," and in southern California I could not talk to someone at a party for 10 minutes without being asked what my birth sign was.)

Ptolemy wrote several books summarizing the knowledge of his time; his *Almagest* dealt with astronomy, his *Geography* with geography, and his *Tetrabiblos* with astrology. The *Almagest* and the *Geography* are historical documents, representing the intellectual achievements of the time but hopelessly outdated now. However, the *Tetrabiblos* is still the basis for current astrological practice.

Perhaps astrology had some real basis when the Ptolemaic theory of the universe was still considered valid. The *Almagest* indicates that Ptolemy felt that the real universe was destined to remain forever mysterious, and it was easy to believe that the planets and the sun

---

[1]A planetarium is a hemispherical theater with a projector at the center. The projector displays the stars as they appear in the real sky. A planetarium should not be confused with an observatory.

might influence people on the centrally located earth. Such a theory
is much less tenable with a Newtonian universe, in which our earth   **4**
is just one piece of rock orbiting around a sun that is 150 million km
away.

How could the other planets, the other rock balls and gas balls,
influence people's lives on the earth? Astrological influences from the
planets cannot be transmitted by any of the forces we know about.
Modern science recognizes four forces: gravitational, electromagnetic,
and strong and weak nuclear forces. The nuclear forces do not act over
astronomical distances. The gravitational force of a delivery table acts
ten times more strongly on a newborn baby than the gravitational
force of the planet Mars, regarded as one of the strongest astrological
influences. The electromagnetic radiation from a 100-watt light bulb
in the delivery room is tens of thousands of times brighter than the
radiation from Venus, the brightest planet. In order to explain the
potency of celestial bodies as determinants of human fortunes, astrologers must appeal to mystical and mysterious cosmic influences.   **5**

The status of astrology as a pseudoscience is confirmed by consid-
eration of the contents of a scientific model. One characteristic of
modern science is its reliance on fundamental physical laws that
describe, in a precise mathetical form, the interactions of objects in
the universe. The theoretical descriptions of these interactions are
then confirmed by comparison with observations. What are the laws
of astrology? When have these laws been made into a concrete model
which can then be tested against reality? Astrologers have rarely made
any statistical tests of their predictions, and those tests that have been
made show that there is no evidence that astrological predictions are
correct.[2]

The persistence of astrology over 2000 years is quite surprising to
me as a scientist. Perhaps it reflects the unconscious desire of many
people to believe in magic; perhaps it comes from people's need for
guidance and comfort in an uncertain world. But whatever comfort is
provided by the horoscopes and fortune telling of the astrologers, any
claim that this reassurance is based on scientific knowledge is false.

[2]See Lawrence E. Jerome, "Astrology: Magic or Science?" and Bart J. Bok, "A Critical
Look at Astrology," *The Humanist* (September–October 1975).

EXERCISE 13

PTOLEMY AND ASTROLOGY

Preview the passage and answer questions 1 and 2. Then, read the passage and answer the remaining questions.

_____ 1. Major details are indicated
  a. in the introduction
  b. by a number or numbers.
  c. by words in italic type.
  d. in first sentences of paragraphs.

_____ 2. Which title best states the expository pattern?
  a. Why Ptolemy Believed in Astrology
  b. The Two-Thousand-Year History of Astrology
  c. The Reasons Astrology Is a Pseudoscience
  d. Ptolemy: Student of Fact and Fantasy

Circle the numbers in front of the questions whose answers are implied by the passage but are not directly stated in it.

_____ 3. To _decipher_ is to
  a. decode something hard to understand.
  b. make various numerical computations.
  c. write using numbers rather than letters.
  d. arrange objects in concentric circles.

_____ 4. _Tenable_ means
  a. very long or large in scope.
  b. very short or small in scope.
  c. logical and defendable.
  d. illogical and indefensible.

_____ 5. _Cosmic,_ in the passage, means
  a. vast.
  b. earthly.
  c. planetary.
  d. universal.

_____ 6. The basis for the current practice of astrology is found in Ptolemy's book
  a. _Tetrabiblos,_ written about 1,850 years ago.
  b. _Tetrabiblos,_ written about 2,000 years ago.
  c. _Astrologica,_ written about 1,850 years ago.
  d. _Astrologica,_ written about 2,000 years ago.

_____ 7. The fundamental belief of astrology is that
  a. it is possible to know future events.
  b. our life events are known at birth.
  c. astrology helps in decision making.
  d. the sun and planets influence human life.

_____ 8. The basic reason that astronomers do not believe in astrology is that
  a. predictions of astrologers are often incorrect.
  b. heavenly influences cannot be sent by a known force.
  c. ancient knowledge is unverified in modern times.
  d. astrology texts were lost in the tenth century.

_____ 9. Evidence of the weak influence of forces from the planets is summarized by saying that
  a. nuclear forces do not act over the long distances between the earth and the planets.
  b. a table and a light bulb have more force on people than the force from the most forceful planet.
  c. the gravitational force of a table is ten times greater than that of the most forceful planet.
  d. the electromagnetic force of a light bulb is ten times greater than that of the brightest planet.

_____ 10. The belief in astrology became indefensible when facts about the universe were revealed by the work of
  a. Isaac Newton.
  b. Albert Einstein.
  c. Giuseppe Piazzi.
  d. Carl Sagan.

Making an Evaluation

The author gives two examples of the influence of astrology on people he has encountered. Write the examples on the following lines.

1. _____

   _____

2. _____

   _____

What is the author's attitude toward these people?

_____

Is it appropriate for an author to express an attitude such as this one in a serious college textbook?

14 THE NEED FOR AFFECTION

In meeting the **need for affection,** the individual attempts to establish and maintain with other people a healthy relationship centered on love and affection. Affection refers to close personal relations involving a need to develop and maintain mutual regard for others.

Close personal and emotional feelings between people can be defined as affection behavior. These feelings involve an element of trust and the sharing of innermost thoughts and personal wishes. Strong positive affectional associations are usually marked by the depth at which feelings are shared in a relationship. In group interaction, affection is manifested by overtures of friendship between members of the group. Affection behavior occurs in situations of love, emotional closeness, personal confidence, and intimacy. Negative affection also exists, and can be characterized by hatred, hostility, alienation, and emotional rejection.

Affection types usually deal with "dyadic" relations—that is, relations between two people. The three personality types associated with affection behavior are the underpersonal, the overpersonal, and the personal.

The *underpersonal* type tends to avoid close personal affiliations with others, maintaining dyadic relations on a superficial, distant level. This person feels most comfortable when others project similar distant and superficial behaviors. Expressions about not getting "emotionally involved" indicate that the desire to keep an emotional distance exists at the conscious level. Unconsciously these individuals fear that no one loves them even though they may be searching for satisfactory love relations. To like people sincerely is difficult for these people because of their overpowering distrust of others and their projected feelings. The feeling of being unlovable persists and is magnified by the fear that if people are allowed to get emotionally close, they will discover traits that make these people so unlovable.

The *overpersonal* individual values close relationships and being liked by others. The need for close emotional relationships is an attempt to relieve anxious feelings about being rejected and unlovable. To satisfy this need, the person may employ direct, overt means to 3 gain approval, by being totally personal, intimate, and confiding. More subtle means are also used, such as manipulative behavior, which is an attempt to envelop friends and to punish subtly any efforts by them 4 to establish other friendships. This person is motivated by a strong desire for affection and tends to be possessive in relationships. Possessiveness helps to cover the anxiety this person feels about being loved and about being unlovable. Thoughts of anticipated rejection contribute to this person's considerable hostility.

The *personal* type has successfully resolved feelings about being a lovable person. These feelings provide this person with the ability to give and share genuine affection with others. Likewise, when this

person is disliked by others, strength is gained from the knowledge
that the potential for being loved remains rewardingly intact.   5

Personality types based upon the above interpersonal needs are interesting and revealing. How easy it is for us to identify individual
personalities and place them in one category or the other. But how
many of those people place us in one of the categories that our personalities might realistically match, but of which we are not con-
sciously aware? Try to assess yourself. What are your needs for inclu-
sion, control, and affection? How do you fit with the personality types
discussed?

EXERCISE 14

THE NEED FOR AFFECTION

Preview the passage and answer questions 1 and 2. Then, read the passage and answer the remaining questions.

_____ 1. Major details are *not* indicated
   a. in the introduction.
   b. by words in italic type.
   c. by a number or numbers.
   d. in first sentences of paragraphs.

_____ 2. Which title best states the expository pattern?
   a. How to Be a More Affectionate Person
   b. Three Personality Types and Affection Behavior
   c. The Effects of Feeling Unlovable
   d. Comparison of Positive and Negative Affection

Circle the numbers in front of the questions whose answers are implied by the passage but are not directly stated in it.

_____ 3. *Overt* means
   a. hidden and unobservable.
   b. open and observable.
   c. expected.
   d. unexpected.

_____ 4. *Subtly* means
   a. slyly and deviously.
   b. honestly and openly.
   c. gently and lovingly.
   d. harshly and angrily.

_____ 5. *Intact* means
   a. thoughtful.
   b. thoughtless.
   c. partial and spoiled.
   d. whole and undamaged.

_____ 6. Affection behavior is
   a. invariably positive.
   b. invariably negative.
   c. either positive or negative.
   d. neither positive nor negative.

_____ 7. In relating to others, underpersonal people are *not* likely to
   a. avoid intimate, emotional involvements.
   b. be distrustful of others' motives.
   c. keep hidden what they dislike about themselves.
   d. pursue close, deep, trusting friendships.

_____ 8. In marriage, overpersonal people are *not* likely to
   a. tell spouses all about themselves.
   b. be jealous of their spouses' friends.
   c. become hostile toward their mates.
   d. provide easygoing companionship for mates.

_____ 9. Individuals feel themselves unlovable when they are the
   a. underpersonal type.
   b. overpersonal type.
   c. underpersonal or overpersonal type.
   d. overpersonal or personal type.

_____ 10. The authors of the passage intend that readers will use the information in it to
   a. analyze what personality types they are.
   b. analyze the personality types of others.
   c. advise friends about their personality types.
   d. advise others how to be better friends.

Making an Evaluation

Keeping in mind that categories in textbooks tend to overlap (see page 152), is the information in the passage useful to you in identifying your personality type with regard to affection behavior?

1. Are you the underpersonal type, preferring superficial, distant relationships?
2. Are you the overpersonal type, tending to be overly confiding and possessive in your close relationships with others?
3. Are you the personal type, sharing affection with others and knowing that you are lovable even if somebody dislikes you?

Do your friends tend to be the same personality type that you are?

15. INTERPRET TABLES AND GRAPHS

Textbooks for natural sciences, social sciences, and many other college subjects include tables and graphs to summarize or illustrate information explained in them.

1. Preview before reading.
2. Locate major details.
3. Find minor details.
4. Identify expository patterns.
5. Infer implied meanings.
6. Make evaluations.
7. **Interpret tables and graphs.**

Information in tables and graphs is interpreted by (1) reading headings, (2) reading labels, (3) comparing data, and (4) deciding the important point of the information presented in them.

TABLES

Tables are well-organized lists of statistical information. Interpret the information in Table 15.1 by answering the following questions.

1. *Read the heading.* The heading follows "Table 15.1" on page 236. What is the information in the table?

_____

_____

2. *Read the labels.* What type of information is listed in the first column on the left of the table?

_____

TABLE 15.1

Percentage share of total income received by each fifth of American families, 1958–1978

	Percent Distribution of Total Income				
Year	Lowest Fifth	Second Fifth	Middle Fifth	Fourth Fifth	Highest Fifth
1958	5.0	12.5	18.0	23.9	40.6
1960	4.8	12.2	17.8	24.0	41.3
1962	5.0	12.1	17.6	24.0	41.3
1964	5.1	12.0	17.7	24.0	41.2
1966	5.6	12.4	17.8	23.8	40.5
1968	5.6	12.4	17.7	23.7	40.5
1970	5.4	12.2	17.6	23.8	40.9
1972	5.4	11.9	17.5	23.9	41.4
1974	5.4	12.0	17.6	24.1	41.0
1976	5.4	11.8	17.6	24.1	41.1
1978	5.2	11.6	17.5	24.1	41.5

Source: U.S. Bureau of the Census.

What information is listed in the other five columns of the table?

_____

3. *Compare the data.* During the period 1958–1978, approximately what percentage of total income was received by the poorest fifth of American families?

_____

During the period 1958–1978, approximately what percentage of total income was received by the richest fifth of American families?

_____

4. *Decide the important point.* What is the important point of the information in the table?

_____

Answer the questions before reading the following explanations.

1. The information in the table is about the percentage share of total income received by each fifth of American families during the period 1958–1978.

2. The information in the first column is about the even numbered years from 1958 through 1978, and the information in the other five columns is about the percentage of total income received by each fifth of American families.
3. During the period 1958–1978, the poorest fifth of American families received about 5 percent of the total income while the richest fifth received about 40 percent of the total income.
4. One important point of the information in the table is that there has been little change in the distribution of total income among poor and rich American families over the twenty-year period represented in the table. Another important point is that approximately 20 percent of families (the highest fifth) receives about 40 percent of the total income while the other 80 percent of families shares the remaining 60 percent of income.

BAR GRAPHS

Bar graphs are usually used to show differences in amounts. Interpret the information in the bar graph (Figure 15.1) by answering the following questions.

1. *Read the heading.* The heading follows "Figure 15.1." What is the information in the bar graph?

FIGURE 15.1

United States loss of life
due to wars

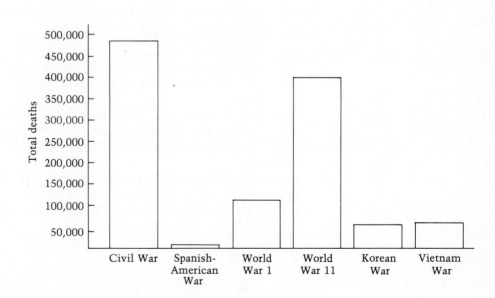

2. *Read the labels.* What information is represented by the numbers from bottom to top on the left of the graph?

_____

What information do the bars in the graph represent?

_____

3. *Compare the data.* Which two wars combined had more deaths than the Civil War?

_____

How many times more Americans died in World War II than in World War I?

_____

4. *Decide the important point.* Considering that the population of the United States was much smaller when the Civil War was fought than when World War II was fought, what is the most important point made by the information in the graph?

_____

_____

Answer the questions before reading the following explanations.

1. The information in the graph is about the loss of life in the United States due to war.
2. The numbers from bottom to top on the left of the graph indicate numbers of deaths, and the bars represent six wars fought by the United States.
3. World War I (100,000+) and World War II (400,000) combined had more deaths than the Civil War (500,000). Also, about four times more Americans died in World War II (400,000) than in World War I (100,000+).
4. Considering that the population of the United States was smaller in the 1860s than in the 1940s, loss of life during the Civil War was proportionately far greater than in any of our other wars.

LINE GRAPHS

Line graphs are usually used to show increases or decreases in amounts. Interpret the information in the line graph (Figure 15.2) by answering the following questions.

FIGURE 15.2

Women as a percent-
age of the total em-
ployed in traditionally
male occupations

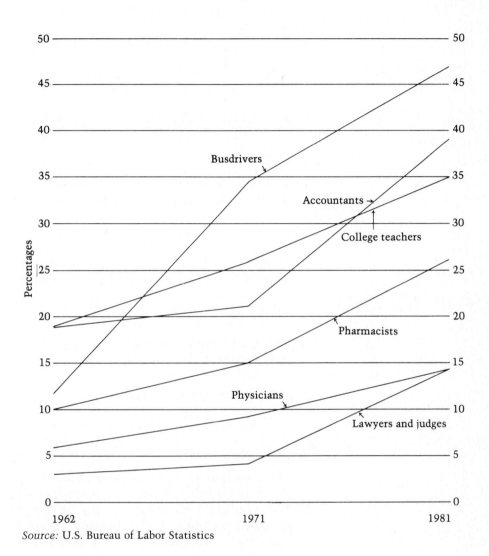

Source: U.S. Bureau of Labor Statistics

1. *Read the headings.* The heading follows "Figure 15.2." What is the important information in the graph?

   _____

   _____

2. *Read the labels.* What information is represented by the numbers from bottom to top on the left and right of the graph?

   _____

What information is represented from left to right across the bottom of the graph?

_____

What type of information is represented by lines in the graph?

_____

3. *Compare the information.* Comparing 1962 to 1981, did the percentage of women employed as physicians double, triple, or quadruple?

_____

Comparing 1971 to 1981, did the percentage of women employed as lawyers and judges double, triple, or quadruple?

_____

4. *Decide the important point.* What is the most important point of the information in the line graph?

_____

_____

Write answers to the questions before reading the following explanations.

1. The information in the graph is about the percentage of women employed in traditionally male occupations during the period 1962–1981.
2. The numbers from bottom to top on the left and right of the graph represent percentages; the numbers across the bottom represent the years 1962, 1971, and 1982; and the lines represent six occupational categories.
3. Comparing 1962 to 1981 the percentage of women employed as physicians slightly more than doubled from 6 percent to 14 percent, and comparing 1971 to 1981 the percentage of women employed as lawyers and judges slightly more than tripled from 4 percent to 14 percent.
4. The important point of the information in the graph is that women made substantial employment gains in traditionally male occupations during the period 1962–1981. However, the graph also reveals that women are still underrepresented in prestigious occupations such as medicine and the law.

INTERPRETING TABLES AND GRAPHS

The following exercises provide practice for interpreting information in tables and graphs. Use the procedures explained in this chapter when you do the exercises: (1) read headings, (2) read labels, (3) compare data, and (4) decide the important point of information in tables and graphs.

EXERCISE 1

TABLE

Read the heading and the labels, compare the data, and decide the important point of the information in the table.

TABLE 15.2

Additional years United States males may expect to live (life expectancy)

Age	Never Smoked Regularly	Cigarettes Smoked by Daily Amount			
		1–9	10–19	20–39	40+
25	48.6	44.0	43.1	42.4	40.3
30	43.9	39.3	38.4	37.8	35.8
35	39.2	34.7	33.8	33.2	31.3
40	34.5	30.2	29.3	28.7	26.9
45	30.0	25.9	25.0	24.4	23.0
50	25.6	21.8	21.0	20.5	19.3
55	21.4	17.9	17.4	17.0	16.0
60	17.6	14.5	14.1	13.7	13.2
65	14.1	11.3	11.2	11.0	10.7

Source: Hammond study. Reprinted by permission of Public Health Service, Department of Health, Education, and Welfare.

1. Comparing men age 25 who never smoked regularly to men age 25 who smoked a pack of cigarettes a day, how many additional years can the nonsmokers expect to live?

   _____

2. Comparing men age 25 who never smoked regularly to men age 25 who smoked two packs of cigarettes a day, how many additional years can the nonsmokers expect to live?

   _____

3. Comparing men age 45 who never smoked regularly to men age 45 who smoked one cigarette a day, how many additional years can the nonsmokers expect to live?

   _____

4. Comparing men age 25 who never smoked regularly to men age 65 who never smoked regularly, how many additional years can the men age 65 expect to live?

_____

5. What is the important point of the information in the table?

_____

_____

EXERCISE 2

BAR GRAPH

Read the heading and labels, compare the data, and decide the important point of the information in the bar graph.

FIGURE 15.3

Percentages of crimes in five categories that are cleared and not cleared by arrest

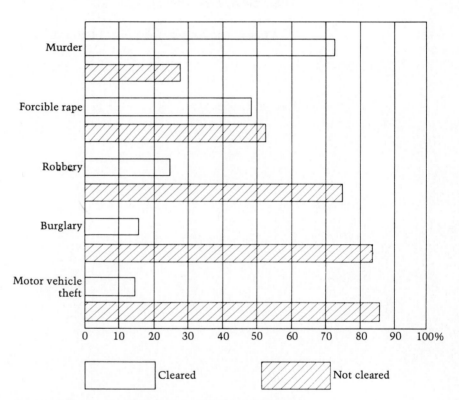

Source: *Crime in the United States: Uniform Crime Reports* (Washington, D.C.: Government Printing Office, 1979), p. 178.

1. What is the only crime for which a majority of incidences are cleared by arrest?

   _____

2. For what crime are approximately an equal number of incidences cleared and not cleared by arrests?

   _____

3. For robbery, approximately _____ percent of incidences are cleared by arrest and approximately 75 percent are not.

4. For burglary and motor-vehicle theft, approximately 85 percent of incidences are not cleared by arrest and approximately _____ percent are cleared by arrest.

5. What is the important point of the information in the graph?

   _____

EXERCISE 3

LINE GRAPH

Read the headings and labels, compare the data, and decide the important point of the information in the line graph.

FIGURE 15.4

Percentages of persons
arrested: 1960–1978

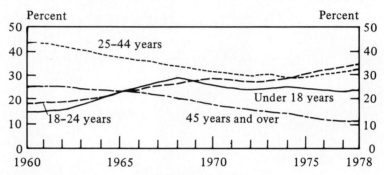

Source: Chart prepared by U.S. Bureau of the Census. Data from U.S. Federal Bureau of Investigation.

1. In 1960 _____ percent of persons arrested were 45 years old or over, but in 1978 they were _____ percent of arrested persons.

2. In 1960 _____ percent of persons arrested were 25–44 years old, but in 1978 they were _____ percent of arrested persons.

3. In 1960 _____ percent of persons arrested were 18–24 years old, but in 1978 they were _____ percent of arrested persons.

4. In 1960 _____ percent of persons arrested were under 18 years old, but in 1978 they were _____ percent of arrested persons.

5. What is the important point of the information in the line graph?

IV. STUDY FOR EXAMINATIONS

In college, test scores are used to compute final course grades, and final course grades are used to compute grade point averages. Those who do well on tests do well in courses and eventually earn degrees.

Some students have difficulty when they take tests because they prepare for tests by reading rather than by studying. *Reading* is the process that is used to understand information presented in writing, but *studying* is the process that is used to learn and remember information. Reading is done using methods that are explained in Chapters 9–15. Studying uses the following procedures.

1. Take good class notes.
2. Decide what to learn.
3. Underline textbooks.
4. Make notes for textbooks.
5. Recite from notes.

The methods for doing these things are explained in Chapters 16–20, which follow.

Chapters 1 and 2 of *RSVP* also include suggestions that are important in studying for tests. Chapter 1 explains basic methods for doing well in courses and improving concentration. Chapter 2 illustrates how to schedule time for studying (see especially pages 24–25).

16. TAKE GOOD CLASS NOTES

Study for examinations begins by taking good class notes.

1. **Take good class notes.**
2. Decide what to learn.
3. Underline textbooks.
4. Make notes for textbooks.
5. Recite from notes.

Class notes usually include explanations about complicated course material, important facts that are not stated in required reading material, and hints about what to study for tests. As a result, they are usually the best source of help for understanding course subject matter and deciding what to study for tests. Attend classes faithfully to take complete and well-organized notes about the explanations, facts, and hints you need to do well when you take examinations.

PREPARE TO TAKE NOTES

Prepare to take class notes by reading assigned material before class to have it fresh in mind when you listen to what instructors have to say about it. When there is insufficient time to read material thoroughly before a class, use methods explained in Chapters 9 and 10 to locate topics and the major details about them. The strategies explained in Chapters 9 and 10 may be used to learn a great deal about printed material quickly.

Before class also care for physical needs that may become sources of discomfort that interfere with concentration. Go to the rest room; have a drink of water; and eat something if you are likely to become hungry before class is over.

In class, sit in the center and front of the room for a clear, uninterrupted view of the teacher. Avoid sitting next to annoying classmates or near windows with a view of activities going on outside of classrooms.

TAKE WELL-ORGANIZED NOTES

Studies of students' class notes reveal that good notes have the characteristics that are illustrated in Figure 16.1. Use the methods good note-takers use to take well-organized class notes.

1. *Use paper that measures 8½ by 11 inches.* Paper this size is usually large enough so that most of the information about a topic is on one page rather than on several.
2. *Begin each day's notes with a heading that includes the name or number of the course, the instructor's name, the date, and the topic of the lecture.* Writing a heading will put you in the proper frame of mind for note-taking. Also, you can use the information later to make certain that you have notes for each class meeting.
3. *Organize notes so major details stand out clearly.* In Figure 16.1, the three major details are written to the left side of the page and they are underlined.
4. *List minor details under major details in an orderly fashion.* In Figure 16.1, some minor details are numbered and others are indicated by stars.
5. *Summarize what teachers say rather than try to write what they say word for word.* It is not possible to record teachers' words exactly; summarize what they say in your own words.

Compare class notes you have taken with the notes in Figure 16.1. When you took notes, did you use these methods that good note-takers use? If not, this chapter explains how you can take better-organized and more complete notes.

LISTEN FOR MAJOR DETAILS

During lectures, make it your goal to find major details and to make them stand out clearly in your notes.

Some teachers directly state major details by using phrases such as "Now I'm going to discuss . . ." and "My next point is . . . ." Instructors also use pauses and repetition to emphasize major details in their lectures.

1. A *pause* in speech is a period of time during which nothing is spoken. When teachers pause while lecturing, this is often a clue that students should write down what was said just before the pause or what will be said after it.
2. When teachers *repeat* statements, this is usually a definite hint that students should record the repeated information in class notes.

Listen for direct statements of major details, pauses, and repeated statements to help in writing major details in class notes.

© 1984 by Houghton Mifflin Company

FIGURE 16.1

251

Well-organized class
notes

Study Skills 101, 9/14/87   Shepherd
                    Taking Good Class Notes

Five characteristics of good notes
    1. Written on 8½-by-11-inch notebook paper.
    2. Heading includes name or number of course, teacher's
       name, date, and lecture topic.
    3. Major details stand out clearly.
    4. Minor details are listed neatly under major details.
    5. They summarize what teachers say.

How to improve listening
    ★ Eliminate environmental distractions. (EX) Don't
      sit near windows or near annoying classmates.
    ★ Eliminate physical distractions.
      1. Visit rest room before class.
      2. Eat before class so you won't get hungry.
      3. Dress so you won't be too warm or cold.
    ★ Eliminate internal distractions. (EX) Don't think
      about what you'll do after class.

Hints for taking and studying notes
    ★ Read about lecture topics before classes.
    ★ Mark things written on chalkboards and about which
      teachers give study hints for special attention
      when studying.
    ★ Review notes as soon after class as possible.
    ★ Study notes thoroughly before tests.

LISTEN FOR MINOR DETAILS

Many lecturers make it clear how many minor details to list under major details in notes by making statements such as these:

- There are *three* basic steps in the hydrologic cycle.
- Sociologists give *four* reasons that upward social mobility is gradual in the United States.
- Let's examine *six* tragic effects of the Civil War.

When instructors make statements such as these, it is clear exactly how many minor details to list under major details.

In other instances teachers make it clear that it is necessary to list minor details without stating the number of details to list. For instance, an instructor may say, "I'm going to talk about some of the problems with starting a small business." In this case, students should write "Problems with starting a small business" in notes and prepare to list the problems. However, they will not know how many problems there are until the teacher states them all.

Minor details in class notes are often lists of the following kinds of information.

advantages	kinds	purposes
disadvantages	categories	functions
causes	characteristics	steps
effects	differences	stages
types	similarities	benefits

Listen for these and similar words during lectures for hints about the kinds of minor details to list in notes.

TAKE COMPLETE NOTES

When you are aware that you have missed information during a lecture, leave a blank space in your notes. When the time is appropriate, raise your hand and ask the question that will help you to make your notes complete. Or make your notes complete after class by (1) talking with the teacher, (2) talking with a classmate who takes good notes, or (3) studying required course reading material.

In case you must be absent from a class, hand copy or photocopy notes taken by one of your classmates while you were absent. Unfortunately, though, the notes your fellow students take are not likely to be very useful to you when you study. They take the kinds of notes that are useful to them, and you take the kinds of notes that are useful to you. This is one of the major reasons it is important to go to classes faithfully.

ATTEND TO THE CHALKBOARD

Anything written on a chalkboard may be used as the basis for a test question. Include in class notes everything that is written on chalkboards and mark it for special attention when you study. You might draw a star or write *Important* in the margin next to the information, or you might mark it with yellow highlighting ink so you will not overlook it when you study for tests.

Following are some of the types of information that instructors write on chalkboards:

- Tables, charts, and diagrams
- Mathematical formulas
- Important terminology
- Persons' names and dates

In high school you may have been expected to learn about people and dates only for history courses. But in college, teachers of business, psychology, chemistry, and other subjects expect students to know the names of people who made important contributions to their disciplines.

Copy everything written on chalkboards in notes and mark it for special attention. You will find that it is often used as the basis for test questions (see page 258).

LISTEN FOR STUDY HINTS

Instructors usually inform students what is especially important to learn by making statements such as the following:

- This is very important.
- I'll probably ask a test question about this.
- You must be able to do these kinds of problems.
- This confuses some students—don't let it confuse you.
- The sequence is important here.

When teachers make statements such as these, write them in notes and mark the information to which they pertain for special attention, in the same way you mark things you copy from chalkboards.

BUILD NOTE-TAKING SPEED

It is not possible to take class notes that include everything teachers say. Good notes are summaries, not word-for-word records of teachers' statements. The methods explained in Chapter 19 for making notes about information presented in books may also be used to summarize information presented orally in lectures.

In addition, build note-taking speed by writing using fewer lines, curves, and flourishes. The following statement is written in a student's usual handwriting.

This is how I write when I'm not taking class notes.

While taking class notes, the student practiced writing using fewer lines, curves, and flourishes. Following is the way she now writes when she takes class notes.

This is how I write when
*   I take class notes.*

This simplified form of handwriting makes it possible for her to write more quickly during her lecture classes.

You may also build note-taking speed by using abbreviations for words that occur often in lectures. Make abbreviations by writing only the first letters of words. For example, write "eq" for "equation," "psy" for "psychology," "chem" for "chemistry," and "impt" for "important."

Also, substitute abbreviations or symbols for common words that occur frequently in lectures. For example,

Common Words	Symbols and Abbreviations
and	&
too, to, two	2
equals	=
North	N
and so on	etc.
example	EX
New York	NY
number	#
dollars, money	$
without	w/o

The best abbreviations are the ones you make up and understand.

Finally, do not worry about spelling when you take class notes. Undue concern about correct spelling will slow you down. You are the only one who reads your notes; you may correct misspelled words after class.

REVIEW NOTES AFTER CLASS

Notes taken in September may contain information that needs to be known for a test in November. If you do not understand your notes in September, you will not understand them in November when you use them to study for a test. Therefore, during the first free time you have following a lecture, reread your notes to make certain that you understand them and that they are complete.

Change your notes in any way that makes them more understandable. Correct misspelled words, fill in missing information, and make other changes that improve them.

STUDY NOTES BEFORE TESTS

It is almost always essential to study class notes thoroughly before tests. When class notes do not help students to do well on tests, either the students take poor notes or their teachers do not give helpful lectures of the kind that most teachers give.

Suggestions for scheduling study time are given in Chapter 2, and methods for studying class notes are explained on pages 258 and 289.

TAKING GOOD CLASS NOTES

The best practice for taking class notes is to *use the suggestions in this chapter to take good class notes for your college courses.* Also, if your school has a learning center or skills laboratory, recorded lectures may be available there for the practice of taking class notes.

EXERCISE 1

EVALUATING LECTURES

Write the names of two of your lecture courses over the columns on the right. Rate lectures in each category using 100 (perfect), 90–99 (excellent), 80–89 (good), 70–79 (satisfactory), 60–69 (passing), or 0–59 (failing). Then find the average for lectures by adding the numbers in each column and dividing the sums by 10.

	1. _____	2. _____
1. Gives well-organized lectures	_____	_____
2. States major details clearly	_____	_____
3. Usually identifies the number of minor details to include in a list	_____	_____
4. Pauses to give students time to write	_____	_____

5. Repeats important
   statements so all
   students can get them
   in notes   _____   _____

6. Encourages students to
   ask questions so their
   notes will be complete   _____   _____

7. Makes good use of the
   chalkboard   _____   _____

8. Informs students what
   is important to learn   _____   _____

9. Seems very interested
   in the subject matter of
   the course   _____   _____

10. Explains difficult ideas
    and concepts so they're
    easy to understand   _____   _____

                     Totals   _____   _____

Divide totals by 10 to find averages.

EXERCISE 2

EVALUATING CLASS NOTES

Write the names of the same lecture courses you wrote in Exercise 1
over the columns on the right. Then rate your class notes for the courses
in each category using 100 (perfect), 90–99 (excellent), 80–89 (good), 70–
79 (satisfactory), 60–69 (passing), or 0–59 (failing). Find the average for
your notes by adding the numbers in each column and dividing the sums
by 10.

                                 1. _____   2. _____

1. I read about lecture
   topics before class.   _____   _____

2. Each day's notes start
   with a complete
   heading.   _____   _____

3. The major details stand out clearly in notes. _____ _____

4. Minor details are neatly listed under major details and they are often numbered. _____ _____

5. Notes summarize rather than repeat word for word what was said. _____ _____

6. Notes include everything written on the chalkboard, marked for special attention. _____ _____

7. Notes include study hints and the information to which they pertain, marked for special attention. _____ _____

8. I ask questions when I need to make my notes complete. _____ _____

9. I practice new ways to write faster when I take notes. _____ _____

10. I review my notes as soon after class as possible. _____ _____

Totals _____ _____

Divide totals by 10 to find averages. Compare ratings for lectures and notes to determine if there are relationships between them. For instance, if you rated lectures for a course high, did you rate your class notes for the course high also?

17. DECIDE WHAT TO LEARN

It is not possible to learn everything on every page of five, six, or more books during the few weeks of a college term. You must decide what you will learn from among the many things that you could learn.

1. Take good class notes.
2. **Decide what to learn.**
3. Underline textbooks.
4. Make notes for textbooks.
5. Recite from notes.

If you make wise decisions about what to learn for tests, you will do better when you take them and you will learn the most important things to know about the subjects you study.

USE CLASS NOTES AS A GUIDE

Since most instructors explain in classes the things that are important to learn, class notes are usually the best guide for what to study for tests. If you use the suggestions in Chapter 16, you will take good class notes and you will mark for special attention information in them that is copied from chalkboards or about which teachers give study hints (see pages 252–253).

It is usually important to learn everything in class notes when studying for a test, and *information in class notes that is also in course reading material is especially likely to be used as the basis for test questions.* Mark it for special attention in class notes *and* textbooks. For instance, if you use a star to mark information for special attention in class notes, place a star in the margin next to the information in class notes *and* in the textbook.

© 1984 by Houghton Mifflin Company

ATTEND TEST REVIEWS

Many instructors give reviews for tests during class or at special times outside of class. Attend reviews, take complete notes, and learn everything that you are told to learn. Teachers give reviews to focus students' attention on learning what is most important. They want to help students; take advantage of the help they give.

ASK WHAT TO STUDY

When instructors do not give test reviews, ask them what to study. Some teachers give suggestions such as "Study everything, including tables, graphs, and footnotes." A general suggestion of this type may be more helpful than it seems. Those who study tables, graphs, and footnotes may answer correctly questions that others answer incorrectly.

Sometimes students ask instructors whether there will be test questions about specific information, and teachers answer by making statements such as "I don't think so" or "probably not." Students often misinterpret answers such as these to mean "You will definitely not be asked to answer a test question about the information." Unfortunately, this is not what the responses usually mean; they usually mean, "I am not certain at this time whether I will ask a question about the information." Teachers are not certain exactly what questions will be on tests until they prepare them. Therefore, it is always wise to learn information about which teachers say they "don't think," "probably won't," or "may not" ask test questions.

TALK WITH YOUR TEACHERS' FORMER STUDENTS

If at all possible, ask former students of your teachers how to study for their tests. Teachers' testing methods seldom change much from year to year. As a result, students who studied with your teachers in the past have answered test questions very much like the ones you will answer. Students who received good grades for the courses you are taking know things that may be very useful to you. They may be eager to explain to you the methods that they used to earn good grades.

EXAMINE TESTS YOUR TEACHERS HAVE GIVEN

Some teachers give students tests to keep. Also, at some schools samples of tests teachers gave in the past are available for students to examine. Ask former students of your teachers if they have copies of tests you may examine. If your teachers' tests are on file for student examination, locate them and study them.

Also, analyze the types of questions on the first test you take for a course; they will give you hints about the types of things to learn for subsequent tests. For instance, if the questions on a first test are mostly about minute details in a textbook, that teacher's other tests are also likely to focus on the same kinds of details—study them for the next test.

LEARN EASY-TO-UNDERSTAND INFORMATION

Some students believe that if they understand information they know it. However, the difference between understanding and knowing is the difference between reading and studying. Reading is done to understand information; studying is done to recall it.

You have no doubt understood everything you have read in *RSVP*. However, you cannot recall most of the information in this book unless you have studied it. For instance, when you read Chapter 16, you understood the methods listed there for making well-organized class notes, but you cannot recall the methods unless you studied them. Without looking back at Chapter 16, list the methods that are used to make well-organized class notes.

1. _____

2. _____

3. _____

4. _____

5. _____

Unless you studied Chapter 16, or looked back at it, you were probably not able to list accurately all five methods for making well-organized class notes.

Learn information that is easy to understand. It is extremely discouraging to lose points on tests for failure to learn information that you could easily have learned.

PRACTICE SKILLS

Some courses require the learning of **skills,** which are abilities acquired through practice. Writing error-free prose, solving mathematical problems, speaking foreign languages, and performing scientific experimentation are a few of the skills taught in colleges.

It is often necessary to practice a skill more than a teacher requests. For instance, when a mathematics textbook provides forty problems of a specific type, a teacher may assign only twenty of them. However, some students may need to do twenty-five, thirty, or all forty problems. Others may even need to locate a book that contains additional problems to have the practice they need to learn how to solve the problems.

If you are an accomplished athlete, musician, ballet dancer, or writer, you know that long hours of practice are necessary to acquire a skill. Provide yourself with the practice you need to develop the abilities taught in mathematics, science, foreign language, and other courses that teach skills.

DECIDING WHAT TO LEARN

The following exercise provides practice in using the suggestions in this chapter to decide what to learn for one of your courses. If you can improve your ability to decide what is most important to learn, you will do better when you take tests. You will also learn the most important things to know about the subjects you study.

EXERCISE 1

DECIDING WHAT TO LEARN

Use the suggestions in this chapter to decide what to learn for one of the courses you are taking. Write the name of the course on the following line.

_____

Answer the following questions about this course.

1. Will you learn everything that is written in your class notes for the course?

_____

2. How much of the information in class notes is similar to information in required course reading material?

_____ almost all

_____ 75 percent or more

_____ 50 percent or less

_____ very little

Will you learn all this information thoroughly?

_____

3. Does the teacher give reviews for tests?

_____

4. If the answer to question 3 is yes, do you attend reviews, take complete notes, and learn everything you are told to learn?

_____

5. If the answer to question 3 is no, do you ask the teacher what is most imporatant to learn when you study for tests?

_____

6. Write the names of two of the teacher's former students with whom you have discussed how to study for the teacher's tests.

_____   _____

7. Are tests the teacher gave in the past available for you to examine? If you don't know, write "I don't know."

_____

8. If the answer to question 7 is yes, have you studied copies of the tests?

_____

9. Write the headings that come before two easy-to-understand discussions in the course textbook.

   a. _____

   b. _____

10. Will you learn about the topics you listed in question 9 and all the other easy-to-understand information in the course before you take a test?

_____

11. If you are supposed to acquire skills for the course, list them on the following lines. If not, write "no skills."

_____

_____

12. If you listed any skills in question 11, will you provide yourself with the practice you need to acquire them?

_____

18. UNDERLINE TEXTBOOKS

Having decided what is important to learn, the third step in studying for examinations is to underline textbooks.

1. Take good class notes.
2. Decide what to learn.
3. **Underline textbooks.**
4. Make notes for textbooks.
5. Recite from notes.

Underlining is the drawing of lines under words in the way illustrated in Figure 18.1. It is usually done with a pen, using a ruler as a guide. Many students prefer to highlight rather than underline because highlighting can be done neatly without using a ruler. **Highlighting** is the marking of books using a felt-tipped pen that contains water-color ink. Yellow is the most popular color. If the passage in Figure 18.1 were highlighted, yellow or some other water-color ink would be over the words that are underlined. (*Underline* is used in *RSVP* to mean "underline or highlight.")

REASONS FOR UNDERLINING

High school students are usually told that they must not mark books. As a result, many of them enter college without having learned an essential skill for efficient study—underlining.

1. When a book is underlined, there is a permanent record of the information to learn in it.
2. When a book is underlined accurately, it is easier to make well-organized notes for learning the information in it.

FIGURE 18.1

An underlined textbook
passage

The Effects of the Civil War on the South

The immediate ravages of war most deeply affected the South, since most of
the fighting took place there with the usual consequences. Crops were
destroyed, homes and farm buildings went up in flames, cities and towns were
occupied. Even before he took Atlanta and began his march through Georgia to
the sea, Sherman wrote to his wife that "We have devoured the land. . . . All
the people retire before us and desolation is behind. To realize what war is one
should follow our tracks." But this was only the most dramatic example of the
misery wrought by the war.

(1)

The relentless pressure of the Federal naval blockade of Southern ports, the
presence on Southern soil of Union armies, the cutting-off of Texas and
Arkansas by Grant's campaign along the Mississippi River, the steady
shrinking of Southern resources chewed up by military demands—all these
combined to ruin the Southern economy and make miserable the lives of the
people. The transportation system broke down, shortages of many goods
developed, coffee disappeared, salt became scarce, and inflation by 1864 led to
butter selling at $25 a pound and flour at $275 a barrel. Impoverishment was
the fate of many, and disease the byproduct of poverty. Women and children
tried to carry on the work of the farms and the shops, but by 1864 the task had
become too great for many, the penalties in suffering too high. One North
Carolina woman wrote to Governor Vance pleading that her husband be
allowed to come home so that her children might be fed: "i would like to know
what he is fighting for he has nothing to fight for i don't think that he is
fighting for anything only for his family to starve." One man wrote to his
brother advising him to desert: "I would advise you to . . . go to the other side
whear you can get plenty and not stay in this one horse barefooted naked and
famine striken Southern Confederacy."

(2)

Examples

Intellectual and cultural life in the South suffered devastating blows under
the impact of the war. Many private plantation libraries were destroyed; the
importation of books was severely limited by the blockade; book publishing
was greatly restricted by lack of paper, some of the books published came out
on coarse brown paper or even wallpaper, and in all cases the number of copies
was far below the demand. Newspapers and periodicals were equally hard hit,
some being forced to suspend publication, others coming out on half-sheets,
mere slips of paper, or wallpaper. Except for a few isolated instances, the
public school system broke down, private academies closed or survived on a
day-to-day basis, colleges closed for lack of private or public funds. The war
was clearly an economic, social, and cultural disaster for the South. Scarcely a
single aspect of life remained unaffected.

(3)

Examples

On the other hand, when a book is not underlined, it is necessary to read
and reread it to find the information that needs to be learned and it is
more difficult to make notes for learning the information.

Some students resist underlining because they cannot, or fear they
cannot, resell marked books. This is a foolish way to economize. Textbooks are expensive, but they are a small cost of attending college in
comparison to tuition, housing, food, transportation, and other expenses.
Almost all successful students underline their books because underlining

saves them valuable study time. Don't resist underlining. Do what successful students do—underline textbooks.

The only students who do not need to underline are the ones who make good notes as they read. If you make well-organized notes for books as you read them, you do not need to underline.

GUIDELINES FOR UNDERLINING

Use the following guidelines to underline books.

1. *Read a section before you underline it.* If you underline *as* you read, you may underline information that you later decide is not very important.
2. *Do not underline too much.* If an entire page is marked, it is the same as if nothing is marked.
3. *Underline information that will help in making good notes.* The purpose of underlining is to make a permanent record that will help in later making notes for learning information. Use techniques explained in Chapter 17 to decide what is important to underline, write in notes, and learn.
4. *Make major details stand out.* Major details are used to make well-organized notes, and it is almost always important to learn them. Sometimes write numbers in the margin as a reminder of how many details will be written in notes and learned (see Figure 18.1).

It may sometimes seem impossible to follow the second guideline: "Do not underline too much." One way to avoid underlining too much is to write "Example" or "EX" in the margin next to examples, as in Figure 18.1. Another method is to underline only key words that identify major details. For instance, if a page in a human anatomy textbook describes all the bones in the hand and arm, underline the names of the bones but not the information about them. Later, use the underlining as a guide for making notes.

UNDERLINING TEXTBOOKS

The best practice for underlining is to *underline the information you want to learn in textbooks you are studying for other courses.*

Since underlining is done for the purpose of making notes, the exercises for underlining are combined with the exercises for making notes at the end of Chapter 19, which follows.

19. MAKE NOTES FOR TEXTBOOKS

Use the underlining in textbooks as a guide for making notes to learn the information in them.

1. Take good class notes.
2. Decide what to learn.
3. Underline textbooks.
4. **Make notes for textbooks.**
5. Recite from notes.

There are three reasons it is important to make notes for learning information in books. First, *writing information in notes often helps to learn it.* To make notes, statements are pondered and restated. In many instances, information is learned as it is processed in this way. Second, *notes reduce the amount of information to learn.* Note-taking condenses information by selecting what is most important in books and summarizing it. As a result, there is much less to learn when studying notes than when studying directly from textbooks. Third, *information in notes is organized for efficient learning.* Information in textbooks is organized to make it understandable to most students, but in good notes the information is organized to make it easier for the note-taker to learn.

Good notes, studied using suggestions in Chapter 20, make it possible to learn information more quickly and thoroughly than is possible using any other method.

GUIDELINES FOR MAKING NOTES

When you make notes for textbooks, write descriptive titles, make major details stand out clearly, and include minor details, which are often examples.

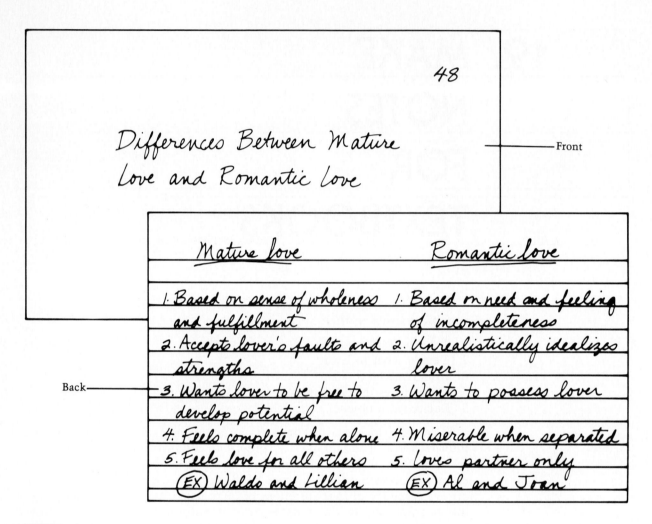

48

Differences Between Mature Love and Romantic Love

Front

Mature love	*Romantic love*
1. Based on sense of wholeness and fulfillment	1. Based on need and feeling of incompleteness
2. Accepts lover's faults and strengths	2. Unrealistically idealizes lover
3. Wants lover to be free to develop potential	3. Wants to possess lover
4. Feels complete when alone	4. Miserable when separated
5. Feels love for all others	5. Loves partner only
(EX) Waldo and Lillian	(EX) Al and Joan

Back

FIGURE 19.1

Notes for the passage
on page 151

Write Descriptive Titles

Write titles for notes that accurately describe the information to be
learned. The notes in Figure 19.1 are for the passage entitled "Romantic
and Mature Love," on page 151. The title for the notes, "Differences
Between Romantic and Mature Love," is more descriptive than the title
for the passage.

EXERCISE 1

WRITING DESCRIPTIVE TITLES

Headings in textbooks are often descriptive titles for notes. When they are not, rewrite them to make them more descriptive.

1. Write a more descriptive title for the passage entitled "Words at Play," on page 169.

   _____

2. Write a more descriptive title for the passage entitled "Energy from the Sun," on page 175.

   _____

3. Write a more descriptive title for the passage entitled "Rabies," on page 179.

   _____

4. Write a more descriptive title for the passage entitled "Relatives," on page 183.

   _____

Make Major Details Stand Out

It is almost always important to learn major details; therefore, make them stand out in notes so it is clear exactly how many major details there are to learn. Notice in Figure 19.1 that the five major details for romantic love and mature love are numbered to stand out clearly.

EXERCISE 2

MAKING MAJOR DETAILS STAND OUT

Referring to the passage entitled "Relatives," on page 183, write the major details in it on the following lines as you would to make them stand out clearly in notes.

Three Types of Relatives

1. _____

   _____

2. _____

   _____

3. _____

   _____

Include Minor Details

Include minor details that explain or help you to understand the major details in notes; they may often be examples. Notice in Figure 19.1 that the minor details are examples of romantic and mature lovers who are friends of the person who made the notes.

In Figure 19.2 on page 272, the major details are the names of the intellectual stages to the left of the margin ("Sensorimotor stage," and so on). The minor details to the right of the margin in Figure 19.2 include facts and examples.

EXERCISE 3

INCLUDING MINOR DETAILS

Complete the following notes by writing minor details on the lines provided. The details may be statements in the passage on page 183, or they may be examples of your secondary and tertiary relatives.

Three Types of Relatives

1. Primary relatives—mother, father, brothers, sisters, husband or wife, sons, and daughters.

2. Secondary relatives—primary relatives of primary relatives

_____

_____

3. Tertiary relatives—primary relatives of secondary relatives

_____

_____

NOTES ON CARDS

Figure 19.1 (page 268) and Figure 19.3 (page 273) illustrate how to make notes on 3-by-5-inch cards or pieces of paper. (*Card* is used in *RSVP* to mean "3-by-5-inch card or piece of paper.")

1. *Write titles on the blank sides of cards.* Notice in Figure 19.1 and Figure 19.3 that titles are written boldly on the blank sides of cards.
2. *Number cards on the blank sides.* Number cards so they can be put back into correct order quickly in case they become disorganized. In Figure 19.3 one card is numbered "14a" to indicate that it is part of a series of five cards that begins with card "14." Cards "14b," "14c," and "14d," for the preoperational stage, concrete operations stage, and formal operations stage are not shown in Figure 19.3 (see Figure 19.2).
3. *Write details on the backs of cards upside-down in relation to titles and numbers on the fronts.* When notes are made in this way, information on the backs of cards is in the proper position for reading when cards are turned over.

Notes on cards may be held together with a rubber band, and notes on slips of paper may be held together with a large paper clip.

NOTES ON NOTEBOOK PAPER

Figure 19.2 illustrates one way to make notes on notebook paper.

1. Write the topics about which you want to learn to the left of the margin.
2. Write details to the right of the margin.
3. Skip a line between sets of details written to the right of the margin.

Notes prepared in this way are tidy, and they may be learned efficiently using methods that are explained in Chapter 20.

FIGURE 19.2

Textbook notes on note-
book paper

Piaget's stages of intellectual development	
1. Sensorimotor stage	★ Birth to age two ★ Does not use language ★ By age two knows objects do not disappear when hidden
2. Preoperational stage	★ Ages two to seven ★ Uses language to label things (Ex) "Kitty" ★ Develops concepts (Ex) Can select the middle-sized doll from among three dolls of different sizes
3. Concrete operations stage	★ Ages seven to eleven ★ Understands classification and sequential order and uses them to solve problems ★ Understands conservation (Ex) Knows a piece of clay does not increase in amount when rolled into a "snake"
4. Formal operations stage	★ Ages eleven to fifteen ★ Engages in abstract reasoning ★ Imagines possibilities in problems ★ Performs experiments ★ Draws valid conclusions by reasoning

ADVANTAGES OF NOTES ON CARDS

Information may be learned from notes on notebook paper or cards, but cards have advantages that notebook paper does not have.

1. *Cards make it possible to integrate class notes and textbook notes easily.* Information in class notes may be copied onto related textbook notes so that all the information about a topic is in one place for efficient study.
2. *Cards make it possible to separate information that has been learned from information that has not been learned.* By separating "learned" notes from "unlearned" notes, attention can be more readily directed toward studying information that has not been learned.
3. *Cards are convenient to study at times it is inconvenient to study notes on notebook paper.* They may be studied while walking from class to class or even while standing on a bus; notes on notebook paper are inconvenient to study at such times.

FIGURE 19.3

Two of five cards for the notes in Figure 19.2

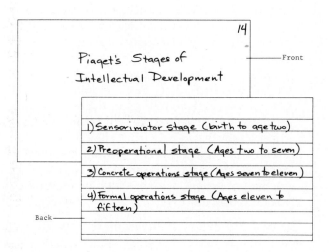

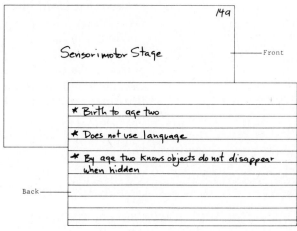

Consider these advantages of cards before deciding whether to make notes on notebook paper or on cards.

NOTES IN CLASSIFICATION CHARTS

Classification charts are charts of the type in Figure 19.4, which are useful for notes about passages that explain how two or more persons, places, or things are alike or different in two or more ways. The notes in Figure 19.4 are based on the following passage.

THE PSYCHOSEXUAL STAGES, ACCORDING TO FREUD

Sigmund Freud proposed that there are five stages in people's psychosexual development. He believed that the success with which individuals deal with the problems of each stage is related to their personality development.

The first stage, which lasts from birth until about one year of age, he called the *oral stage*. During this time the infant's pleasure centers around the mouth in eating, biting, chewing, and sucking. The *anal stage*, which lasts from age one year to age three, is the time when the young child finds pleasure in holding and letting go of waste matter from the body. This is the important time of toilet training. The *phallic stage* begins at age three and continues until age six. It is during this time that the child, male or female, derives pleasure from primary sex organs to a great degree. Beginning at age six and continuing until about age eleven, the child passes through what Freud called the *latency period*. During this time the child denies affection and attraction for the parent of the opposite sex and identifies strongly with the parent of the same sex. Adolescence marks the beginning of the *genital stage*, which is the awakening of sexuality and the desire for heterosexual love.

The notes in Figure 19.4 summarize the information about the psychosexual stages under headings that explain the two ways in which the stages differ from one another: "Age" and "Characteristics." The notes also emphasize the sequence in which the stages occur.

When you have difficulty making good notes for information, ask this question about it: "Does this information explain how two or more persons, places, or things are alike or different in two or more ways?" If the answer to this question is yes, make notes in a chart of the type illustrated in Figure 19.4.

The Psychosexual Stages, According to Freud

	Age	Characteristics
Oral Stage	Birth to 1 year	Gets pleasure from mouth by sucking, eating, biting, and chewing.
Anal Stage	1 year to 3 years	Gets pleasure from holding and letting go of body waste.
Phallic Stage	3 years to 6 years	The child derives pleasure from his or her own primary sex organs.
Latency Period	6 years to about 11 years	Child denies attraction for parent of opposite sex and identifies with parent of the same sex.
Genital Stage	Adolescence	Awakening of sexuality and desire for heterosexual love.

FIGURE 19.4

Textbook notes in a classification chart

FIGURE 19.5

A map for the passage
on page 179

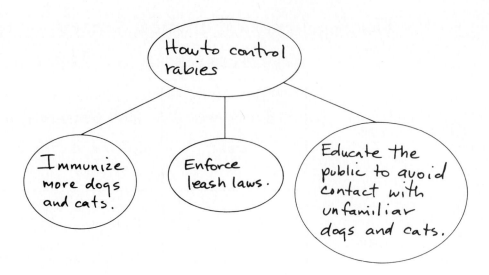

NOTES IN MAPS

Some students report that they learn efficiently from notes in **maps,**
which are diagrams such as the one shown in Figure 19.5 for the passage
entitled "Rabies," on page 179. The main thought of the passage is in
the center circle and the major details are summarized in circles con-
nected to it. Experiment with making maps; you may find them useful.

UNDERLINING AND MAKING NOTES

The best practice for underlining and making notes is to *underline and
make notes for learning information in textbooks you are studying for
other courses.*

Underlining is good when it helps you to make good notes. Notes are
good when they have descriptive titles; when they make the major details
stand out; and when they include minor details, which are often examples. Evaluate your notes by asking the following questions about them:

- Can I write a more descriptive title?
- Can I make the major details stand out more clearly?
- Have I included too few or too many minor details?

If the answer to each of these questions is no, the notes are the best you
can make. If the answer to any question is yes, improve your notes.

The following exercises provide practice in making notes on cards and
notebook paper and in preparing classification charts.

EXERCISE 4

HUMAN MOTIVATION (page 185)

Underline the passage named above and make notes for it on the form for an index card, below (see Figure 19.3).

Can you write a more descriptive title?
Do the major details stand out, and are they numbered?
Did you include minor details?

EXERCISE 5

CONFLICT (pages 141–143)

Underline the passage named above and make notes for it in the chart below (see Figure 19.4).

	Number of Alter-natives	Positive or Negative?	Example	Resolution
Approach-approach	Two	Positive	Datson or Toyota?	One choice becomes more posi-tive than the other

EXERCISE 6

DEATH AND DYING (pages 144—145)

Underline the passage named above and make notes for it on the form for an index card, below (see Figure 19.3).

Can you write a more descriptive title?
Do the major details stand out, and are they numbered?
Did you include too few or too many minor details?

EXERCISE 7

HELPFULNESS (pages 157–159)

Underline the passage named above and make notes for it on the lines, below (see Figure 19.2).

EXERCISE 8

MAKING ETHICAL DECISIONS (pages 199–200)

Underline the passage named above and make notes for it on the lines below (see Figure 19.2).

EXERCISE 9

PROPAGANDA (pages 203–204)

Underline the passage named above and make notes for it on the chart below (see Figure 19.4).

	Definition	Example
Transfer and Testimony	A sales pitch given for a product by a famous person	
Bandwagon		"Everybody else is doing it, you should too."

EXERCISE 10

SYPHILIS (pages 215–216)

Underline the passage named above and make notes for it on the lines below (see Figure 19.2).

EXERCISE 11

THE SELECTION OF EMPLOYEES (pages 223–224)

Underline the passage named above and make notes for it on the lines below (see Figure 19.2).

EXERCISE 12

THE NEED FOR AFFECTION (pages 231—232)

Underline the passage named above and make notes for it on the form for an index card, below (see Figure 19.3).

Can you write a more descriptive title?
Do the major details stand out, and are they numbered?
Did you include minor details?

20. RECITE FROM NOTES

Reciting is the final and most important component of the process used to study for examinations.

1. Take good class notes.
2. Decide what to learn.
3. Underline textbooks.
4. Make notes for textbooks.
5. **Recite from notes.**

Reciting is the act of repeating information silently or aloud to learn and remember it. Students who spend most of their study time reciting rather than reading do better on tests because reciting gives practice answering test questions. For instance, when students recite information about human anatomy, they practice answering questions that appear on human anatomy tests; reading about human anatomy does not provide this valuable practice.

RECITE, DON'T MEMORIZE

Actors memorize their parts in plays to speak them word for word, but students recite to learn and remember information, not to memorize it. Use the following procedures for reciting from well-organized notes.

1. Read the title of the information to be learned and turn it into a question.
2. Try to answer the question silently or aloud to yourself without reading it.
3. Read the information in notes to make certain that you recited it correctly. If you did not, reread the information and then immediately try to recite it again.

Repeat these procedures at later times until you recall the information accurately.

A student needed to learn the information in Figure 20.1 for a business course. She recited it by reading the title, "Types of Advertising," and by turning the title into the following question: "What types of advertising are there?" After several attempts, she recited the information in the following way.

AN EXAMPLE OF RECITING

Primary demand, selective, and institutional advertising. Primary demand advertising sells a product without trying to sell any particular

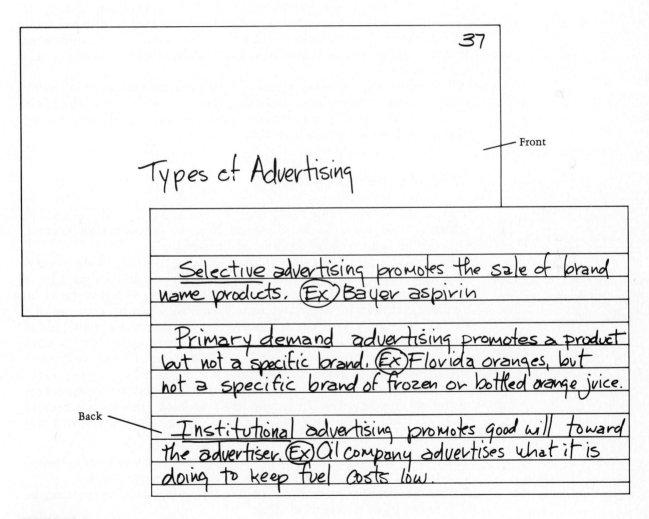

FIGURE 20.1

Notes for a business textbook

brand name product . . . sells things made out of cotton without selling specific products, such as Arrow shirts or Cannon towels. Selective advertising is used to sell specific brand name products, such as Cannon towels and Skippy peanut butter. Institutional advertising tries to increase good will toward the advertiser . . . as when Mobil Oil sponsors a movie on public television.

Compare this example of recitation to the notes in Figure 20.1 to notice that they are different in several respects. First, the student organized her thoughts by naming the three types of advertising. Second, she did not recite the information about the three types of advertising in the same sequence in which they are listed in her notes. Third, the explanations she gave while reciting are not word-for-word duplications of statements in the notes. Fourth, the examples she gave while reciting are not identical to examples in the notes. She recited correctly, showing that she had learned the information in the notes, not that she had merely memorized words.

If students did not recite, we would have few doctors, lawyers, architects, accountants, teachers, and other professionals to serve the needs of society. It is reciting that makes it possible to remember information that is used to answer test questions.

SCHEDULE TIME FOR REVIEW

Methods for scheduling study time for examinations are explained in Chapter 2, on pages 24–25. Time needs to be scheduled for reading, underlining, note making, reciting, and reviewing.

We tend to forget 30 to 40 percent of what we "learn" within twenty-four hours after learning it. For example, after reciting for an hour, a student had "learned" the information on twenty of eighty cards he prepared to study for a physics test. However, when he reviewed the twenty "learned" cards the following day, he discovered that he had forgotten information on six of them. What happened to him is what happens to most of us; we forget 30 to 40 percent of what we "learn" within twenty-four hours after learning it.

Review is the repeated reciting of information to counteract the effects of normal forgetfulness. To review notes on cards, maintain a deck of "learned" cards and a deck of "unlearned" cards. Then, each time you recite:

1. Begin by reviewing the deck of "learned" cards. If you have forgotten information on a card, put it back in the "unlearned" deck.
2. Then, recite the "unlearned" cards, attempting to move as many as you can into the "learned" deck.

Continue in this way until you can accurately recite all the information twenty-four hours after all the cards are in the "learned" deck.

To review notes on notebook paper, place checks in pencil next to information as you "learn" it. Then, each time you recite:

1. Begin by reviewing checked information, and erase checks next to information you have forgotten.
2. Then, recite the information that is not checked, attempting to place checks next to as much of it as you can.

Continue in this way until you can accurately recite all the information twenty-four hours after placing checks next to it.

Attempting to move as many cards as possible into a "learned" deck, or to check as much information in notes as possible, makes studying a kind of game. Those who view studying as a challenging game to play and win enjoy studying more and learn more.

PREPARE CLASS NOTES FOR RECITING

It is almost always important to learn everything in class notes before a test or examination. When reciting from notes on cards, combine information about a topic in class notes and a textbook on the same card so all the information is in one place for efficient learning.

When reciting from notes on notebook paper, summarize class notes in the format illustrated on page 272. Or, if class notes are neat and do not need to be summarized, highlight the titles for information in them and use the highlighted titles to stimulate recall. For instance, if "Types of Advertising" is a title for information in class notes, highlight it. Use it for reciting just as the student used the front of the index card for reciting in Figure 20.1 on page 287. When titles in class notes are not descriptive, write more descriptive ones, placing them in the left margin if necessary.

USE MNEMONICS

Mnemonic (ni-mon'ik) means "to help the memory." The jingle "*i* before *e*, except after *c*" is a mnemonic rhyme for remembering a spelling principle. The following discussions explain three types of mnemonic devices that are helpful for learning information: acronyms, sentences, and visualizations.

Acronyms

An **acronym** is a word made from the initial letters of other words. For instance, *homes* is an acronym made from the initial letters of the Great Lakes: *H*uron, *O*ntario, *M*ichigan, *E*rie, and *S*uperior. *Homes* may be used to remember the names of the lakes: *H* recalls *Huron*, *O* recalls *Ontario*, and so on.

An acronym may be a nonsense word. For instance, "Death and Dying," on pages 144–145, explains the emotional stages terminally ill people often experience when they learn they are about to die. The stages are:

Denial
Anger
Bargaining
Depression
Acceptance

The nonsense acronym DABDA may be used to learn the stages in the correct sequence: *D* recalls *Denial*, *A* recalls *Anger*, and so on.

Sometimes it is not possible to create an acronym using the initial letters of key words. These are the three methods for making ethical decisions that are explained in a passage on pages 199–200.

Fixed rules
Greatest good for the greatest number
Situational ethics

The letters FGS cannot be arranged to spell a word or an easy-to-remember nonsense word. However, by adding another letter enclosed in parentheses, the acronym F(i)GS may be used to recall the three methods for making ethical decisions. *F* recalls "Fixed rules," *G* recalls "Greatest good for the greatest number," and *S* recalls "Situational ethics." The parentheses around the *i* serve as a visual reminder that there are three, not four, methods for making ethical decisions.

Sentences

A mnemonic sentence is a sentence in which the initial letters of words in the sentence are the same as the initial letters of words that need to be recalled. Following is a well-known mnemonic sentence:

My	Very	Earthy	Mother	Just	Served	Us	Nine	Pizzas.
e	e	a	a	u	a	r	e	l
r	n	r	r	p	t	a	p	u
c	u	t	s	i	u	n	t	t
u	s	h		t	r	u	u	o
r				e	n	s	n	
y				r			e	

This sentence may be used to recall the sequence of the planets, starting with the one nearest the sun and proceeding to the one farthest from the sun. The sentence is much easier to remember than the letters MVEMJSUNP—the initial letters of the names of the planets.

Mnemonic sentences may be devised for almost any list. For instance, these are the four defense mechanisms explained in the passage on pages 127–128:

Rationalization
Projection
Sublimation
Compensation

It is not possible to make an acronym from the letters *RPSC*, but many mnemonic sentences may be made from them. For example:

Roger plays soccer competently.
Real people sell candy.
Rats please some customers.

Memory experts claim that mnemonic devices are easier to remember when they are funny, fanciful, or ridiculous. According to this theory, "Rats please some customers" should be the easiest of the sentences to remember. When you make mnemonic devices, make ones that are easy to recall.

Visualizations

A **visualization** is anything that can be pictured in the mind to aid the recall of information. Often a visualization is an example in the form or a person, place, thing, event, or set of circumstances.

The notes, "Types of Advertising," in Figure 20.1 on page 287, include three visualizations, which are examples of things.

Type of Advertising	Visualization
Selective (which promotes the sale of a brand name product)	Bayer aspirin
Primary demand (which promotes a product but not a specific brand)	Florida oranges
Institutional (which promotes good will toward the advertiser)	Oil company advertises how it keeps fuel costs low.

The visualizations help in learning and remembering the differences among the three types of advertising.

Also, the four types of social mobility explained on page 124 can be remembered using visualizations such as the following.

Type of Social Mobility	Visualization
Horizontal (from one status to a similar status)	When I changed jobs from pumping gas to parking cars.
Vertical (from one status to a higher or lower status)	When I changed jobs from parking cars to being a management trainee for an insurance company.

Intragenerational (horizontal or vertical mobility during an individual's career)	When I changed jobs from pumping gas to parking cars *or* from parking cars to being a management trainee for an insurance company.
Intergenerational (horizontal or vertical mobility from one generation to the next)	My grandfather was a laborer, but my father supervises skilled factory workers.

Visualizations are often extremely useful for increasing understanding of information and learning it.

PRACTICE RECITING

The best practice for the suggestions in this chapter is to *recite information in notes you make to study for tests in your college courses.*

You may also practice reciting information in notes to prepare for tests your instructor may give you about information in *RSVP.*

The following exercises provide practice for making mnemonic acronyms, sentences, and visualization.

EXERCISE 1

STAGES OF PREGNANCY (pages 123–124)

Write visualizations for learning and remembering what occurs during each of the three trimesters of pregnancy.

1. First trimester _____

   _____

2. Second trimester _____

   _____

3. Third trimester _____

   _____

EXERCISE 2

MEASURES OF CENTRAL TENDENCY (pages 128–129)

Following is a visual display that may be used to remember and learn the differences between the mean, median, and mode.

$$\underset{\text{mode}}{2 + 2} + \underset{\text{median}}{3} + 5 + 8 \quad = \quad \frac{20}{5} \quad = \quad \underset{\text{mean}}{4}$$

Devise a similar display of your own, and write it in the space provided below.

EXERCISE 3

SQ3R (pages 153–154)

What is the mnemonic device for remembering the five steps of the study procedure that are explained in the passage?

EXERCISE 4

LOW-LEVEL CLOUDS (pages 155–156)

Write a sentence or other device for recalling the four types of low-level clouds: stratus, cumulus, nimbostratus, and stratocumulus.

EXERCISE 5

HELPFULNESS (pages 157–158)

Write a mnemonic sentence using the italicized letters *N*, *S*, *R*, *C*, and *M*, for recalling the following outline.

I. *N*ormative explanation
   A. *S*ocial responsibility
   B. *R*eciprocity
II. *C*ost analysis approach
III. *M*ood approach

_____

_____

EXERCISE 6

TYPES OF ADVERTISING (page 165)

Write an acronym for remembering the three types of advertising: *S*elective, *P*rimary demand, and *I*nstitutional.

_____

EXERCISE 7

RABIES (page 179)

Use the italicized letters *I*, *l*, and *E* to write an acronym for recalling the three measures that can be taken to control rabies.

*I*mmunize more dogs and cats
Enforce *l*eash laws
*E*ducate the public about the danger of rabies

_____

EXERCISE 8

HUMAN MOTIVATION (page 185)

Write visualizations for learning and remembering the five human needs.

1. physiological _____

_____

2. safety _____

_____

3. belongingness _____

_____

4. esteem _____

_____

5. self-actualization _____

_____

EXERCISE 9

TESTS OF ABNORMALCY (page 181)

Use the italicized letters *f, s, d* and a vowel enclosed in parentheses to write an acronym for recalling the three tests of abnormalcy.

Test of *f*requency
Test of *s*ocietal standards
Test of *d*egree of disability

_____

EXERCISE 10

THE SELECTION OF EMPLOYEES (pages 223–224)

Use the italicized letters *I, A, T,* and *P* to write a sentence for recalling the steps for selecting employees in the correct sequence.

*I*nterview
*A*pplication
*T*esting
*P*hysical examination

_____

_____

V. USE GOOD TEST-TAKING METHODS

Teachers of most college courses are required to give tests and to consider test scores when they assign final course grades for students. It is the responsibility of teachers to give tests, and most of them take the responsibility seriously.

Some instructors give only a midterm and a final examination; students who do poorly on one of the tests usually receive low final course grades. Other teachers give many tests because they want to make certain students learn what they teach and to give them chances to earn good course grades even if they do not do well on one or two tests. When you have teachers who give many tests, keep in mind that they are trying to help you to learn and to do your best in their courses.

Considering the importance that is attached to test scores, it is surprising that little attention is given to teaching students how to do their best when they take tests. But test-taking is a skill that can be learned in the same way the skills of reading and writing are learned. The chapters in this part of *RSVP* explain basic methods for taking any test and specific strategies for answering five types of questions that appear often on college tests: true-false, multiple-choice, matching, fill-in, and essay questions.

21. BASIC TEST-TAKING METHODS

Chapters 16–20 explain what to do *before* taking tests, and this chapter explains basic methods to use *while* taking them.

1. Read directions and follow them.
2. Plan how to use test time.
3. Answer the easiest questions first.
4. Usually answer all questions.
5. Check answers carefully.
6. Don't share answers.
7. Learn from incorrect answers.

Specific strategies for answering true-false, multiple-choice, matching, fill-in, and essay questions are explained in Chapters 22–26.

READ DIRECTIONS AND FOLLOW THEM

Test directions are sometimes important to teachers for reasons that are not obvious to students. For instance, one instructor types the following direction at the beginning of his multiple-choice tests.

Show your answers on the answer sheet by clearly printing capital letter A, B, C, or D.

Before students answer questions, he draws this direction to their attention; prints capital letters A, B, C, and D on the chalkboard; and informs students that he will deduct 10 points from the test scores of those who do not follow the direction. However, some students who do not follow the direction complain that the teacher is "unfair" when he deducts 10 points from their test scores. Is he?

Test directions are also sometimes very different from what students expect. The directions for the test in Figure 21.1 on page 302 state that only two of four questions are to be answered. If students answer all four questions, only the first two answers will be graded. Those who write C

FIGURE 21.1

An essay test

Test: Mass Communication

Answer any two of the following four questions. Each answer has a value of 50 points. You have 50 minutes to write your answers.

1. What part should the media play in changing the public's attitudes and opinions?
2. Compare the importance of movies as a mass medium in the 1940s to their importance today.
3. What issues and problems would each of the following disciplines emphasize in studying mass communication: psychology, sociology, and linguistics?
4. What questions and issues are of concern when studying broadcasting from a content point of view?

---

answers for the first two questions and B answers for the third and fourth questions will receive grades of C, not B.

DECIDE HOW TO USE TEST TIME

Since instructors seldom allow unlimited time to answer test questions, it is necessary to decide how to use the available time. Decisions about using time are made by finding answers to the following questions.

1. How much time do I have?
2. How many questions must I answer?
3. What is the point value for each answer?

For instance, students who take the essay test in Figure 21.1 have fifty minutes to answer two questions that have a value of fifty points each. Since each answer accounts for half the test grade, they should plan to spend about half the time (twenty-five minutes) answering each question.

EXERCISE 1

PLANNING TEST-TAKING TIME

Practice planning test-taking time by answering the following questions.

1. You have 50 minutes to solve 10 mathematical problems, which have a value of 10 points each. How many minutes should you spend solving each problem?

    _____

2. You have 100 minutes to answer four essay questions. One answer has a value of 40 points and three answers have a value of 20 points each. How many minutes should you plan to spend answering the 40-point question?

    _____

    How many minutes should you plan to spend answering each of the 20-point questions?

    _____

3. You have 60 minutes to answer 25 multiple-choice questions and 10 short-answer questions. The multiple-choice questions have a value of 2 points each and the short-answer questions have a value of 5 points each. How many minutes should you plan to spend answering the 25 multiple-choice questions?

    _____

    How many minutes should you plan to spend answering each short-answer question?

    _____

ANSWER THE EASIEST QUESTIONS FIRST

One of the simplest and most beneficial test-taking strategies for you to use is to answer the easiest questions first. There are at least four benefits in using this strategy.

1. All questions that can be answered correctly are answered correctly in case time runs out before you can answer all the questions.

2. Answering easy questions correctly may increase your confidence that you will also answer more difficult questions correctly.
3. Answers to difficult questions are often recalled while writing answers to easier ones.
4. Test questions are sometimes interrelated so that answers to some difficult questions are located while answering easier ones.

When you answer true-false or multiple-choice questions, read a question twice and answer it or move on to the next question. When you have read each question twice and answered as many as you can, reread the first unanswered question twice again and answer it or move on to the next unanswered question. Work through the test in this way as many times as necessary to select an answer to each question. When you are uncertain about the correct answer to a true-false or multiple-choice question, use suggestions in Chapters 22 and 23 to guess at the answer.

Also answer the easiest questions first when you write answers to essay questions or solve mathematical problems. For instance, if you have sixty minutes to write four answers to essay questions which have a value of 25 points each, you should plan to spend about fifteen minutes writing each answer. However, if you answer the two easiest questions first, you may answer them in fewer than thirty minutes. You will then have more than thirty minutes to answer the two more difficult questions.

USUALLY ANSWER ALL QUESTIONS

Answer all questions on a test unless you are told not to. For instance, if you take an essay test with directions of the type illustrated in Figure 21.1, do not answer all the questions. At other times, answer all test questions even if you must guess at some answers—you may guess correctly.

When you guess at the answer to a true-false question you have a 50 percent chance of guessing the correct answer; there is a 50 percent chance it is "true" and a 50 percent chance it is "false."

When you guess at the answer to a multiple-choice question that has four possible answers (a, b, c, or d), you have a 25 percent chance of guessing the correct answer. There is a 25 percent chance the answer is a, a 25 percent chance the answer is b, and so on. Guessing one correct answer can make an important difference when a test is graded. If a test has 40 questions of equal value ($2.5 \times 40 = 100$), those who answer 31 questions correctly receive grades of C+ ($2.5 \times 31 = 77.5$) but those who answer 32 questions correctly receive grades of B− ($2.5 \times 32 = 80$).

CHECK ANSWERS CAREFULLY

Do not rush when you take tests because other students finish before you or because you want to finish before others. Instead, spend time answering questions correctly and checking answers after you write them to make certain that they are correct.

However, take care when you check answers to true-false and multiple-choice questions. Some students have the tendency to change correct answers to incorrect ones! When you change answers to these types of questions, cross out the original answers but leave them visible so that when the test is reviewed you can analyze whether you changed correct answers to incorrect ones. By using this procedure you will soon learn whether you should change answers only when you are absolutely certain that they are incorrect.

DON'T SHARE ANSWERS

Students who have not studied may ask you to show them your answers during tests or they may read your answers without asking permission. If other students read your answers, you may be accused of cheating. People who allow others to read their answers are as guilty of cheating as those who read them. Therefore, during tests always sit so that other students cannot see your answers and you cannot see what other students write.

LEARN FROM INCORRECT ANSWERS

Test-taking is a skill, and skills are improved by making mistakes and learning not to make them. For instance, if you are an expert automobile driver, you have learned not to make the mistakes you made while you were learning to drive. Similarly, you may become an expert test-taker by learning not to make mistakes that you now make when you take tests.

When tests are returned to you, analyze them to understand why you answered questions incorrectly. You may decide that you did not plan test-taking time carefully enough or that you did not study class notes as thoroughly as you should have. Try not to make the same kind of mistake in the future.

EXERCISE 2

USING BASIC TEST-TAKING METHODS

Write the names of two courses for which you have recently taken tests over the columns on the right. Then, write "yes" or "no" on the lines for the statements listed on the left.

1. _____   2. _____

1. I read the test directions and followed them exactly.

2. I planned carefully how I would make the best use of test-taking time.

3. I answered the easiest questions first.

4. I picked up extra points by guessing at the answers to some questions.

5. I checked answers carefully after I wrote them.

6. I was careful not to let any classmate see my answers during the test.

7. I studied incorrect answers when the test was returned and learned how I can do better on the next test the teacher gives.

8. I answered correctly all questions about information in class notes.

9. I answered correctly all
   questions about
   information written on
   the chalkboard.   _____   _____

10. I answered correctly all
    questions about
    information the teacher
    said was important to
    learn.   _____   _____

22. TRUE-FALSE
QUESTIONS

True-false questions are statements that test-takers must decide are either true or false. They are well-suited for testing whether students have learned specific facts such as the following.

T   F   The United States entered World War II in 1941.

The United States either entered World War II in 1941 or it did not. It did; the statement is true.

ASSUME STATEMENTS ARE TRUE

The basic strategy for answering true-false questions is to assume that they are true. For instance,

T   F   Cavendish discovered hydrogen in 1766.

If you must answer this question on a chemistry test, assume it is true unless, by considering what you have learned, you decide it is false. If you must guess whether the statement is true or false, guess it is true. There is a *tendency* for true-false tests to include more true statements than false ones; in the long run, you will guess more correct answers if you guess they are true than if you guess they are false.

Also, keep in mind that a statement is false if any part of it is false. The italicized words in the following statements make them false.

T   F   Cavendish *created* hydrogen in 1766.

T   F   Cavendish discovered the *composition of air* in 1766.

T   F   Cavendish discovered hydrogen in *1866*.

Answer true-false questions using information you learned while studying class notes and required reading material. When you must guess answers to them, guess they are true.

ABSOLUTE DETERMINERS

Absolute determiners are words such as *all, none, always, never, everybody, nobody, only,* and *invariably;* they tend to appear in false statements. On the other hand, statements that include words such as *few, often, sometimes, most, many,* and *usually* tend to be true. The italicized word in the following sentence suggests it is false.

T   F   Businesses *always* adopt and use new technology.

This statement is false, but the following statement is true.

T   F   Successful large businesses *usually* adopt and use new technology.

When only successful large businesses are considered, it is true that they *usually* adopt and use new technology.

Compare the following false and true statements, paying attention to the words printed in italics in them.

False Statements	True Statements
1. *All* children love cheeseburgers.	1. *Many* children love cheeseburgers.
2. Men are *never* nurses.	2. Men are *seldom* nurses.
3. Parents *invariably* love their children.	3. Parents *usually* love their children.
4. *Nobody* reads dictionaries for pleasure.	4. *Few people* read dictionaries for pleasure.

When you answer true-false questions, remember that words such as *all, never, invariably,* and *nobody* tend to be in false statements. Words such as *many, seldom, usually,* and *few* tend to be in true statements.

REASONS

True-false questions that state reasons tend to be false either because they state an incorrect reason or because they do not state all the reasons. Statements of reasons are often indicated by the word *reason, because,* or *since.* For example,

T   F   The *reason* many teachers give multiple-choice tests is that it is easy to write multiple-choice questions.

T   F   Many teachers give multiple-choice tests *because* it is easy to write multiple-choice questions.

T   F   *Since* it is easy to write multiple-choice questions, many teachers give multiple-choice tests.

These statements are false; multiple-choice questions are not easy to write.

Qualifying words such as *one* and *partly* may make an otherwise false statement true. For example,

T   F   *One reason* many teachers give multiple-choice tests is that they are easy to grade.

T   F   Many teachers give multiple-choice tests *partly because* they are easy to grade.

When you answer true-false questions, remember that statements of reasons tend to be false unless they are qualified in some way.

ANSWERING TRUE-FALSE QUESTIONS

When you answer true-false questions, assume they are true unless, by considering what you have learned, you decide they are false. If you must guess whether a statement is true or false, guess it is true. In addition, keep the following hints in mind:

1. Statements with an absolute determiner tend to be false.
2. Statements of reasons tend to be false.

The following exercises provide practice for learning how to select more correct answers to true-false questions; the answers to the questions in the exercises are correct according to the sources upon which they are based. Use what you learn by doing the exercises to answer more true-false questions correctly on college tests.

EXERCISE 1

TRUE-FALSE QUESTIONS

The following statements are true except for those that have an absolute determiner or that state a reason. Circle T in front of true statements and F in front of false statements. Also, underline the word in a statement that causes you to decide it is false.

T   F   1. The latent content of a dream is the underlying meaning of a dream.

T   F   2. Color blindness is found only in men, never in women.

T   F   3. Those who have strong self-awareness are likely to cope efficiently with anxiety.

T   F   4. Sigmund Freud's id, ego, and superego represent the unconscious, the rational, and the conscience.

T   F   5. Sleep was not scientifically investigated until recently because there was no interest in this subject until after World War II.

T   F   6. All the fears of young babies are fears they learned.

T   F   7. Sigmund Freud, Havelock Ellis, and Magnus Hirschfeld were famous nineteenth-century sex researchers.

T   F   8. The reason group health insurance policies are better than individual policies is that they are less expensive and cover more types of illness and injury.

T   F   9. Americans today enjoy longer life spans solely because of genetic factors.

T   F   10. College freshmen are more romantic than college seniors.

T   F   11. The decision to commit suicide is never sudden or impulsive.

T   F   12. Most parents who abuse their children actually need them and love them.

EXERCISE 2

TRUE-FALSE QUESTIONS

The following statements are true except for those that have an absolute determiner or that state a reason. Circle T in front of true statements and F in front of false statements. Also, underline the word in a statement that causes you to decide it is false.

T   F   1. In the early nineteenth century, native-born women did not strike over the deteriorating conditions in textile mills because they were fearful of losing their jobs.

T   F   2. Black slaves in the South knew more about how to cultivate rice than did their white masters.

T   F   3. The annexation of the Dominican Republic was the only successful foreign policy of Grant's administration.

T   F   4. During colonial times, the extended family was probably more important among black families than among white families.

T   F   5. The war against Mexico was supported by public opinion in all sections of the United States.

T   F   6. The French navy played an important role in the victory over Cornwallis at Yorktown.

T   F   7. The capitol of the United States was designed to symbolize the separation of the three branches of government.

T   F   8. The reason Napoleon sold Louisiana to the United States is that he feared we would take it by force.

T   F   9. Discrimination against blacks in the North completely disappeared during the Civil War.

T   F   10. The great majority of whites in the South did not own slaves, but a majority of political offices were held by slave owners.

T   F   11. The purpose of the Removal Act of 1830 was to relocate native Americans to areas west of the Mississippi River.

T   F   12. In the late part of the nineteenth century, factory production increased because of the growing size of the labor force.

EXERCISE 3

TRUE-FALSE QUESTIONS

The following statements are true except for those that have an absolute determiner or that state a reason. Circle T in front of true statements and F in front of false statements. Also, underline the word in a statement that causes you to decide it is false.

T   F   1. When students disagree with answers to test questions, it is wise for them to discuss disagreements with teachers in private rather than at the times answers are reviewed.

T   F   2. In the adult world, those who conform always avoid becoming deviant.

T   F   3. Polyandry is the form of polygamy in which one wife has two or more husbands.

T   F   4. The reason for underlining textbooks is that if they are underlined there is no need to make notes on the information in them.

T   F   5. We do not know for certain what causes lightning.

T   F   6. In 1932, at the height of the depression, there were more than 2 million people traveling around the country living on charitable handouts or by begging.

T   F   7. The way you communicate with others now will definitely not change much in the future.

T   F   8. Threat of imprisonment is an effective deterrent to white-collar crime.

T   F   9. One effective way to protect against rabies infection is to immunize dogs and cats by vaccinating them regularly.

T   F   10. Those who experience intense anxiety invariably separate themselves from the company of others.

T   F   11. Since women have less education than men, they earn less money than men.

T   F   12. Laws do nothing to diminish discrimination because it is not possible to legislate morality.

EXERCISE 4

TRUE-FALSE QUESTIONS

The following statements are true except for those that have an absolute determiner or that state a reason. Circle T in front of true statements and F in front of false statements. Also, underline the word in a statement that causes you to decide it is false.

T   F   1. The reason the government protects consumers is that consumer lobbyists fought for this protection.

T   F   2. A company suffers a loss when expenses exceed revenues.

T   F   3. The three main issues in the consumer movement are product performance safety, information disclosure, and environmental protection.

T   F   4. All workers prefer to hear negative comments from their supervisors than to hear no comments at all.

T   F   5. Disposable income is used to purchase necessities such as food, clothing, and shelter and for luxuries and saving.

T   F   6. Using the accepted criteria for professions, selling today is definitely a profession.

T   F   7. Markup pricing is not used often by retailers because it complicates the process of deciding what prices to charge for merchandise.

T   F   8. There are approximately 25,000 different occupations available for workers in the United States.

T   F   9. Inflation soared in the early 1970s due to policies of President Nixon.

T   F   10. There is a tendency for young people to consider as necessities many products that adults categorize as luxuries.

T   F   11. Salespeople have always enjoyed high prestige in their communities.

T   F   12. Employers frequently give preemployment physical examinations to prospective employees.

EXERCISE 5

TRUE-FALSE QUESTIONS

The following statements are true except for those that have an absolute determiner or that state a reason. Circle T in front of true statements and F in front of false statements. Also, underline the word in a statement that causes you to decide it is false.

T   F   1. A zygote is formed by the union of a male sperm and a female egg.

T   F   2. The health care system in the United States is solely disease oriented.

T   F   3. Psychologists agree that our value systems are always formed by the time we are six years old.

T   F   4. During the second trimester of pregnancy, fetal heartbeats are about 120 to 140 beats per minute compared to maternal heartbeats of 70 to 80.

T   F   5. Nimbostratus clouds in the sky indicate that it is likely to rain.

T   F   6. New Delhi is a better location for the capital of India than Calcutta because it is a better outlet for international commerce and trade.

T   F   7. The impact of the sun's energy on the earth is regulated by the ocean.

T   F   8. The right hemisphere of the brain is believed to be nonverbal.

T   F   9. Secondary syphilis lasts for about three to six months and it can be diagnosed by blood tests.

T   F   10. The reason Tropical Africa has a very good agricultural economy is that there is a very long growing season there.

T   F   11. In the 1920s, agriculture was the only sector of the American economy that was consistently healthy.

T   F   12. The reason the Urals are the traditional boundary between Europe and Asia is that the physical conditions on either side of these mountains are very different.

EXERCISE 6

TRUE-FALSE QUESTIONS

The following statements are true except for those that have an absolute determiner or that state a reason. Circle T in front of true statements and F in front of false statements. Also, underline the word in a statement that causes you to decide it is false.

T   F   1. When measuring liquid, one liter is equal to one cubic decimeter.

T   F   2. Genoa, Hamburg, and Rotterdam are the largest port cities in Italy, Germany, and Holland.

T   F   3. In colonial America, bills of exchange were good substitutes for money because their value did not depend on the reputations of the merchants who used them.

T   F   4. All lower-class people accept the success goal but reject the use of legitimate means for achieving success.

T   F   5. Since the Kinsey studies of human sexuality were done a long time ago and have been widely criticized, they have lost almost all of their value.

T   F   6. The Old Testament does not report an incident in which a woman was put to death for sleeping with a man other than her husband.

T   F   7. In the 1920s, the Congress was the only branch of the federal government that was supportive of business.

T   F   8. President Truman fired Douglas MacArthur because the general insisted on a negotiated settlement to the Korean War.

T   F   9. Of the slaves who were taken from Africa, about 6 percent of them were brought to the United States.

T   F   10. Prejudice is based solely on fear, ignorance, and cultural conditioning.

T   F   11. Married couples who do not have children tend to be happier than married couples with children.

T   F   12. The Eighteenth Amendment to the Constitution made it illegal to manufacture, transport, or sell alcoholic beverages.

23. MULTIPLE-CHOICE QUESTIONS

Multiple-choice questions are incomplete statements followed by possible ways they may be completed or they are questions followed by possible answers. For example,

1. A speech that has as its purpose to inform how to plan a successful party must use
   a. narration.
   b. persuasion.
   c. exposition.
   d. argumentation.

The incomplete statement or question that begins a multiple-choice question is called the **stem.** This is the stem:

1. A speech that has as its purpose to inform how to plan a successful party must use

The choices that are given for answers are called **options.** These are the options:

   a. narration.
   b. persuasion.
   c. exposition.
   d. argumentation.

Options are written so that one is the correct answer and the others are **distractors.** The correct answer to this question is option *c;* options *a, b,* and *d* are distractors. The correct answer is supposed to be selected by students who know it. Other students are supposed to be distracted and select one of the incorrect options—one of the distractors.

Multiple-choice questions are popular among college teachers because they can be used to test all aspects of students' knowledge and ability to reason using information they have learned. Also, when answers are recorded on answer sheets, multiple-choice tests are easy to grade. For these reasons, you may answer many multiple-choice questions during your college career.

317

ELIMINATE THE DISTRACTORS

The basic strategy for answering a multiple-choice question is to eliminate the distractors.

Multiple-choice questions are prepared by first writing a stem and the correct answer. For instance,

1. A speech that has as its purpose to inform how to plan a successful party must use
   a. exposition.
   b.
   c.
   d.

The question-writer then fills in the distractors and decides whether to locate the correct answer following *a, b, c,* or *d.*

The correct way to answer a multiple-choice question is to analyze it for the purpose of eliminating the distractors. A question-writer includes distractors to deceive students who do not know or who are uncertain about the correct answer. When you answer multiple-choice questions, consider the method that is used to prepare them, and eliminate the distractors to select the option that is the correct answer.

ABSOLUTE DETERMINERS

Chapter 22 explains that absolute determiners tend to be found in false true-false questions; in multiple-choice questions, absolute determiners tend to be in distractors. Circle the letter in front of the correct answer to the following question.

2. Which of the following is true about LCU scores?
   a. People with lower scores generally have better health.
   b. People with higher scores always have better health.
   c. Losing a loved one never raises LCU scores.
   d. LCU scores are invariably related to career problems.

In options *b, c,* and *d,* the words *always, never,* and *invariably* suggest they are distractors. In option *a,* the word *generally* suggests it is the correct answer, and it is.

UNFAMILIAR TERMS OR PHRASES

Unfamiliar terms or phrases are often included in distractors. Circle the letter in front of the correct answer to the following question.

3. Freud believed that dreams
   a. always have one clear meaning.
   b. can be interpreted on different levels.
   c. invariably predict future events.
   d. reveal various synergetic dissonances.

You should have eliminated option *d* as a distractor because it includes the unfamiliar phrase "synergetic dissonances." You should also have eliminated options *a* and *c* because they contain the absolute determiners *always* and *invariably*. Option *b* is the correct answer.

Some students select distractors with unfamiliar terms or phrases because they reason "If I don't know it, it must be right." However, if they have studied for tests, it is not likely that correct answers will include terms or phrases that are unfamiliar to them.

JOKES AND INSULTS

Options that are jokes or insults are usually distractors. Circle the letter in front of the correct answer to the following question.

4. A common reason students give for dropping out of college is that they
   a. find that other students have inferior ability.
   b. don't like their teachers' abusive language.
   c. lack the desire to become educated people.
   d. decide that something else interests them more.

The statements in options *a*, *b*, and *c* are either ridiculous or insulting; you should have eliminated them and selected option *d* as the correct answer.

HIGH AND LOW NUMBERS

When options are series of numbers that go from high to low, the high and low numbers tend to be distractors. Circle the letter in front of the correct answer to the following question.

5. Approximately what percentage of the population of the United States has been found to have some degree of mental impairment?
   a. 50 percent
   b. 65 percent
   c. 80 percent
   d. 95 percent

You should have eliminated the high and low numbers in options *a* and *d* as distractors and made your choice between options *b* and *c*. According to the source upon which this question is based, the correct answer is option *c*.

"ALL OF THE ABOVE"

When "all of the above" is an option, it tends to be the correct answer. Circle the letter in front of the correct answer to the following question.

6. Silver is used to make
   a. jewelry.
   b. knives and forks.
   c. film for photography.
   d. all of the above

If you know that silver is used to make jewelry and knives and forks, you must select "all of the above" as the correct answer even if you do not know that it is also used to make film for photography. If you select option *a*, you do not include knives and forks; if you select option *b*, you do not include jewelry. You must select option *d* to include options *a* and *b* in your answer. Option *d* is the correct answer.

MORE COMPLETE OR INCLUSIVE STATEMENTS

More complete or inclusive statements tend to be correct answers. Circle the letter in front of the correct answer to the following question.

7. Weight is likely to be most variable for a group of
   a. men who are football linebackers.
   b. women who are ballet dancers.
   c. people who are jockeys.
   d. people who are college students.

Football linebackers tend to include only heavy people; women ballet dancers and jockeys tend to include only light people. College students, on the other hand, include people who are heavy, light, and medium in weight. The statement in option *d* is more inclusive; option *d* is the correct answer.

TWO SIMILAR-LOOKING ANSWERS

When two options are similar looking, the correct answer is often one of the two similar-looking options. Circle the letter in front of the correct answer to the following question.

8. In the brain, language functions are associated mainly with the
   a. left hemisphere.
   b. right hemisphere.
   c. cerebellum.
   d. corpus callosum.

You should have eliminated options *c* and *d* as distractors and made your choice between the two similar-looking options—options *a* and *b*. Option *a* is the correct answer.

ANSWERING MULTIPLE-CHOICE QUESTIONS

When you answer multiple-choice questions, make it your goal to eliminate the distractors that question-writers include to deceive students who do not know or who are uncertain about answers. Also, keep the following outline in mind.

Clues for Multiple-Choice Questions

I. These types of options tend to be distractors
   A. Ones with absolute determiners
   B. Unfamiliar terms or phrases
   C. Jokes and insults
   D. High and low numbers
II. These types of options tend to be correct answers
   A. More complete or inclusive statements
   B. "All of the above"
   C. One of two similar-looking answers

The following exercises provide practice for learning how to select more correct answers to multiple-choice questions. The answers to the questions in the exercises are correct according to the sources upon which they are based. Use what you learn by doing the exercises to answer more multiple-choice questions correctly on college tests.

EXERCISE 1

MULTIPLE-CHOICE QUESTIONS

Use the clues summarized on page 321 to select the correct answers to the following questions.

_____ 1. The most frequent criticism of the behavioral approach to personality is that it
   a. is never supported by scientific research.
   b. gives a mechanistic view of human behavior.
   c. attends only to past events and experiences.
   d. is always of immeasurable practical value.

_____ 2. Examine this: /p/. This represents
   a. the sound of "p."
   b. a homograph.
   c. graphemic notation.
   d. morphemic code.

_____ 3. After the Civil War, Reconstruction legislatures in the South were successful in
   a. making reforms in the prison system.
   b. integrating the public school system.
   c. improving facilities for the handicapped.
   d. achieving all of the foregoing.

_____ 4. The major problem with selling beverages in throwaway cans is that these types of containers
   a. create costly litter and garbage disposal problems.
   b. are expensive to produce and to dispose of.
   c. utilize a great deal of increasingly costly metal.
   d. require much expensive energy to produce.

_____ 5. A dietitian studied the eating habits of a group of children over a ten-year period. The type of research done by the dietitian is called
   a. latitudinal.
   b. longitudinal.
   c. child-centered.
   d. comparative.

_____ 6. The syntax of language includes
   a. phrases.
   b. clauses.
   c. sentences.
   d. phrases, clauses, and sentences.

_____   7. Studies of embryos have found that the fetus usually begins
             to move as early as
             a. 8 weeks following conception.
             b. 16 weeks following conception.
             c. 24 weeks following conception.
             d. 32 weeks following conception.

_____   8. In medieval times, women of nobility
             a. always married men younger than themselves.
             b. invariably joined religious orders.
             c. managed households when husbands were absent.
             d. pursued only domestic responsibilities.

_____   9. The median is a measure that is similar to
             a. the average.
             b. a coefficient.
             c. a histogram.
             d. the skewness.

_____ 10. Before 1860 in the United States, there were improvements
             in all the following *except*
             a. roads.
             b. farms.
             c. bridges.
             d. telephones.

_____ 11. The burning of fossil fuel is causing a build-up of carbon
             dioxide that may eventually
             a. affect the global radiation balance.
             b. create a warming trend on earth.
             c. irreversibly alter world ecosystems.
             d. all of the above

_____ 12. The number of words per minute in a radio commercial
             should not exceed
             a. 100.
             b. 150.
             c. 200.
             d. 250.

_____ 13. The loss of all sensation in the hand would most likely
             result from
             a. aphasia.
             b. hallucinations.
             c. damage to afferent spinal nerves.
             d. damage to efferent spinal nerves.

EXERCISE 2

MULTIPLE-CHOICE QUESTIONS

Use the clues summarized on page 321 to select the correct answers to the following questions.

_____ 1. In the colonial American family, the status of women was
   a. better than that of American men.
   b. better than that of British women.
   c. lower than that of slaves and servants.
   d. of no interest to American men.

_____ 2. Most psychologists agree that
   a. institutionalized children never succeed in life.
   b. fatherless boys always become homosexuals.
   c. unloved infants usually have personality problems.
   d. those abused as children always abuse their children.

_____ 3. The biosphere consists of
   a. air above the earth.
   b. the earth's surface.
   c. bodies of water on earth.
   d. air, earth surface, and water bodies.

_____ 4. Approximately what percentage of drinkers in the United States become alcoholics?
   a. 5 percent
   b. 10 percent
   c. 20 percent
   d. 25 percent

_____ 5. Members of one's family of orientation are
   a. blood relatives.
   b. affinal relatives.
   c. tertiary relatives.
   d. misogynistic relatives.

_____ 6. What is the relationship between finger ability and finger workload on a standard typewriter keyboard?
   a. .80
   b. .60
   c. .40
   d. .20

_____ 7. Mentally healthy people
            a. never change their goals.
            b. are always happy when alone.
            c. are sometimes afraid or anxious.
            d. never examine their mistakes.

_____ 8. Most Jewish immigrants to the United States came from
            a. Western Europe.
            b. Eastern Europe.
            c. the Middle East.
            d. Africa and Asia.

_____ 9. Disagreements about money in marriage result because a marriage partner is struggling for
            a. power.
            b. self-esteem.
            c. love or appreciation.
            d. any of the above

_____ 10. Ultraviolet light is damaging to microbial cells chiefly because of its effects on
            a. DNA.
            b. RNA.
            c. cell walls.
            d. ribosomes.

_____ 11. "Thwart" means about the same as
            a. stop.
            b. icon.
            c. flout.
            d. abut.

_____ 12. Refuge to victims of persecution has been given by
            a. France.
            b. Switzerland.
            c. Great Britain.
            d. all of the above

_____ 13. Spherical bacteria that usually grow in chains are called
            a. diplococci.
            b. vibrios.
            c. staphylococci.
            d. streptococci.

_____ 14. Our sexual attitudes develop
            a. solely from what we learn from our parents.
            b. from positive and negative sexual experiences.
            c. through having positive sexual experiences.
            d. through having negative sexual experiences.

EXERCISE 3

MULTIPLE-CHOICE QUESTIONS

Use the clues summarized on page 321 to select the correct answers to the following questions.

_____ 1. The difficulty of reading material is sometimes estimated by studying the lengths of
a. words.
b. sentences.
c. paragraphs.
d. words and sentences.

_____ 2. Educators refer to individuals of extremely low intelligence as
a. idiots.
b. morons.
c. imbeciles.
d. totally dependent.

_____ 3. The perceived size of a car driving away down a straight highway
a. depends solely on its distance from the viewer.
b. remains the same whether it is close or far away.
c. is totally unaffected by prior learning.
d. is invariably a function of retinal articulation.

_____ 4. In the 1840s the great potato famine in Ireland resulted from
a. unusually wet weather.
b. unusually dry weather.
c. a sudden growth in population.
d. a disease that killed potatoes.

_____ 5. The word "misfortune" and the phrase "it's more fun" are most similar with regard to their
a. syntax.
b. letters.
c. phonemes.
d. morphemes.

_____ 6. During the last 40 years of the 1800s, the value of consumer goods
a. remained constant.
b. almost doubled.
c. almost tripled.
d. almost quadrupled.

_____ 7. Student speeches are most impressive when the information in them is based on
     a. two authoritative sources.
     b. a variety of authoritative sources.
     c. authoritative sources and original thought.
     d. exclusively on opinions and original thought.

_____ 8. Artists of the romantic period
     a. revolted against techniques of classicism.
     b. despised and rejected creativity.
     c. were completely disinterested in classical art.
     d. were more interested in love-making than art.

_____ 9. Napoleon was admired by French
     a. peasants.
     b. soldiers.
     c. businessmen.
     d. all of the above

_____ 10. Genocide, the mass killing of a national or ethnic group,
     a. is reported in the Bible.
     b. has been committed only by whites.
     c. has never occurred in the twentieth century.
     d. is found always in Eastern countries.

_____ 11. A woman has an anxiety reaction that causes her to worry unduly about her cat. This worry interrupts her life so that she does not leave home more than twice a week. This woman is
     a. obsessive-compulsive.
     b. a dipsomaniac.
     c. somewhat abnormal.
     d. a fruitcake.

_____ 12. Brazil was colonized by
     a. Indians.
     b. North Americans.
     c. a heterogeneous group of Europeans.
     d. a homogeneous group of Europeans.

_____ 13. Some societies attempt to keep romantic love from influencing people, whom they marry by
     a. arranging child marriages.
     b. the use of chaperones.
     c. ridiculing romantic love.
     d. all of the above

| EXERCISE 4 |

MULTIPLE-CHOICE QUESTIONS

Use the clues summarized on page 321 to select the correct answers to the following questions.

_____ 1. Some bacterial cells secrete viscous envelopes, which often indicate that they can produce disease. This envelope is called a
a. pilus.
b. mesosome.
c. capsule.
d. nucleoid.

_____ 2. Children learn about the values of their society from
a. their parents.
b. their teachers.
c. the mass media.
d. all of the above

_____ 3. Between 1870 and 1910 American women gained greater independence and, as a result, more of them
a. divorced their husbands.
b. became prostitutes.
c. quit their jobs.
d. committed suicide.

_____ 4. When adding suffixes that begin with vowels to words that end with *e*
a. always drop the *e.*
b. never drop the *e.*
c. usually drop the *e.*
d. always change *e* to *i.*

_____ 5. Partners in a marriage are likely to be similar in
a. height and weight.
b. hair and skin color.
c. general health.
d. size, coloring, and health.

_____ 6. Which of the following statements about ability is true?
a. People differ in their types of abilities.
b. All people are equal in their abilities.
c. There is only one basic type of ability.
d. Ability never changes over one's lifetime.

_____ 7. All known viroids are
       a. plant parasites.
       b. animal parasites.
       c. nonpathogenic.
       d. single NRAs.

_____ 8. Studies of workers' attitudes have found that
       a. most workers feel they should have better jobs.
       b. many would rather have better jobs than more pay.
       c. workers are motivated by conflicting drives.
       d. all of the above

_____ 9. The endomorphic body type is characterized by
       a. quite noticeable softness.
       b. a roundness of appearance.
       c. a tendency toward shortness.
       d. softness, shortness, and roundness.

_____ 10. On the average, what percentage of the retail price of a
product pays for its distribution to stores?
       a. 6 to 9 percent
       b. 19 to 22 percent
       c. 33 to 36 percent
       d. 47 to 58 percent

_____ 11. More doctors are males than females probably because
       a. women do not want prestigious jobs.
       b. of established occupational expectations.
       c. males make better doctors than females.
       d. most women "crack" easily under pressure.

         12. Mary runs three miles every day because it makes her feel
good about herself. She is motivated by
       a. an extrinsic reward.
       b. an intrinsic reward.
       c. a psychological need.
       d. peer-group pressure.

_____ 13. The base used in most logarithmic calculations is
       a. 1.
       b. 10.
       c. 100.
       d. 1000.

_____ 14. The abbreviation SEM refers to a type of
       a. serological technique.
       b. anaerobic bacteria.
       c. microscope.
       d. avian embryo.

EXERCISE 5

MULTIPLE-CHOICE QUESTIONS

Use the clues summarized on page 321 to select the correct answers to the following questions.

_____ 1. The people who left the Old World to settle in what is now the United States did this because they
  a. hoped they would find gold.
  b. wanted to spread Christianity.
  c. wanted to acquire land.
  d. all of the above.

_____ 2. Products are
  a. goods.
  b. services.
  c. ideas.
  d. goods, services, and ideas.

_____ 3. How many English colonies were established in North America in the seventeenth century?
  a. 2
  b. 3
  c. 12
  d. 13

_____ 4. Which of the following statements is _false_ with regard to vitamins?
  a. Tomatoes are a source of vitamin C.
  b. They make people more beautiful or handsome.
  c. Not all known vitamins are needed for health.
  d. Grown men have the least need for vitamin D.

_____ 5. Studies of the relationship between intellectual ability and occupational choice have demonstrated
  a. a range of intelligence among workers in a job.
  b. that the two factors are invariably unrelated.
  c. all unskilled laborers have inferior intelligence.
  d. every job has clear-cut intellectual requirements.

_____ 6. The term "competence," in biology, is related to
  a. transformation.
  b. transduction.
  c. the operon model.
  d. none of these

_____ 7. The objective of learning how to play the piano while sing-
ing occurs in the
a. motor domain.
b. cognitive domain.
c. affective domain.
d. motor and cognitive domain.

_____ 8. Even if no special buffering agents were added to a nutrient,
what substances in the medium would serve as a buffer?
a. lipids
b. purines
c. proteins
d. nucleic acids

_____ 9. The conscious mind
a. evaluates everything it accepts.
b. can help us to succeed or fail.
c. acts only on positive orders.
d. never changes after age twenty.

_____ 10. Pesticides are potentially harmful to life on earth because
they
a. do not disappear from the environment.
b. are passed through the ecosystem.
c. may concentrate in the food chain.
d. all of the above

_____ 11. The first book published in the New World was printed in
a. Peru in 1473.
b. New York in 1486.
c. Mexico in 1539.
d. Massachusetts in 1626.

_____ 12. On June 21, the sun is found directly over the
a. Tropic of Cancer.
b. Tropic of Capricorn.
c. Equator.
d. North Pole.

_____ 13. In R factors, R stands for
a. RNA.
b. ribosomes.
c. resistance.
d. rhizopods.

_____ 14. In the United States, most women deliver babies in
a. taxicabs.
b. hospitals.
c. airports.
d. abortion clinics.

24. MATCHING QUESTIONS

Matching questions present two lists of items and require test-takers to associate items in one list with items in the other list. For example, the following matching question requires matching operas and their composers.

_____ 1. *Dido and Aeneas*   a. Puccini

_____ 2. *Don Giovanni*   b. Mozart

                                     c. Monteverdi
_____ 3. *La Tosca*
                                     d. Purcell
_____ 4. *Tristan and Isolde*   e. Wagner

_____ 5. *Orfeo*

A question similar to this one may be asked in a music appreciation course.

CROSS OUT MATCHED ITEMS

The basic strategy for answering matching questions is to use one list as the starting place for making all matches and to cross out items as they are matched. When the statements in one list are longer than items in the other list, use the list with the longer statements as the starting place to make all matches.

It is extremely difficult to guess correct answers to properly written matching questions. For instance, if you guess at the composers of the operas, you are not likely to guess more than one correct answer.

However, when matching questions are poorly written, logical clues may be used to guess answers. Use logical clues to guess the answers to the poorly written matching question in Figure 24.1 (page 334) before reading the following explanations of the answers to it.

FIGURE 24.1

A matching question

Psychology

Match items in the second column with items in the first column, using items in the second column one time only.

_____ 1. located in the ear	a. James-Lange Theory
_____ 2. behaviorist	b. parapraxis
_____ 3. childhood crisis	c. organ of Corti
_____ 4. measures capacity to learn	d. James B. Watson
	e. convergent thinking
_____ 5. tally of scores	f. to trust others
_____ 6. study of an individual	g. frequency distribution
_____ 7. feelings are the result of emotional behavior	h. ideographic study
	i. aptitude test
_____ 8. leading to one answer	

---

1. The ear is part of the body and organs are located in the body (c).
2. The suffix -*ist* indicates that *behaviorist* refers to a person, and James B. Watson is a person (d).
3. It makes sense that children must learn to trust (f).
4. Tests measure abilities or learning (i).
5. A tally is used to keep records of amounts and frequency refers to amounts (g).
6. The word *study* appears in only one item in the list on the right (h).
7. This statement sounds more like a theory than any other statement in list on the left (a).
8. Thinking (e) leads to answers, and there is no logical reason to match this item with *parapraxis* (b).

ANSWERING MATCHING QUESTIONS

When you answer matching questions, use one list as the starting place for making all matches and cross out items as you match them. When statements in one list are longer than items in the other list, use the list with the longer statements as the starting place for making matches. Also, use logical clues to guess at correct answers.

The following exercises provide practice in answering matching questions; the answers to the questions are correct according to the sources upon which they are based. Use what you learn by doing the exercises to answer more matching questions correctly on college tests.

EXERCISE 1

MATCHING QUESTIONS

It is extremely difficult to guess correct answers to well-written matching questions. If you are unfamiliar with the facts tested by the following question, you should make no more than one correct match by guessing at answers. In order to understand how difficult it is to guess the answers to matching questions, match the items in the right column to the names in the left column. Use all but one of the items in the right column, and use an item one time only.

_____ 1. Democritus	a.	Law of Triads
_____ 2. Van Helmont	b.	Naming of cathode rays
_____ 3. Proust	c.	Conceived of the atom
_____ 4. Berzelius	d.	Discovered sulfanilamide
_____ 5. Döbereiner	e.	Discovered DDT
_____ 6. Zeidler	f.	Law of Definite Composition
_____ 7. Gelmo	g.	Discovered element 106
_____ 8. Urey	h.	First atomic pile
_____ 9. Goldstein	i.	Modern symbols for elements
_____ 10. Fermi	j.	Discovered deuterium
	k.	Foundations of chemical physiology

EXERCISE 2

MATCHING QUESTIONS

Use logical clues to locate the correct answers to the following poorly written matching question.

_____ 1. Indentured servant

_____ 2. Largest city on eve of the Revolution

_____ 3. He established the American factory system

_____ 4. She advocated better care for the insane

_____ 5. State where Prohibition was strongest

_____ 6. Number of Southern slaves in 1860

_____ 7. Painters of American life

_____ 8. The Fourteenth Amendment

_____ 9. Contribution of black musicians

_____ 10. Needed for frontier farming

_____ 11. Describes U.S. policy toward Indians

_____ 12. Average yearly income in 1890

_____ 13. Percent of population living in cities in 1910

_____ 14. Popular nineteenth-century entertainment

_____ 15. Year the Great Depression started

_____ 16. President Roosevelt's solution to the Depression

a. Maine

b. Made blacks citizens

c. Thirty-eight

d. Barbed wire

e. Temporary laborer

f. Currier and Ives

g. 1929

h. $486

i. Samuel Slater

j. 4,000,000

k. Dorothea Dix

l. Duplicity

m. Melodrama

n. The New Deal

o. Jazz

p. Philadelphia

© 1984 by Houghton Mifflin Company

25. FILL-IN
QUESTIONS

Fill-in questions are statements with deleted portions that test-takers must supply. For instance,

> There are _____ morphemes in the word "unthankful."

The correct answer is "three"; the morphemes are *un-*, *thank*, and *-ful.*

DECIDE THE TYPE OF ANSWER

The basic strategy for answering a fill-in question is to decide the type of answer that is wanted and to give that type of answer. For instance, the type of answer wanted for the question about "unthankful" is a number such as "two," "three," or "four." What type of answer is wanted for the following question?

> After reading _____ , President Theodore Roosevelt ordered an investigation of the meat-packing industry.

You should have decided that the type of answer wanted for this question is the name of a book, magazine, newspaper, or other written material. However, it is extremely difficult to guess the answer to the question; it is a book entitled *The Jungle.*

When you are uncertain what type of an answer is wanted, ask a teacher for clarification. For instance,

> The Boer War was fought in _____ .

If you are uncertain what type of an answer is wanted for this question, you might ask a history teacher: "Do you want me to give the place where the war was fought or the time when it was fought?" Prepare your question carefully. Don't, for example, point to a question and ask a teacher "What do you mean?" Request clarification by asking questions that help teachers understand why you are confused.

LOOK FOR THE "AN" CLUE

Sometimes the word "an" just before a write-on line is a clue to the correct answer. For instance,

Compliments satisfy an _____ need.

The word "an" just before the write-on line suggests that the correct answer is a word that begins with a vowel sound such as those represented by *a, e, i, o,* and *u.* Those who have studied human needs know they are of five basic types: physiological, safety, belongingness, esteem, and self-actualization. The correct answer is *esteem.* However, few instructors give this clue to answers. The "an" clue is usually eliminated by writing *a(an), a(n),* or *a/an* instead of *an.*

ANSWERING FILL-IN QUESTIONS

When you answer a fill-in question, decide what type of an answer is wanted and give that type of answer. Also, remember that the word *an* just before a write-on line may be a clue that the answer is a word that begins with a vowel sound, such as those represented by *a, e, i, o,* and *u.*

The following exercises provide practice for answering fill-in questions; the answers to the questions are correct according to the sources upon which they are based. Use what you learn by doing the exercises to write more correct answers to fill-in questions on college tests.

EXERCISE 1

FILL-IN QUESTIONS

The basic strategy for answering fill-in questions is to decide the type of answer that is wanted. Decide the types of answers wanted for the following questions, in the way illustrated in the first question.

College is attended by ___a number___ percent of American young people.

1. It was _____ who said, "A man with God is always in the majority."

2. It was so they could read _____ that colonial children were taught reading.

3. It is among the _____ that the practice of wife-lending has been reported most often.

4. Until _____ slavery existed in some form in the world.

5. A _____ waiting period for obtaining a marriage license is required by most states.

6. _____ was the first institution of higher learning to admit women as students.

7. It is to purchase their children a _____ that is the greatest motivation for most middle-class parents to save money.

8. There are about _____ unmarried adults in the United States.

9. An acre of government land cost _____ beginning in 1820.

10. In the nineteenth century, _____ and teaching were the most acceptable occupations for genteel women.

11. It was in _____ that the most serious northern draft riots took place in 1863.

12. A(n) _____ killed 300,000 people in Bangladesh on November 13, 1970.

13. One belief of _____ is that life in all its forms is an aspect of the divine.

14. _____ was the first chief justice of the United States.

EXERCISE 2

FILL-IN QUESTIONS

The following questions are based on information in Chapters 21–25. Write as many correct answers as you can without looking for the answers in this book.

1. Students should guess about _____ correct answers when they guess at the answers to twenty true-false questions.

2. Students should guess about _____ correct answers when they guess at the answers to twenty multiple-choice questions with the choices *a, b, c,* and *d.*

3. "Assume it is _____ ," is the basic strategy for answering a true-false question.

4. "All kids love candy," contains a(n) _____ .

5. The word "reason," "because," or "_____" may indicate that a reason is stated in a true-false question.

6. True-false questions tend to be false when they state reasons or when they include a(n) _____ .

7. The statement or question that begins a multiple-choice question is called the _____ .

8. The words or statements that follow the letters *a, b, c,* and *d* in a multiple-choice question are called _____ .

9. The words or statements that follow the letters *a, b, c,* and *d* in a multiple-choice question are either a correct answer or they are a(n) _____ .

10. A multiple-choice question is prepared by first writing a(n) _____ and by then writing _____ .

11. The correct answer is *a* about _____ times on a properly prepared multiple-choice test that consists of forty questions with the options *a, b, c,* and *d.*

12. "Eliminate the _____ ," is the basic strategy for answering a multiple-choice question.

13. Jokes and insults tend to be _____ in multiple-choice questions.

14. "All of the above" tends to be a(n) _____ in a multiple-choice question.

15. Unfamiliar terms tend to be _____ in multiple-choice questions.

16. One of two similar-looking answers tend to be a(n) _____ in a multiple-choice question.

17. High or low numbers tend to be _____ in a multiple-choice question.

18. A more complete answer tends to be a(n) _____ in a multiple-choice question.

19. The basic strategy for answering matching questions is to use _____ as the starting place to make all matches and to _____ items as they are matched.

20. "Decide what _____ of answer is wanted," is the basic strategy for answering a fill-in question.

26. ESSAY QUESTIONS

Essay questions require written answers that are usually a paragraph or more in length. They are answered by studying in the way explained in Chapters 16–20, by planning test-taking time using methods explained on pages 302–304, and by using the suggestions in this chapter.

1. Understand direction words.
2. Answer all parts of questions.
3. Write well-organized answers.
4. Write complete answers.
5. Proofread answers.

Read the directions for the essay test in Figure 26.1. Notice that students are to answer only three of the five questions; if they answer more than three questions, only the first three will be graded (see pages 301–302).

Answers to essay questions are usually written in **bluebooks,** which are small booklets that contain lined paper. At one time the covers of these booklets were always blue, but today covers of bluebooks may be blue, yellow, pink, green, or some other color.

Some teachers give take-home or open-book tests. A **take-home test** may be test questions that students actually answer "at home" or test questions that they study "at home" but answer in class. The questions on take-home tests are usually more difficult than the questions on tests students see for the first time in class. Also, teachers tend to grade answers to take-home test questions strictly.

An **open-book test** is a test during which students may refer to textbooks, and sometimes to notes, as they answer questions. The term "open-book" suggests students may copy answers to test questions from books; however, open-book tests seldom include questions for which answers can be copied. Whatever benefit students gain by referring to books is directly related to how thoroughly they studied. Prepare for an open-book test just as you would for any other type of test.

Use the suggestions that follow, together with the suggestions in Chapter 21, when you answer essay questions.

American History Test

Write your answers to the following questions in the booklet which you have been given. Answer any two of the 25-point questions and one of the 50-point questions. You have sixty minutes to write your answers.

Answer Two (25 points each)

1. Why did the American colonists place strong emphasis on the importance and value of work?
2. Compare white and black servitude in colonial America.
3. Discuss how Benjamin Franklin was influenced by the religious revival.

Answer One (50 points)

4. Compare the class structure in colonial America with the class structure in contemporary America and explain why these two class structures are similar or why they are different.
5. Discuss the motives of those who emigrated to colonial America and compare their motives to the motives of those who emigrate to America today.

FIGURE 26.1

Essay test for an American history course

UNDERSTAND DIRECTION WORDS

The first step in answering essay questions is to interpret the meanings of direction words correctly. **Direction words** are words in essay questions that inform students what type of answers to write. Direction words are italicized in the following questions.

Compare white and black servitude in colonial America.

Discuss how Benjamin Franklin was influenced by the religious revival.

Explain the success of Eliza Pinckney.

Before taking an essay test, learn the meanings of all the direction words in Figure 26.2 on page 344. Pay special attention to the often-misinterpreted meanings of *compare*, *criticize*, and *justify* and notice that *describe*, *explain*, and *illustrate* have two meanings.

FIGURE 26.2

Meanings of direction words

Direction Words	Meanings	Sample Essay Questions
Discuss	Write as much as you can.	Discuss test-taking skills.
Describe	Write as much as you can.	Describe early-American family life.
	Write about the subject so it can be visualized.	Describe a nutritious diet.
Explain	Write as much as you can.	Explain totalitarianism.
	Discuss reasons.	Explain why we entered World War II.
Compare	Discuss similarities and differences.	Compare democracy and communism.
Contrast	Discuss differences.	Contrast Catholicism and Protestantism.
Criticize or Evaluate	Discuss good and bad points and conclude if it is more good or bad.	Criticize (or evaluate) the death sentence.
Justify	Discuss good and bad points and conclude that it is good.	Justify U.S. expenditures on military defense.
Diagram	Draw a picture and label its parts.	Diagram the parts of the human ear.
Illustrate	Draw a picture and label its parts.	Illustrate the parts of the human eye.
	Give a long, written example.	Illustrate the use of the SQ3R study formula.
Enumerate	Make a numbered list.	Enumerate good and bad listening habits.
List	Make a numbered list.	List good and bad manners for business settings.
Outline	Make a numbered or well-organized list.	Outline the basic test-taking strategies.
Summarize	Briefly state.	Summarize the accomplishments of President Truman.
Define	Give the meaning.	Define "psychopath."
Relate	Discuss the connection between (or among) them.	Relate television viewing to reading habits.
Trace	Discuss in a logical or chronological sequence.	Trace the path by which blood flows through the human body.

ANSWER ALL PARTS OF QUESTIONS

Failure to answer all parts of questions is a major reason for essay test grades that are lower than they should be. The first of the following questions has one part, but the second question has two parts.

Explain the functions of the endocrine glands.

Explain the functions of the endocrine glands and make a diagram that shows the locations of these glands in the human body.

The answer to the second question must include everything that is included in the answer to the first question *and* a diagram of the type illustrated in Figure 26.3.

When essay questions are clearly written, it is usually easy to find all the parts of them. For instance,

Explain five propaganda techniques and give an example of each of them.

Clearly, answers to this question must include (1) explanations of five propaganda techniques and (2) examples of how each of the techniques is used.

Unfortunately, essay questions are not always clearly written. When you cannot understand an essay question, ask the teacher who wrote it for clarification. It is appropriate for you to assume that your teachers want you to understand their test questions.

FIGURE 26.3

A diagram for an answer to an essay question

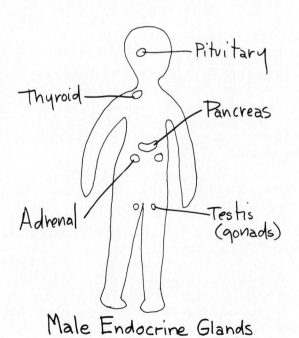

WRITE WELL-ORGANIZED ANSWERS

After you have interpreted the direction words and identified all parts of an essay question, prepare to write a well-organized answer to it. Well-organized answers are written by planning the major points, by writing clear introductions, and by making the major points stand out clearly (see Figure 26.4 on page 347 and Figure 26.5 on page 348).

Plan the Major Points

Sometimes the major points to include in an answer are stated in an essay question. For instance,

> Explain the differences among the following four types of conflict: approach-approach, avoidance-avoidance, approach-avoidance, and double approach-avoidance.

The major points to include in an answer are stated in the question; they are the four types of conflict.

However, major points for answers are often not stated in questions. Notice in Figure 26.4 that the question does not state the four types of conflict; to answer the question, students must recall how many types of conflict there are and their names.

It is often helpful to make lists of major points before writing answers. The lists may be written on the back of a page on which test questions are printed or on a page in the back of a bluebook.

Write Clear Introductions

The introduction for an essay answer should be a summary of the answer. After deciding what the major points will be, summarize them in the introduction for the answer. The introduction to the answer in Figure 26.4 summarizes the four major points in the answer.

An answer may have only one major point to state in an introduction. For instance,

> Explain whether you believe that the positive values of the American people outweigh their negative values or that their negative values outweigh their positive values.

Notice in Figure 26.5 that the introduction for the answer to this question states: "As an American, I would like to believe that our positive values outweigh our negative values, but I cannot." Another student may have written, "The positive values of the American people clearly outweigh their negative values." Whichever point of view is taken, it should be clearly stated in an introduction. Other statements in answers should explain the reasoning behind the position stated in the introduction.

<u>Question</u>

Explain the types of conflicts that people often experience and how each
type of conflict is ordinarily resolved.

<u>Answer</u>

The four types of conflict that people commonly experience are the
approach-approach, avoidance-avoidance, approach-avoidance, and the
double approach-avoidance conflict.

1. The approach-approach <u>conflict</u> exists when a person must choose between
two attractive possibilities (a vacation in England or a vacation in
France). The conflict is resolved when one possibility becomes more attractive
than the other. If a vacation in France will include visits with friends and the trip
to England will not, then France may become the more attractive choice.

2. The avoidance-avoidance <u>conflict</u> exists when a person must choose between
two <u>un</u>attractive possibilities (having a tooth pulled or having root canal work
done on it). The conflict is resolved when one possibility becomes less attractive
than the other. If having a tooth pulled becomes more unattractive, then root canal
work may become the more attractive choice.

3. The <u>approach-avoidance conflict</u> exists when one possibility is both attractive and
unattractive (dessert tastes good, but it's fattening). This type of conflict often
causes unhappiness because it is often not resolved. For example, some people
are unhappy throughout their lives because they must choose whether to eat
fattening food or to be healthfully slim.

4. The <u>double approach-avoidance conflict</u> exists when two possibilities are both
attractive and unattractive. For example, a man must choose between getting
married and remaining single. Marriage is attractive to him because it will provide
companionship, but it is unattractive to him because it will create many financial
responsibilities; the single life is attractive to him because he has few financial
responsibilities, but it is unattractive to him because he is lonely without
companionship. This type of conflict frequently has no resolution. For example, many
of the people who marry later get a divorce.

FIGURE 26.4

An essay question and
answer

<u>Question</u>

Explain whether you believe that the positive values of the American people outweigh their negative values or that their negative values outweigh their positive values.

<u>Answer</u>

As an American, I would like to believe that our positive values outweigh our negative values, but I cannot.

Admirable traits of Americans cannot be denied. However, over the years we have lost many of the qualities for which we were once admired. We used to be willing to delay gratification; our grandparents worked hard and saved their money so that they might eventually own a home or send their children to college. Today, the saving habits of Americans are shameful. We spend our money and use credit to acquire gadgets, and we consume more of the earth's resources per person than any other country. At the same time, most of the people in the world are suffering poverty and millions are dying from starvation.

But I believe that our greatest failing is to care for the needs of all the members of our society. The cost of health care is so outrageously high that a short stay in a hospital can put a family in debt for years. We do not systematically provide for the health care of our people. Also, most of us are forced to retire at age sixty-five with an insufficient income to maintain a reasonable standard of living. Millions of Americans are inadequately fed, clothed, housed, and otherwise cared for. Even the education of our citizens has an increasingly low priority; when cities must cut budgets, schools often suffer first and most.

I believe that our unwillingness to care for the basic needs of large numbers of our citizens is an overwhelming weakness in our value system. Until our country adopts policies that show we respect each member of the society, I must conclude that our negative values outweigh our positive values.

FIGURE 26.5

An essay question and answer

Make Major Points Stand Out

Notice in Figure 26.4 that major points are numbered and underlined to make them stand out clearly and that in Figure 26.5 paragraphs begin with sentences that summarize the thoughts developed in them.

When major points stand out clearly, it is easier to proofread answers for completeness and it is easier for teachers to grade them. If you make it easier for teachers to grade your answers, they may show their appreciation by giving your answers higher grades than they give for answers that are written in ways that make it difficult to find major points in them.

WRITE COMPLETE ANSWERS

Answers to essay questions should include as much relevant information as possible. One way to write complete answers is to write to an uninformed reader; the other is to write more than you think you need to write.

Write to an Uninformed Reader

If you tend to write answers to essay questions that are too short, write them thinking they will be read by a friend or relative rather than by a teacher. The thought that your answers will be read by a person who is uninformed about them may help you to write more complete answers and to explain your thoughts more carefully.

This method was used to write the answers in Figure 26.4 and Figure 26.5. The person who wrote them had his teen-age sister in mind. He believed that if his answers were complete enough for his teen-age sister to understand, they would also be complete enough to satisfy his instructor. Write to a friend or relative, rather than to a teacher, when you answer essay questions.

Write More Than You Think You Need to Write

The students who receive the highest grades for essay answers are the ones who include the most relevant information in them. It is almost always better to include too many facts and details than to include too few. Whenever you are uncertain whether to include a relevant piece of information or example, include it.

Sometimes teachers mislead students by saying they want short answers when they mean that they do not want to read long-winded answers filled with irrelevant comments. Instructors want to read answers with statements, facts, details, and examples that answer questions. They give the highest grades for answers that have the most relevant information in them. When teachers really want short answers, they give an instruction such as this one: "I will give a grade of F for any answer that is longer than 150 words." Include all relevant information in your answers unless a teacher tells you that you will be severely penalized for writing everything that is relevant to answers.

An essay test may be printed on sheets of paper with spaces on the paper for writing answers. When a space is not large enough for a complete answer, continue it on the back of the page. For instance, if there is not enough space to write a complete answer to a third question, write as much as you can in the space provided and the word "over" in parentheses. Then, on the other side of the page write "3" and complete the answer.

PROOFREAD ANSWERS

You cannot do your best writing when you answer essay questions under the pressure of time limitations; however, your answers should be as well written as possible. Therefore, plan for time to proofread answers after you write them. When proofreading, check for incomplete thoughts and places where additional information or examples can be added. Any improvements you can make to answers while proofreading them will benefit you when they are graded.

WHAT TO DO IF TIME RUNS OUT

It is essential to plan test-taking time carefully when answering essay questions (see pages 302–304). However, no matter how carefully you plan, there will be instances when you do not have enough time to write a complete answer to a question on an essay test. If you write no answer, a teacher will assume that you do not know the answer, and if you write a very short answer, a teacher will assume it is the best answer you can write. In the first case you will receive no credit; in the second case you will probably receive less credit than you should.

One solution to this problem is to write an outline for the answer you would write if you had sufficient time, show it to the teacher, and request additional time to write the complete answer. Another solution is to simply tell a teacher that you did not have enough time to write an answer. A reasonable teacher will offer a solution to this problem.

ANSWERING ESSAY QUESTIONS

Study for essay tests using the methods that are explained in Chapters 16–20, and answer essay questions using the suggestions in Chapter 21 and this chapter.

   I. Understand direction words
  II. Answer all parts of questions
 III. Write well-organized answers
     A. Plan the major points
     B. Write clear introductions
     C. Make major points stand out
 IV. Write complete answers
     A. Write to an uninformed reader
     B. Write more than you think you need to write
  V. Proofread answers

The following exercises provide practice for developing the skills that are used to answer essay questions.

EXERCISE 1

PLANNING TEST-TAKING TIME

Use the point values for answers to questions to plan how test-taking time should be distributed for answering the questions on the following two essay tests.

Principles of Ecology: Test 3

Write your answers to the following questions in the booklet which you have been given. Each answer has a maximum value of twenty points in computing test grades. All test booklets will be collected in sixty minutes.

1. Explain the options for assuring adequate food supply as world population increases.

2. Compare the clear-cutting of timber with selective cutting of timber and give examples when each method is most beneficial.

3. Diagram and label a city that has the multiple nuclei structure.

4. List the characteristics and conditions that make a species susceptible to extinction.

5. Summarize the effects of air and water pollution.

---

1. How should test-taking time be distributed when answering questions on this ecology test?

_____

_____

_____

_____

There is another problem on the next page.

INTRODUCTION TO PSYCHOLOGY
Mid-term Exam

Write answers to any two questions in Group A and to any two questions in
Group B. The answers to questions in Group A have a maximum value of fifteen
points each and the answers to questions in Group B have a maximum value of
thirty-five points each. You have ninety minutes to write answers.

Group A

1. Explain the major functions of the pituitary, thyroid, and adrenal
   glands.

2. Describe the characteristics of each of the stages of sleep.

3. List the three explanations for the causes of obesity and state which
   explanation seems most reasonable to you.

Group B

4. Contrast the nativists' and empiricists' views of how people perceive the
   world. Cite research that supports each viewpoint and explain which
   position is most reasonable to you.

5. Explain under what conditions people learn most efficiently and discuss
   the effects of learning on motivation, distribution of practice, and
   overlearning.

6. Discuss the mental-testing controversy, summarize the arguments and
   research that support both sides of the controversy, and list the
   implications of the controversy for educational policy.

2. How should test-taking time be distributed when answering the questions on this psychology test? (Use approximate numbers.)

_____

_____

_____

_____

EXERCISE 2

DIRECTION WORDS

Learn the meanings of the direction words in Figure 26.2, and write them on the lines beneath the following sample essay questions. The first one is done to illustrate what you are to do.

Discuss three types of social mobility.

Write as much as you can

1. *Describe* the four types of low-level clouds.

2. *Explain* what causes some people to be helpful to others.

3. *Compare* romantic and mature love.

4. *Contrast* properly and improperly written matching questions.

5. *Criticize* this statement: "All college teachers should correct spelling and grammatical errors in written work they receive from students."

6. *Evaluate* the three methods that may be used to make ethical decisions.

7. *Justify* the use of prisons as a deterrent to crime.

8. Make a *diagram* that shows the functioning of the right and left hemispheres of the brain.

_____

9. *Illustrate* the norm of social responsibility and the norm of reciprocity.

_____

_____

10. *Enumerate* the reasons for the enactment of Prohibition.

_____

11. *List* the steps in the selling process.

_____

12. *Outline* clues for identifying distractors and correct answers in multiple-choice questions.

_____

13. *Summarize* the methods for improving listening.

_____

14. *Define* "anagram" and "palindrome."

_____

15. *Relate* Ptolemy to modern-day beliefs in astrology.

_____

16. *Trace* the stages of syphilis.

_____

_____

EXERCISE 3

ANSWERING ALL PARTS OF QUESTIONS

To receive full credit, an answer to an essay question must respond to all parts of it. Number the parts of the following questions in the way that is illustrated for the first question.

① Discuss the three types of social mobility and ② give two examples of each type.

1. Identify three ways to measure central tendency and illustrate each of them.

2. Discuss three methods for making ethical decisions, enumerate the problems associated with each method, and evaluate which method is the most difficult one to use.

3. Is the women's liberation movement a continuation of the women's rights movement, or are they two different movements? Defend your answer.

4. Discuss the differences between modern and traditional dating, identify differences you consider to be most important, and hypothesize how dating may be different twenty years from now.

5. How did each of the following men challenge the accepted religious views during the Age of Enlightenment: Toland, Bayle, Hume, and Voltaire?

6. Contrast the nativists' and empiricists' views of how people perceive the world. Cite research that supports each of the viewpoints and explain which position is most convincing to you.

7. Explain the United States' failure to ratify the Treaty of Versailles in 1919 and the consequences of this.

8. Discuss social class, stating the approximate percentages of people in each class and considering the following: occupations, attitudes, and goals.

EXERCISE 4

ESSAY QUESTIONS

Write a well-organized and complete answer to the following question: *Explain the five steps in studying for examinations and illustrate how you used each of them in preparing for a test you have taken.* Proofread your answer.

EXERCISE 5

ESSAY QUESTIONS

Write a well-organized and complete answer to the following question: *Summarize the basic strategies for taking any test and the specific strategies for answering true-false, multiple-choice, matching, and fill-in questions.* Proofread your answer.

EXERCISE 6

ESSAY QUESTIONS

Write a well-organized and complete answer to the following question: *Discuss the methods that may be used to write well-organized and complete answers to essay questions.* Proofread your answer.

GLOSSARY

Words within the definitions that are printed in italics are defined in this glossary.

Absolute determiner. A word such as "all," "none," "always," or "never," which tends to appear in false statements, such as "All children love candy."

Acronym. A word made from the initial letters of other words. "Scuba" is an acronym made from the initial letters of the following words: s(elf)-c(ontained) u(nderwater) b(reathing) a(pparatus).

Appendix. The part of a book that contains any supplementary materials or information; usually located in the back of a book, following the last chapter.

Associate degrees. Degrees offered by two-year colleges, usually the A.A. (Associate of Arts), A.S. (Associate of Science), or A.A.S. (Associate of Applied Science).

Authoritative. Said of information that is written by people who are experts on the subjects about which they write.

Bachelor's degrees. Degrees offered by four-year colleges, usually the B.A. (Bachelor of Arts) or B.S. (Bachelor of Science).

Bar graph. A drawing in which straight lines are used to show differences in amounts. A bar graph may be used to show differences in the amounts of tar content of various brands of cigarettes.

Bluebooks. Booklets, not necessarily blue, containing lined paper, in which students write essays or answers to *essay questions.*

Catalogue. A booklet published by a college or university that includes information about *curriculums,* courses, and other important facts.

Categories. Divisions created to organize facts and concepts so that they are more easily understood. Biology textbooks explain the categories or types of animals and plants.

Causes. Explanations that help in understanding why things are as they are. History textbooks explain the causes or reasons for wars of the past.

Classification chart. A format for taking notes to learn information that explains how two or more persons, places, or things are alike or different in two or more ways.

Combining form. A word form that combines with words or other combining forms. For example, "micro-" in "microfilm" and "bio-" and "-logy" in "biology" are combining forms.

Comparison. A statement of similarities or differences between or among persons, places, or things.

Concentration. The ability to focus thought and attention.

Context. A sentence, paragraph, or longer unit of writing that may reveal the meaning of an unfamiliar word.

Contrast. A statement of differences between or among persons, places, or things.

Copyright page. The page following the *title page* of a book, which states the year a book was published.

Course guide. Same as *course outline.*

Course outline. A paperback book that summarizes the information that is usually taught in a college course, such as an introductory psychology or chemistry course.

Credits. Units given for completion of study that applies toward a college *degree.*

Curriculum. The courses and other requirements for a particular *degree.*

Definition. The explanation of the meaning of a word. Most of the statements in this *glossary* are definitions.

Degrees. Ranks given to students who have successfully completed requirements in *curriculums,* usually *associate degrees, bachelor's degrees, master's degrees,* or *doctoral degrees.*

Direction word. A word in an *essay question* that informs test-takers what type of answer they are to give. The direction word "diagram" usually indicates that students are to draw a picture and label its parts.

Distractor. An *option* for a *multiple-choice question* that is not the correct answer.

Doctoral degrees. The highest *degrees* offered by colleges and universities, such as the Ph.D. (Doctor of Philosophy) and Ed.D. (Doctor of Education).

Effects. The consequences of actions, events, or circumstances. Ecology textbooks explain the effects of pollution on the environment.

Essay questions. Test items that require students to give written answers that are usually one paragraph or more in length.

Etymology. Information enclosed in brackets in a dictionary entry that explains the origin of a word.

Evaluate. To analyze the pros and cons of something for the purpose of arriving at a conclusion about its merits.

Example. In a dictionary entry, a phrase or sentence that illustrates how a word is used.

Fact. Things that are known or regarded, as a result of observation, to be true.

Fill-in questions. Test items that are statements that have a deleted portion that test-takers must supply: "There are ____ letters in the English alphabet."

Glossary. A list of words and their definitions; usually located in the back of a book just in front of the *index.* This is a glossary.

GPA values. Values given to *letter grades* so that *grade point averages* may be computed. The following values are used at many colleges: A, 4.00; B, 3.00; C, 2.00; D, 1.00; and F, 0.00.

Grade point average (GPA). A number that usually ranges from 0.00 to 4.00 and that indicates a student's average course grade.

Highlighting. The act of marking important words or sentences in a book using a pen that contains water-color ink.

Hour. A unit, usually less or more than sixty minutes, that designates time spent in classroom, laboratory, or conference for a course.

Imply. To hint, suggest, or otherwise indicate indirectly.

Incomplete grade (INC). A grade given at many colleges when students are doing passing work but have not completed all course requirements. Usually an INC grade is changed to F or some other grade if incomplete work is not completed within a specified time.

Index. An alphabetically arranged listing of subjects and the page numbers on which they are discussed in a book; usually located at the very end of a book.

Infer. To use known facts, information, or evidence to arrive at a conclusion.

Introduction. The part of a book that gives the author's explanations of why a book was written. It often includes a summary of the purposes, philosophy, or contents of a book and is usually located right after the *table of contents.* This information may also be located in a *preface.*

Letter grade. A grade such as B+, C, or D− that designates the quality of work students do. Letter grades have the following meanings at many schools: A, excellent; B, good; C, satisfactory; D, passing; and F, failing.

Line graph. A drawing in which lines are used to show increasing or decreasing amounts. A line graph may be used to show increases or decreases in the number of students enrolled at a college over a period of years.

Major detail. Information that is subordinate to, or beneath, topics discussed in printed materials or lectures. Compare with *minor detail.*

Map. A diagram or other drawing that shows the relation between a topic and major details or among a topic, *major details,* and *minor details.*

Master's degrees. Degrees that rank higher than *bachelor's degrees* but lower than *doctoral degrees,* usually the M.A. (Master of Arts) or M.S. (Master of Science).

Matching questions. Test items that present two lists and require test-takers to associate words or statements in one list with words or statements in the other list.

Methods. The procedures, processes, or ways of doing something. Mathematics textbooks explain methods for solving mathematical problems.

Minor detail. Information that is subordinate to, or beneath, *major details* discussed in printed materials or lectures.

Mnemonic. That which aids the memory. "Use *i* before *e* except after *c*" is a mnemonic for remembering a spelling principle.

Multiple-choice question. A test item written in a format that requires test-takers to select the correct answer from among four or five possible answers, or *options.*

Number grade. A grade such as 91, 85, or 68 that designates the quality of work students do. Many colleges agree on the following correspondences between number grades and *letter grades*: A, 90–100; B, 80–89; C, 70–79; D, 60–69; and F, 0–59.

Open-book test. A test during which students may refer to books, and sometimes notes, as they write answers to questions.

Option. In a *multiple-choice question,* one of the choices from which a correct answer is selected; one option is a correct answer and the others are *distractors.*

Preface. See *introduction.*

Prefix. A letter or letters joined to the beginning of a word. The "re-" in "rewrite" is a prefix.

Prerequisite. A requirement that must be completed before a

course may be taken. For instance, the prerequisite for an intermediate algebra course may be a course in elementary algebra.

Preview of a book. The examination of the major features of a book, such as the *table of contents, introduction, appendix,* and *glossary.*

Preview of a chapter. The quick examination of introductory paragraphs, headings, pictures, tables, and other features of a chapter to learn what major topics it discusses.

Primary source. A firsthand source of information. A motion picture starring Marilyn Monroe is a primary source of information about her appearance on screen. Contrast with *secondary source.*

Reading. The process used to understand information that is presented in writing. Contrast with *studying.*

Reciting. The act of repeating information silently or aloud to learn it and to be able to recall it.

Registrar. The title of a person at a college who is responsible for registering students in courses and for maintaining their academic records on *transcripts.*

Review. The repeated *reciting* of information to learn it or the practicing of *skills* to acquire them.

Scan. To read for the purpose of locating printed information quickly. For instance, one scans when reading a telephone book to locate a telephone number.

Secondary source. A statement made about a *primary source.* A motion picture review describing Marilyn Monroe's ap-

pearance on screen is a secondary source about her appearance.

Section. One of two or more classes for the same course. For instance, a college may offer several classes (or sections) of a freshman writing course.

Sequence. The order in which things follow each other in time, space, rank, or some other dimension. History textbooks explain the historical sequences in which important events occurred.

Skill. An ability acquired as a result of training and practice; reading and writing are skills.

Stem. The part of a *multiple-choice question* that comes before the first *option,* or choice for an answer.

Studying. The process used to learn and remember information. Contrast with *reading.*

Subject label. In dictionary entries, a term printed in italics to indicate the field of knowledge to which a definition pertains.

Suffix. A letter or letters joined to the end of a word. The "-ish" in "babyish" is a suffix.

Table. A presentation of statistical information arranged in well-organized columns and rows.

Table of contents. A list that shows the page numbers on which chapter headings and subheadings of a book appear; usually located right after the *title page* of a book.

Take-home test. A test for which students are given questions that they answer at home or study at home before they answer them in class.

Terminology. Words or phrases that are used with specific meanings when a subject is discussed. *Stem, option,* and *distractor* are terminology used to discuss the subject of *multiple-choice questions.*

Theory. A possible but not certain explanation of why things are the way they are.

Title page. The page at the beginning of a book that gives information about the title, author, and publisher.

Transcript. The official record of courses taken, grades received, and *grade point averages*—a report card.

True-false question. A test item that is a statement that test-takers must decide is true or false.

Tutor. A person who gives individual instruction to students.

Underlining. The act of drawing lines under important words or sentences in a book.

Visualization. An image that can be pictured in the mind and

used to recall information. If you picture in your mind the room where you sleep, you can use the image to recall information about the room.

Withdrawal grade (W). A grade given at many colleges so that students may drop courses when they have good reasons for so doing. Usually W grades do not lower *grade point averages* when they are requested within specified time limits.

Scott and William Powers, *Interpersonal Communication*, pp. 39–40. Copyright © 1978 by Houghton Mifflin Company. Adapted by permission.

Pages 128–129: "Measures of Central Tendency" from Gary Belkin and Ruth Skydell, *Foundations of Psychology*, p. 24. Copyright © 1979 by Houghton Mifflin Company. Adapted by permission.

Page 130: "Packaging Functions" from William M. Pride and O. C. Ferrell, *Marketing*, 3rd ed., pp. 158–159. Copyright © 1983 by Houghton Mifflin Company. Used by permission.

Pages 130–131: "Money Management" from Robert L. Williams and James D. Long, *Toward a Self-Managed Life Style*, 2nd ed., pp. 262–263. Copyright © 1979 by Houghton Mifflin Company. Adapted by permission.

Page 134: Figure 11.1 from James F. Shepherd, *College Study Skills*, 2nd ed., p. 94. Copyright © 1983 by Houghton Mifflin Company. Used by permission.

Pages 141–143: "Conflict" from Gary Belkin and Ruth Skydell, *Foundations of Psychology*, pp. 321–322. Copyright © 1979 by Houghton Mifflin Company. Adapted by permission.

Pages 144–145: "Death and Dying" from Michael S. Haro et al., *Explorations in Personal Health*, p. 66. Copyright © 1977 by Houghton Mifflin Company. Adapted by permission.

Page 146: "Improving Your Listening Skills" from Barry L. Reece and Rhonda Brandt, *Effective Human Relations in Business*, pp. 49–50. Copyright © 1981 by Houghton Mifflin Company. Adapted by permission.

Pages 147–148: "Theories About Lightning" from Joseph S. Weisberg, *Meteorology*, 2nd ed., p. 213. Copyright © 1981 by Houghton Mifflin Company. Adapted by permission.

Pages 149–150: "The Great Depression" from G. D. Lillibridge, *Images of American Society*, Vol. II, pp. 231–233. Copyright © 1976 by Houghton Mifflin Company. Adapted by permission.

Page 151: "Romantic and Mature Love" from Joann S. Delora et al., *Understanding Human Sexuality*, pp. 333–336. Copyright © 1980 by Houghton Mifflin Company. Adapted by permission.

Pages 153–154: "SQ3R" from Richard G. Warga, *Personal Awareness*, 2nd ed., pp. 185–186. Copyright © 1979 by Houghton Mifflin Company. Used by permission.

Pages 155–156: "Low-Level Clouds" from Joseph S. Weisberg, *Meteorology*, 2nd ed., pp. 102–106. Copyright © 1981 by Houghton Mifflin Company. Used by permission.

Pages 157–159: "Helpfulness" from Gary Belkin and Ruth Skydell, *Foundations of Psychology*, pp. 469–470. Copyright © 1979 by Houghton Mifflin Company. Adapted by permission.

Pages 159–161: "Prisons" from pp. 517–518 in *An Introduction to American Government*, 3rd Edition by Kenneth Prewitt and Sidney Verba. Copyright © 1979 by Kenneth Prewitt and Sidney Verba. By permission of Harper & Row, Publishers, Inc.

Pages 162–163: "Phonemes" from L. Dodge Fernald and Peter S. Fernald, *Introduction to Psychology*, 4th ed., p. 489. Copyright © 1978 by Houghton Mifflin Company. Used by permission.

Page 167: "Odd-Even Pricing" from William Pride and O. C. Ferrell, *Marketing*, 2nd ed., pp. 436–437. Copyright © 1980 by Houghton Mifflin Company. Adapted by permission.

Page 169: "Words at Play" from James F. Shepherd, *College Vocabulary Skills*, 2nd ed., pp. 55–56. Copyright © 1983 by Houghton Mifflin Company. Used by permission.

Page 171: "Television" from Mary Beth Norton et al., *A People and a Nation: A History of the United States*, Vol. II, pp. 880–881. Copyright © 1982 by Houghton Mifflin Company. Adapted by permission.

Page 175: "Energy from the Sun" from Joseph S. Weisberg, *Meteorology*, 2nd ed., pp. 120–121. Copyright © 1981 by Houghton Mifflin Company. Used by permission.

Page 177: "Prohibition" from G. D. Lillibridge, *Images of American Society*, Vol. II, pp. 226–227. Copyright © 1976 by Houghton Mifflin Company. Adapted by permission.

Page 179: "Rabies" from Neal Buffaloe and Dale Ferguson, *Microbiology*, 2nd ed., p. 407. Copyright © 1981 by Houghton Mifflin Company. Adapted by permission.

Page 183: "Relatives" from James F. Shepherd, *College Study Skills*, 2nd ed., pp. 162–163. Copyright © 1983 by Houghton Mifflin Company. Used by permission.

Page 185: "Human Motivation" from Wayne N. Thompson, *Responsible and Effective Communication*, pp. 123–124. Copyright © 1978 by Houghton Mifflin Company. Adapted by permission.

INDEX

STUDY SCHEDULE*

	SUN	MON	TUE	WED	THU	FRI	SAT
8–9							
9–10							
10–11							
11–12							
12–1							
1–2							
2–3							
3–4							
4–5							
5–6							
6–7							
7–8							
8–9							
9–10							
10–11							

* Use pencil so that you can make changes.